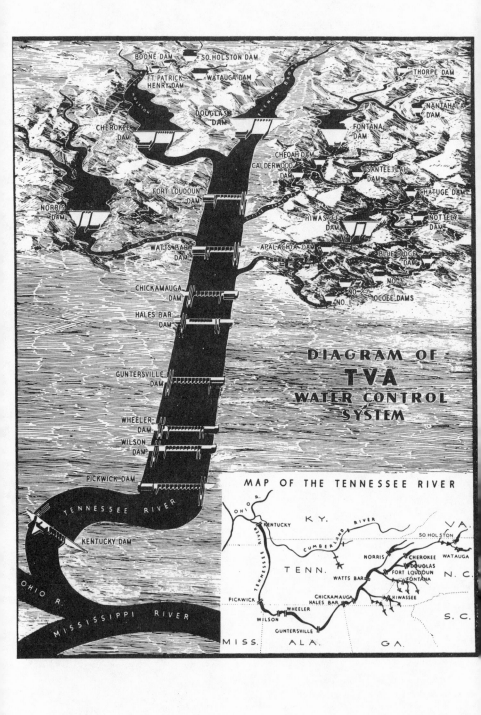

TVA

DEMOCRACY
ON THE MARCH

TWENTIETH ANNIVERSARY EDITION

by

DAVID E. LILIENTHAL

former Chairman,
Tennessee Valley Authority

GREENWOOD PRESS, PUBLISHERS
WESTPORT, CONNECTICUT

Library of Congress Cataloging in Publication Data

Lilienthal, David Eli, 1899-
   TVA : democracy on the march.

   Reprint of the 1954 20th anniversary ed. published
by Harper, New York.
   Bibliography: p.
   Includes index.
   1. Tennessee Valley Authority.
HN79.A135L54   1977   353.008'23'09768   77-7348
ISBN 0-8371-9584-5

To the memory of pioneers of the TVA

GEORGE W. NORRIS

L. N. ALLEN
EUGENE L. BISHOP
C. H. GARITY
CLAIR C. KILLEN
THOMAS D. LEBBY
HARCOURT A. MORGAN
THEODORE B. PARKER
NED H. SAYFORD
WILLIAM L. STURDEVANT

They built for the People of The United States

CONTENTS

TVA REVISITED:
AUTHOR'S NOTE TO THE EDITION OF 1953

This book was originally written, in 1943, as a testament of the writer's faith in certain central principles of working democracy, as they had been exemplified and practiced in the functioning of the experiment known as TVA.

At the time of that writing TVA was ten years old. Since then, another ten years have come and gone. It seems timely to take another look at the principles and precepts which TVA represents and of which the valley of the Tennessee is a living demonstration.

In the course of revisiting TVA as a private citizen, I examined in detail not only the way in which the TVA operates today, and the changed facts about the valley itself, but more especially whether the principles underlying this experiment still seem valid and viable, for it was as a personal interpretation of these principles that my book had been chiefly concerned.

In the rereading of what I had written ten years ago, and assessing those words in the light of today, a decade later, two things are most striking.

First, the impressive and almost incredible changes in the *physical* facts about the TVA, the valley and the life of its millions of people. The unprecedented rate of economic growth and development that occurred in the first decade of the TVA period has proved to be no flash in the pan, no short-lived burst of energy followed by a static period.

Second, the principles, as I understood them, that I described in this book a decade ago—principles of self-government, of decentralized grass-roots administration, of local and individual participation in the valley's development—in the light of today seem to me as sturdy and workable as ever; the need for their observance is greater today than ever before; their practical value, in the TVA of 1953, seems to me to confirm the earlier judgment of their worth and soundness; their applicability, with sensible adaptation, to other regions seems just as clear.

The task, therefore, of revising, and in many instances completely rewriting portions of this book, at TVA's twentieth year of life, has been largely a matter of sketching into the picture some of the more salient recent facts about the river and its control; the story of added billions of kilowatt hours of electric power and their use in valley homes, farms, and industry; the new industrial developments of the past decade; the added acres marked by good husbandry of the land; the way in which, more and more, the recreational assets of the valley have been developed—and so on. I have examined and included in this revision and rewriting only enough of such current evidence—by way of recent data, new illustrations, indications of changes in activities—to satisfy myself about the personal judgments recorded in this book a decade ago.

The figures that record further headway in the valley have changed; some of the valley programs have changed in scope, emphasis, and content. For example, TVA is now building a huge system of coal-burning electric plants, and is becoming one of the largest users of coal in the country. The basic proposition, however, about the nature of the "great change," as I tried to describe it ten years ago, remains, so it seems to me, validated by the added years of trial.

This book was not originally designed and written as a comprehensive exposition of the TVA *as a project*. The revised edition does not depart from that concept. I wrote, out of my own experience, about this valley because I believed it to represent "a demonstration of the vitality of democracy," a story that "reveals the promise and the hope of tomorrow for men everywhere"; that what had been done in this one region could be made to happen in "almost any of the thousand other valleys where rivers run from the hills to the sea." Since then millions of people in faraway lands have come to share this confidence. Worldwide interest in the TVA, manifested in many interesting ways, has so increased that it is now commonly stated that, the world over, the TVA is probably the best known single demonstration of modern American democracy.

Still another development of the past ten years has impressed me. I refer to the maintenance, in full force and freshness, of high standards of technical and managerial competence and integrity in the TVA organization. This is only another way of saying that TVA is today run by able and good human beings. There continues to be not even the faintest whisper of a suspicion that politics have crept in, or any shadow of doubt (even in the minds of those who oppose TVA in principle) that there has been in TVA any dishonesty in the handling of its funds, favoritism in dealings with the public, or tawdry and degrading episodes of petty graft or insensibility to the ethics of public trust. The caliber of the men who are responsible for TVA has not declined, nor the spirit of dedication to the public service diminished, though this has been common in the history of administrative agencies, after the excitement and novelty of the pioneer days are over. It is my judgment that TVA now has as strong a Board of Directors as at any time in its history, men with qualifications of judgment and records of achievement that rival those of any corporate executive committee in the country.

There has been some change in the staff, of course, over the years. With the exception of the men who, almost literally, died on the job (to whose memory this book is dedicated), the TVA today is staffed, in its major posts, largely by men who were in the organization ten years ago; some of the most important positions are filled by men who entered the TVA's service in the very beginning, in 1933 to 1935. That some of the ablest engineers and executives to be found anywhere, carrying huge responsibility at a fraction of the salaries they could easily command in industry, should elect to carry on with the TVA is a reflection of the great resources of love of country and devotion to principle one finds everywhere in this land.

TVA now has grown up. It has been through fires of public scrutiny and attack as have few American enterprises, private or public. It has come through this testing with the support and approval of almost the whole of the people of the valley, and, by all accounts, with the respect of a very large proportion of public opinion through the country, without regard to party or region.

In his message to Congress recommending the establishment of the TVA experiment, President Roosevelt said: "If we are successful here we can march on, step by step, in a like development of other great natural territorial units within our borders."

But if TVA is such a good thing, if it has been "successful," why have there been no other TVAs?

Certainly not because the record of TVA has persuaded the country to put an end to large federal expenditures for river and resource development in other valleys. As a matter of fact the scale of federal expenditures in support of resource development, such as the TVA has undertaken, has increased enormously since TVA was established; but the developments have not been administered by regional agencies like TVA. Apparently, then, opposition to spending federal taxpapers' money does not account for the fact that there are no more TVAs.

By all odds the most stupendous single demand for public expenditure in the history of this or any other country's rivers—over eleven billions of dollars for the direct benefit of one region, to be put up by American taxpayers everywhere—is involved in the Missouri Valley's projected development.[1] This comes from those who in the name of "states' rights" are the most vigorous opponents of a federal agency such as TVA to adminster the undertaking; I refer to the Governors of Missouri River states. No suggestion that the Missouri Valley states finance this states' rights project has been advanced. Opposition to an MVA, it is evident, is not due to a reluctance to use federal funds for that valley's development.

Nor can the fact that there have been no other TVAs be credited or attributed to the power and influence of the historical opponents of TVA, the privately owned electric companies. There has never been a greater expansion in the development of hydroelectric power by the federal government than since the advent of the TVA. This expansion, all through the country, continues and is at a greater rate today than ever, with bipartisan support. However much (or little) the TVA example contributed to this expansion of federal water power development, it is certainly not true that the fact that

[1] Of this total, six billions has already been authorized by Congress.

there are no more TVAs is because TVA has demonstrated the un-wisdom of more federal hydroelectric developments.

There was a time when it was argued, in opposition to the adoption of the TVA idea in other valleys, that TVA constituted an impairment of state and local government. Vigorous assertions to the contrary by the Governors of the Valley states, and the cumulative record of actual operations of TVA, have largely dispelled this contention. A student of public administration has recently put it this way:

> No more ridiculous allegation has been made, in all the extravagant and acrimonious debate about the valley-authority question, than the repeated charge that the TVA represents an attack upon states rights and local government. People who make such statements are either ignorant of its history or purposeful prevaricators. Indeed, precisely the opposite criticism would have much more cogency: namely, that TVA has delegated too much of its responsibility to state and local agencies and has refrained from the imposition of sufficient controls and checks.[2]

A somewhat similar comment would seem to lie against the argument that TVA is "socialistic," and that therefore the "experiment" should not be repeated in other regions. The effort to portray the TVA as antagonistic to private competitive business does not stand up in the light of the record of the TVA's stated purposes, and the quite remarkable results of the TVA program in terms of the growth and health of free competitive enterprise throughout the Valley; to this story a considerable portion of this book is devoted. Moreover, it is well known that in this region live the traditionally most individualistic people of any part of the country. The business men of the Valley, who live in close daily contact with the TVA, almost without exception consider it as a stimulant to free enterprise; this they have proudly told the country on many occasions. Speaking in 1953 of a visit he made to the Tennessee Valley in 1951, the new Secretary of the Interior (then the Governor of Oregon) Hon. Douglas McKay is reported as saying of TVA that it "must have done a good job because the people seem to like it."[3]

[2] Charles McKinley, *Uncle Sam in the Pacific Northwest* (University of California Press, 1952), p. 526.

[3] Article by Charles Bartlett, Chattanooga, Tennessee *Times*, February 10, 1953.

As I see the matter at this twenty-year milestone of the TVA experiment, to understand why there is still today only one TVA, one must understand clearly *what TVA is*. It was the purpose of this book, in its original form, to seek to make this plain; it is the purpose of this revision to underline TVA's essential meaning.

If one understands what TVA is, it is possible, I believe, to comprehend more clearly the answer to the question: Why are there no other TVAs?

TVA is an effective effort to decentralize the functioning of the federal government, to reverse the trend toward centralization of power in Washington, to delegate, dilute, and withdraw federal power *out of Washington* and back into the regions and states and localities, insofar as the development of natural resources is concerned.

The majority of the original Board of Directors and succeeding Boards, with the approval of Congress, set out to provide a demonstration that greater and greater centralization in the Washington bureaus and departments was not inevitable; that a practical way could be worked out for regional decentralization that would work. That effort largely succeeded.

TVA therefore represents a major experiment in the reorganization of the federal government. That effort began not at the top (as most do) but at the grass roots, in a single region of moderate and manageable size for so ambitious and difficult an assignment. This book is largely about the results of that reorganization.

That such an experiment would meet the combined opposition of an alliance of all the Washington bureaucracy was a foregone conclusion. And it did. It continues to face that bureaucratic hostility today. It will have to withstand the united front of the Washington bureaucracies in the new Administration of 1953. For if the TVA experiment in decentralizion were ever repeated, in essentials, in other regions, one after another, the power and influence of the Washington departments—from Cabinet officers down—would be immeasurably diminished. No centralized authority in the history of the world has ever submitted to such a defeat without a long and a bitter fight.

The real reason, then, why there are "no more TVAs" is the great bi-partisan power of the Washington bureaucracy. Bureaus of the

Departments of Interior and Agriculture, and the Army Corps of Engineers, have so used their political power as to make more TVAs impossible, and thereby have preserved their "vested interest" in the jurisdiction and prerogatives of their bureaus. For they have seen that if other regional agencies, embodying the TVA idea, were created, many of their functions that are now centered in Washington would be unified and coordinated regionally, and in large measure would be delegated or turned back to the states and localities, as has happened in the Tennessee Valley since 1933.

The TVA came into being after an uphill battle extending over many years prior to 1933. But with this sole exception these Washington agencies have been able to defeat every proposal for unified valley development since the earliest days of conservation forty-five years ago. And, as a consequence, lack of coordination, expensive rivalries, "improvident use" of resources, and floods of ever-increasing magnitude continue to be the story in such a major river basin as that of the Missouri, comprising one-sixth of the land area of the country.

This long-continued triumph of vested bureaucratic power over the sound principle of unified management has not been because the failures of the centralized Departments have not often been made known and vigorously attacked. On the contrary, for almost half a century, from the days of the administration of President Theodore Roosevelt to that of President Dwight D. Eisenhower, the basic unsoundness of the present system has been pointed out and criticized by plain citizens, by independent engineers, and by a long succession of public Commissions of inquiry.

No longer ago than February 2, 1953, President Eisenhower, in his first State of Union Message, called for "a strong Federal program in the field of resource development" to include "the water and minerals, public lands and standing timber, forage and wild life of this country." The new President noted, however, that there "has been much criticism, some of it apparently justified, of the confusion resulting from overlapping Federal activities in this entire field of resource-conservation;" he called for its correction, as several of his predecessors have done.

President Theodore Roosevelt's attack on this same "confusion"

—both of thinking and of administration—is the basis of his fame as the founder of modern conservation. On February 26, 1908, he transmitted to Congress the Report of the Inland Waterways Commission, which he had appointed in an effort to put an end to project-by-project river development by a multitude of uncoordinated agencies. In his message President Roosevelt criticized the "piece-meal execution of projects" dealing with our rivers, soils and forests; he agreed with his Commission's view that coordination of the various bureaus engaged in these matters was essential. He concluded with the statement: "We shall not succeed" in our efforts to make "the best use of our rivers or for exercising foresight in their development . . . until the responsibility for administering the policy and executing and extending the plan is definitely laid on one man or group of men who can be held accountable."

Since that day many Commissions have examined into the obvious mismanagement of our basic river and resource programs; they have, one after another, repeated the refrain of Theodore Roosevelt's criticism and analysis. One of the most thorough-going and biting of such attacks is the report of a Task Force on Natural Resources of the Hoover Commission. More recently, the classic Report of the Cooke Commission (the President's Water Resources Policy Commission) dated December 11, 1950, set out the affirmative thesis of valley-wide unified development at length, with great literary skill and with overwhelming evidence.

The most recent condemnation of the present system of river valley development is contained in a 300 page Report made to President Eisenhower on February 20, 1953, by the Missouri Basin Survey Commission. This bi-partisan commission, composed of eleven residents of the Missouri Valley states—Governors, Senators, Representatives and private citizens—for a year held hearings throughout the vast area of the Missouri Basin. "Time and again at the hearings," the Commission told the President, "the people expressed their strong belief that the resource program now in progress lacks the coordination and balance essential to genuine multiple purpose planning, and even threatens at times to make improvident use of the region's limited supply of water." The Report continues: "the Commission's findings affirm the contentions that there is lack of balance and lack of coordination in the present efforts. *Upon this foundation the Commission has determined unanimously that the coordination and direction of the development of the basin's resource potential should be entrusted to a new agency created for that purpose. This agency, properly invested with essential powers, would coordinate and direct the program as a single resource project."* (My italics)

Although no other regional TVAs have actually been created, it is evident that the demonstration in the valley of the Tennessee has had a considerable influence, as an example and a pattern, for valley development elsewhere in this country, as well as abroad. This is not the only instance in which an "experiment" proved its value not by exact repetition, in the same form, but in other and varied ways. The great American "experiment," our Constitution and Bill of Rights, has had a profound influence upon the free institutions of mankind, though in no significant instance have the exact form and content been repeated.

This is not the place to trace in particular the marks of TVA's example, as a measure of its influence as an experiment. One instance, and the most obvious example, may be cited, however, namely, the impact of the central TVA theme of the *unity* of the river and the land and the people in any program of valley development.

That theme is one of which the Tennessee Valley is today a living exemplification, as a visitor sees it today in all new-found beauty and vigor of land and forest. The lesson of unity is not only written in the technical development plans of other agencies; more significantly, this kind of thinking of the unity of resources has begun to find its way into the minds of millions of the everyday people of other American valleys. While it has its ironic side, it is on the whole reassuring to note how some of the most vigorous opponents of an MVA in the Missouri Valley have adopted the very words that convey the essential concept of regional development, along TVA principles, such terms as "unity of resources," "multipurpose development," and so on, a far cry from their pork-barrel, project-at-a-time terminology of ten years ago.

TVA has demonstrated certain inescapable realities. One of these is that those responsible for the development of the river must see the task as a unit, and not on the old and discredited levee-by-levee,

dam-by-dam basis, so long supported by an alliance of Congressmen, Washington departments, and favored contractors.

If, however, one admits that a river must be seen as a unit—and
the implications of this concept I try to spell out, concretely, in
this book—then those who are responsible for developing it must
also be a *managerial unit,* with unified responsiblity for all parts
of the integrated whole undertaking, ranging from the location of
the site to considerations of public health. Where the river flows
through several states, this unity can be achieved through a federal
authority, or conceivably (though not as a practical matter is this
attainable) by an agency created by a compact between the states,
with federal approval as the Constitution provides. But it really does
not matter whether that managerial unit is called a Valley Authority
or a Valley Commission, or what Richard G. Baumhoff has described
in his book *The Dammed Missouri Valley* as an "Anti-Authority
Authority" (p. 291), is actually not of any consequence. Certainly it
is not important at all that the TVA experience that demonstrated
the practical wisdom of such a unified managerial approach to a
river's development is given "credit" for this advance in thinking.
The result is what is important.

Similarly with progress toward governmental decentralization.
The time may well come when the atmosphere in Washington and
in the country favors such decentralization, not only in words but
by deeds. Such may be the case in 1953, with the coming in of a
new national Administration. The TVA experience, related in this
book, of the "how" of decentralization, against a background of
actual operating results, may prove of value. It can be of practical
value to those in responsible posts who espouse the idea of stronger
state and local governments as contrasted with federal centralization, and really intend to do more than make speeches on the subject. But the TVA example can also be an embarrassment to those
in responsible federal office who, being in a position to do something concrete toward federal decentralization, prefer an excuse for
inaction in a reiteration of the difficulties of decentralization. The
TVA example removes that excuse.

That such an example of actual decentralization exerts an influence by example rather than through the creation of "other"

valley regional administrations is not a matter of importance. What *is* important is that the living example of the valley of the Tennessee contributes to the sum total of democratic achievement in this difficult area in the art of self-government.

D. E. L.

23 Beekman Place
New York City
February 26, 1953

PREFACE TO THE FIRST EDITION

This is a book about tomorrow.

My purpose in writing it today is to try to cut through the fog of uncertainty and confusion about tomorrow that envelops us. The fog is caused largely by words, words without reality in the world as it actually is; to dispel this murkiness we must *see the reality behind the words.*

This book then is about real things and real people: rivers and how to develop them; new factories and new jobs and how they were created; farms and farmers and how they came to prosper and stand on their own. My purpose is to show, by authentic experience in one American region, that to get such new jobs and factories and fertile farms our choice need not be between extremes of "right" and "left," between overcentralized Big-government and a do-nothing policy, between "private enterprise" and "socialism," between an arrogant red-tape-ridden bureaucracy and domination by a few private monopolies. I have tried in these pages to express my confidence that in tested principles of democracy we have ready at hand a philosophy and a set of working tools that, adapted to this machine age, can guide and sustain us in increasing opportunity for individual freedom and well-being.

This confidence that *it can be done,* that the fog, and the fears its shadowy shapes engender, will vanish if we look at the reality and not the words, is based on ten years of experience in the Tennessee Valley. Here the people and their institutions—among them the regional development corporation known as TVA—have provided just such a demonstration of the vitality of democracy. It is that ten years of actual experience—that background for this book—that reveals the promise and the hope of tomorrow for men everywhere.

I am an administrator and not a professional writer. This book bears the literary marks of that deficiency. I have had to do the writing, moreover, while carrying on my work, often in the midst of those recurrent "crises" that make up the life of any administrator. And I recognize that in writing about the Tennessee Valley Authority I cannot be wholly objective. No one can be so absorbed in this work as for a decade I have been and remain thus passionless about a task so altogether heartening. The reader, then, is warned at the outset that he will find no tone of Olympian neutrality in this book. For this I make no apology, for I believe the world badly needs conviction; it has had too much of a kind of impartiality that is inevitably irresponsible. In this book there are convictions stated and conclusions pressed.

This book does not purport to be a full account of the TVA. Except by way of the briefest inventory. I have not described the engineering and technical aspects of that enterprise nor the effect of the changes in the Tennessee Valley upon the lives of particular individuals, in some ways the most interesting part of the TVA story. There is little in this book on the public power issue, although that has been the center of most controversy about the TVA in the past: for this valley that issue appears to be settled.

What I have set down in this book is a statement of my faith, and the facts and reasons that support it.

I believe men may learn to work in harmony with the forces of nature, neither despoiling what God has given nor helpless to put them to use. I believe in the great potentialities for well-being of the machine and technology and science; and though they do hold a real threat of enslavement and frustration for the human spirit, I believe those dangers can be averted. I believe that through the practice of democracy the world of technology holds out the greatest opportunity in all history for the development of the individual, according to his own talents, aspirations, and willingness to carry the responsibilities of a free man. We have a choice: to use science either for evil or for good. I believe men can make themselves free. These convictions have been fortified as I have seen them take on substance and become part of the life of this valley and of its people; and it is of this that I write in this book.

The interpretation of the TVA that I have set down is essentially a personal one, for every man necessarily sees his experiences through his own eyes. But in forming the views and ideas written into this book I am deeply in debt to many men and women, and most of all to the people who live in this valley—and that includes of course the men and women of the TVA, associates and co-workers of mine. For this reason I have dedicated the book to them —builders for democracy—farmers, managers, architects, engineers, construction workers, chemists, merchants, accountants, preachers, many different kinds of people—in the spirit of the tablets we have put upon TVA's dams, upon which appear no named hierarchy of Board of Directors or engineers, but simply the legend: "Built for the People of the United States."

A number of friends, among them TVA Board and staff colleagues, have reviewed all or parts of the manuscript, and made helpful suggestions and criticisms, for which I am grateful. I am specially and deeply indebted to two associates. At every stage of the writing Gordon R. Clapp, General Manager of TVA, has contributed ideas, criticism, editorial suggestions, and the stimulus of his clear and seminal intelligence. I am likewise specially indebted to Marguerite Owen, TVA's Washington Representative, for the benefit of her rare critical judgment, for substantial editorial assistance and many productive suggestions. My special thanks are due to Marion Reames, whose skill and patience carried this book through the many stages of its writing, from my shorthand first drafts to the last typed revision.

In the writing of this book as in everything I have undertaken in the past twenty years I have relied greatly upon the perceptive judgment of my wife, to whom I am infinitely grateful.

What the TVA owes to Senator George W. Norris the country well knows; indeed without him there would be no TVA; his statesmanship and integrity are deeply engraved upon every chapter of TVA's legislative history. And in the years since TVA was created its administrators have been privileged to draw deeply from those well-springs of wisdom and sagacity that mark Senator Norris as one of the great men of America's history. I want too to record the very special debt that is owing to my colleague of the whole period covered by this account, Harcourt A. Morgan, the noblest and most comprehending man I have ever known. He is a great teacher of fundamentals—for a whole valley.

Finally, in addition to the impersonal words that appear in the text of this book, I want to add a word of appreciation to the President of the United States; not only for his unfailing support of TVA's basic principles of conservation and decentralization, for the establishment of which he was largely responsible, but even more for his years of warmhearted and friendly counsel and encouragement.

D. E. L.

Pine Road
Norris, Tennessee
October 6, 1943

T V A

Democracy on the March

Chapter 1

ONE VALLEY—AND A THOUSAND

THIS book was written in the valley of a great American river, the Tennessee. It is about that river, and that valley; about the soil of its farms, the white oak and pine on its mountain slopes, the ores and minerals that lie buried in its hills. It is about the rain that falls so violently upon its fields, and the course the water follows as it seeks out first the streams and then the river itself. This book is about the people of this valley region, the men who work the land, the men who roll the silver sheets of aluminum, who run the cotton gins, and stand behind the counter in the general stores. It is about the women who tend the spindles or stir the kettles or teach the children in the schools.

This is the story of a great change. It is an account of what has happened in this valley since 1933 when Congress set the Tennessee Valley Authority to the task of developing the resources of this region. It is a tale of a wandering and inconstant river now become a chain of broad and lovely lakes which people enjoy, and on which they can depend, in all seasons, for the movement of the barges of commerce that now nourish their business enterprises. It is a story of how waters once wasted and destructive have been controlled and now work, night and day, creating electric energy to lighten the burden of human drudgery. Here is a tale of fields grown old and barren with the years, which now are vigorous with new fertility, lying green to the sun; of forests that were hacked and despoiled, now protected and refreshed with strong young trees just starting on their slow road to maturity. It is a story of the people and how they have worked to create a new valley.

I write of the Tennessee Valley, but all this could have happened in almost any of a thousand other valleys where rivers run from the hills to the sea. For the valleys of the earth have these things in common: the waters, the air, the land, the minerals, the forests. In Missouri and in Arkansas, in Brazil and in the Argentine, in China and in India there are just such rivers, rivers flowing through mountain canyons, through canebrake and palmetto, through barren wastes—rivers that in the violence of flood menace the land and the people, then sulk in idleness and drought—rivers all over the world waiting to be controlled by men—the Yangtze, the Ganges, the Ob, the Parana, the Amazon, the Nile. In a thousand valleys in America and the world over there are fields that need to be made strong and productive, land steep and rugged, land flat as a man's hand; on the slopes, forests—and in the hills, minerals—that can be made to yield a better living for people.

And in foreign but no longer distant lands, in the cities and the villages in those thousand valleys, live men of a hundred different tongues and many racial strains. As you move across the boundaries men have drawn upon their maps, you find that their laws are different, as are their courts and passport regulations, and what they use for money. Different too are the words you hear, the color of men's skin, the customs in the home and in the market. But the things the people live by are the same; the soil and the water, the rivers in their valleys, the minerals within the earth. It is upon these everywhere that men must build, in California or Morocco, the Ukraine or Tennessee. These are the things they dig for and hew and process and contrive. These are the foundation of all their hopes for relief from hunger, from cold, from drudgery, for an end to want and constant insecurity. A thousand valleys over the globe and our valley here are in this way the same: everywhere what happens to the land, the forests, and the water determines what happens to the people.

The Tennessee River had always been an idle giant and a destructive one. Today its boundless energy works for the people who live in this valley. This is true of but few of the thousands of rivers the world over. But it can be true of many, perhaps most. The job will be begun in our time, can be well along toward fulfillment within the life of men now living. There is almost nothing, however fantastic, that (given competent organization) a team of engineers, scientists, and administrators cannot do today. Impossible things can be done, are being done in this mid-twentieth century.

Today it is builders and technicians that we turn to: men armed not with the ax, rifle, and bowie knife, but with the Diesel engine, the bulldozer, the giant electric shovel, the retort—and most of all, with an emerging kind of skill, a modern knack of organization and execution. When these men have imagination and faith, they can move mountains; out of their skills they can create new jobs, relieve human drudgery, give new life and fruitfulness to worn-out lands, put yokes upon the streams, and transmute the minerals of the earth and the plants of the field into machines of wizardry to spin out the stuff of a way of life new to this world.

Such are the things that have happened in the Tennessee Valley. Here men and science and organizing skills applied to the resources of waters, land, forests, and minerals have yielded great benefits for the people. And it is just such fruits of technology and resources that people all over the world will, more and more, demand for themselves. That people believe these things can be theirs—this it is that constitutes the real revolution of our time, the dominant political fact of the generation that lies ahead. No longer do men look upon poverty as inevitable, or think that drudgery, disease, filth, famine, floods, and physical exhaustion are visitations of the devil or punishment by a deity.

Here is the central fact with which today's statesmanship must contend. The political promises that will be made and the great popular movements that have come into being deal with the demands of people for the ever larger harvest that science and nature, devoted to a common purpose, can be made to yield. The terms under which the people of the world receive the products of technical advance, such as those that have come to this valley, are at the vortex of the cyclonic forces of our century.

This is the right time for telling of such things. In the desperation of war, miracles were wrought in laboratories and with machines. Seeing the reality of things they had never dreamed could happen, men the world over were deeply stirred; they began to think of tomorrow, to think of it with longing tinged with fear and uncertainty, livened with hopes for the future.

A great restlessness and acute dissatisfaction with their present lot have seized large areas of the world; peoples who for centuries were without hope now demand an earnest of good faith as to their future—things that they can see, can themselves experience. As even the more obtuse conventional politicians are beginning to learn, people seem less and less beguiled by abstractions and vague eloquence; their thinking is less complicated but closer to life than that of the intellectual on the lecture platform or the political leader drafting a manifesto.

In the recesses of men's thoughts they seem not so concerned with generalizations and exhortations as with quite concrete desires: sixty acres of land, how it can be brought back to fertility; how to get the crop to the best kind of market; how to get a job at a new kind of factory machine at good pay; about a pleasant town where the kids can have bicycles; about electric lights and heated schools and churches and hospitals for the ill; no more flooding out every spring; long Diesel barges on the river to carry off the warehoused wheat; refrigerators and irrigation canals and an end to the malaria mosquitoes. The word spreads that these and many other such things can be theirs; that the inventors and engineers and chemists can make them happen. The word has spread to the crossroad towns in the Ozarks, the trailer camps in Detroit, the boarding houses in Fall River; to men in the oil fields across the Rio Grande, the collieries in Wales, the shops of Leeds and Manchester; even to the villages on the Ganges and the caves beneath Chungking.

Our faith is sustained by the inspiring words of great leadership, by the pledges of freedom and prosperity and democracy. But it is when the words unbend—when they come into men's homes, to their farms, their shops—that they come alive to men. Do the words mean that a livelihood will not always be won at the cost of such drudgery for men and women, will not always be so skimpy and bitter? What of the soil of their land—will it always be so starved? What of the metal that could be made of the minerals, and the houses of the forests; what of the gadgets to pump the water that for so long the women have carried in buckets day after day? What of the river that flows through the valley—what great things would happen if its flow could turn the wheels of new factories? This is a job of building for the new skills of young engineers and chemists and the Army-trained mechanics; a job for the architects and engineers with ideas about new kinds of cities, for the physicians with ideas for new kinds of hospitals and revolutions in nutrition.

The inspiring principles—is this what they mean? To give them such a meaning takes more than words and promises, however eloquent and honestly uttered. This is a job of work to be done, a job for which there is already some experience and more than enough talent and skill. The words of promise can be made to come true. Here is the Grand Job of This Century.

But everything depends upon *how* this job is done.

The spirit in which the task is undertaken; its purpose, whether for the welfare of the many or the few; the methods chosen—these will determine whether men will live in freedom and peace, whether their resources will be speedily exhausted or will be sustained, nourished, made solid beneath their feet not only for themselves but for the generations to come.

The physical achievements that science and technology now make possible *may bring no benefits*, may indeed be evil, unless they have a moral purpose, unless they are conceived and carried out for the benefit of the people themselves. Without such a purpose, advances, in technology may be disastrous to the human spirit; the industrialization of a raw material area may bring to the average man only a new kind of slavery and the destruction of democratic institutions.

But such a moral purpose alone is not enough to insure that resource development will be a blessing and not a curse. Out of TVA experience in this valley I am persuaded that to make such a purpose effective two other principles are essential.

First, that resource development must be governed by the unity of nature herself.

Second, that the people must participate actively in that development.

The physical job is going to be done; of that I think we can be sure. But if, in the doing, the unity of nature's resources is disregarded, the price will be paid in exhausted land, butchered forests, polluted streams, and industrial ugliness. And, if the people are denied an active part in this great task, then they may be poor or they may be prosperous but they will not be free.

Is it inescapable that such a task of resource development be carried on only by highly centralized government direction? Must it inevitably be run by a privileged élite of managers or experts or politicians? Yes, say the defeatists about democracy, the cynics, the disillusioned and frustrated liberals, the believers in force, the disbelievers in men. Can it be done in no other way than by gutting the resources of nature, by making the countryside hideous, by maiming the forests, fouling the streams, ignoring the unity of land and water and men? Yes, that is "the way things are," say the greedy, the short-sighted, the unperceptive.

The experience in this valley gives the lie to such answers and to those who utter them. The whole point of the TVA experience that I shall seek to make plain in this book is that the best way, perhaps the only way the job can be done effectively, is by observing the unity of nature, by following democratic methods, by the active daily participation of the people themselves.

What is going on in the Tennessee Valley and what I shall describe in this book is specific, graphic, particular, something that can be seen, appraised, analyzed. One demonstration is worth much generalized discussion and tall talk. TVA was initiated frankly as an experiment; it has been administered in the spirit of exploration and innovation. But it is no utopian Brook Farm experiment; no endeavor to escape into a simpler past or a more romantic future. TVA and this valley face the facts of the present with all its complexities and difficulties.

The methods of democratic development represented by the TVA are distinctive, but their roots lie deep in the soil of American tradition and common experience. They are methods that differ from those customarily employed both by private enterprisers and public agencies. Nevertheless the TVA experiment has been carried on under the existing rules of the game of American life. It required no change in the Constitution of the United States. Congress has maintained full control. Property rights and social institutions have undergone no drastic amendment. In short, the valley's change has gone forward under typical and traditional American conditions, rather than under non-existent "ideal" conditions that would not or could not be duplicated.

The breadth of purpose and the distinctive methods of the TVA— these it is that constitute the most important part of the enterprise.

It is these that will have the greatest usefulness to other Americans and to the increasingly large number of responsible men in other nations who are concerned with problems essentially similar to those that faced this valley in 1933.

It is upon such purposes and methods that our answers to issues of peace and freedom will turn. All else—"principles" of economics and finance, dollars and pounds sterling, tariffs and taxation, unemployment insurance, health programs, new gadgets and plastics and chemicals and electronic devices, democratic government, even essential international arrangements—will depend upon the decisions we make and the course we follow tomorrow in the fundamental activity of developing the resources in the soil, the air, the water, and within the earth, through modern skills of science and organization.

Chapter 2

A RIVER IS PUT TO WORK FOR THE PEOPLE

THIS is an entirely different region from what it once was. You can see the change almost everywhere you go. You can see it in the copper lines strung along back country roads, in the fresh paint on the houses those electric lines were built to serve. You can see it in new electric water pumps in the farmyards, in the community refrigerators at the crossroads, in the feed grinders in the woodsheds. You can see the factories that stand today where there were worn-out cotton fields and rows of tenant shacks a few years ago. You can see new houses, by the thousands, on the edges of the towns—new houses of the men who take away as much cash from a few trips to the payroll window as they used to earn in a year.

You can see the change best of all if you have flown down the valley from time to time, as I have done so frequently. From five thousand feet the great change is unmistakable. There it is, stretching out before your eyes, a moving and exciting picture. You can see the undulation of neatly terraced hillsides, contrived to make the beating rains "walk, not run, to the nearest exit"; you can see the grey bulk of the dams, stout marks across the river now deep blue, no longer red and murky with its hoard of soil washed from the eroding land. You can see the barges with their double tows of goods to be unloaded at new river terminals. And marching toward every point on the horizon you can see the steel crisscross of electric transmission towers, a twentieth-century tower standing in a cove beside an eighteenth-century mountain cabin, a symbol and a summary of the change. These are among the things you can see as you travel through the Tennessee Valley today. And on every hand you

8

will also see the dimensions of the job yet to be done, the problem and the promise of the valley's future.

A technical man will observe much that will interest him, for the Tennessee Valley Authority represents a substantial technical achievement, a record written over a wide area in concrete and steel, and in land revived and forests renewed. Here one can see what modern science can do in a few years to change the face of the earth and the waters. That technical story has been recorded with painstaking care and great detail and published in the many volumes of scientific reports by TVA's engineers, agronomists, town builders, chemists, biologists, foresters, public health experts, architects.

These technical reports will interest the experts. The average citizen will measure the change through reports of another kind: in the records of new private industries established in the valley, of failing enterprises revived, more money in people's hands, fewer tax delinquencies, increased bank deposits, a greater volume of buying at the stores—trends clearly established before the war. The citizen may read of the change in records of new public library service or state parks established where none had been before, more hospitals, new county health units, less tuberculosis and malaria and other "low-income diseases." He may read of the number of miles of lines built to bring power to the farms of the area and the rapid increase in the amount of electricity used by the people—unprecedented in this country. He may reflect on the better quality of food produced and the increased yield per acre on the land, or analyze the ton-miles of traffic increase on the river. He may figure the potential value of the millions of seedlings planted in farm woodland and forest. He may see the newly created "Great Lakes of the South," the beauty of their thousands of miles of wooded shoreline unmarred, deep blue waters set among high mountains and abounding with game fish.

Such sights and such records reflect the ways in which, as this beautiful valley has changed, the lives of several million fellow Americans have also changed.

The story of the change begins with the river. On the map the river's five mountain tributaries, each a considerable stream—the French Broad, the Holston, the Hiwassee, the Little Tennessee, the

Clinch—are clearly set off from the broad main stem, the Tennessee itself, a major river of great volume, fed by the heaviest rainfall in eastern America. The map shows that main stem as a deep crescent, its source and eastern tip in the Appalachian Mountains, the dip of the crescent slicing off the northern third of Alabama, the western tip arching northward through the flat red lands of western Tennessee and Kentucky. The river flows not in one general direction, but in three; it moves southward first, then its middle course is westward, and its lower reaches turn back toward the north. A river that "flows up the map," as visitors to TVA almost invariably remark, seems to be water flowing perversely uphill, making its way more than 650 miles from Knoxville in Tennessee, in sight of the virgin timber in the Great Smoky Mountains, the highest peaks in eastern North America, to Paducah in the lowlands of Kentucky where across the broad Ohio you can see the fields of Illinois.

The valley through which the river flows actually lies in seven historic states of the Old South: the western part of the seacoast states of North Carolina and Virginia; the northern parts of Georgia, Alabama, and Mississippi; the western half of Kentucky from its southern jointure with Tennessee north to the Ohio River; and almost of the whole of the wide reaches of the state of Tennessee. Less exactly, the region reaches from the mountains about Asheville west to the sluggish Mississippi at Memphis, and north and south from the old steamboat whistle landings on Ohio's shores to the cotton fields of Mississippi and the flambeau of the furnaces at Birmingham—an area all told about the size of England and Scotland, with a population of about 6,000,000 persons.

This is the river system that thirty dams of the TVA integrated system now control and have put to work for the people. To do that job twenty new dams, several among the largest in America, were designed and constructed. Five dams already existing have been improved and modified. Five more major dams owned by a private corporation are, by agreement, operated as a part of the system. One of TVA's carpenters, a veteran who worked on seven of these dams, described this to me as "one hell of a big job of work." I cannot improve on that summary. It is the largest job of engineering and construction ever carried out by any single organization in all our history.

In heat and cold, in driving rain and under the blaze of the August sun, tens of thousands of men have hewed and blasted and hauled with their teams and tractors, clearing more than 175,000 acres of land, land that the surface of the lakes now covers. They have built or relocated more than 1300 miles of highway and almost 200 miles of railroad. With thousands of tons of explosives and great electric shovels they have excavated over 30,000,000 cubic yards of rock and earth to prepare the foundations of these dams—an excavation large enough to bury twenty Empire State buildings. To hold the river the men of the TVA have poured and placed concrete, rock fill, and earth in a total quantity of 113 million cubic yards.

To comprehend these figures requires a few comparisons. This 113 million cubic yards of material is more than twelve times the bulk of the seven great pyramids of Egypt. Of these materials, the concrete alone poured into the TVA dams is two and a half times as much as used in all the locks and structures of the Panama Canal; is four times as much as in Hoover Dam; 1,200,000 cubic yards greater than in the Grand Coulee Dam; would build more than seven dams as large as Soviet Russia's great Dneiper Dam. The Grand Coulee Dam is the largest single masonry structure yet built, and Hoover Dam the second largest. Hoover was in the process of construction for five years and took the combined efforts of six of our largest private building contractor firms. Grand Coulee took eight years to build, and ten major private construction firms were engaged on it.

Thirty-five Hoover dams or ten Grand Coulee dams could have been built with the total materials required for completion of this valley's dams, the work of a single organization. The TVA's employees in 1942 were simultaneously designing and building a dozen dams and improving four others, were erecting the South's largest steam electric plant, and building large chemical and munitions factories, with a total of 40,000 men and women at work.

A decade later, in 1952, a total of 21,000 men and women were at work, building two dams, installing ten additional generators in existing dams, and erecting six huge coal-burning electric generating plants, some of which will be among the largest in the world.

The work of the builders has made of the river a highway that is carrying huge amounts of freight over its deep watercourses. In

1952 more than 800 million ton-miles of traffic moved through locks, designed in co-operation with the Army Corps of Engineers and operated by them, which raise the barges from one lake's level to another. In 1928 only a little more than 46 million ton-miles of traffic moved on the river; in 1933 the figure was 32 million. This was mostly sand and gravel moving in short hauls between adjacent areas, and some forest products.

Today huge modern towboats, powered by great Diesel engines, move up and down the channel, pushing double columns of barges, and the cargo is no longer limited to raw materials. Billets of steel and cotton goods come from Birmingham headed north, grain from the Midwest, millions of gallons of gasoline, oil, machinery, merchandise, automobiles, military vehicles. In 1951, with more than 580 million ton-miles carried, savings were $8,000,000.

Quiet cotton towns of yesterday are now busy river ports. And, as always has been true of water transportation, new industries are rising along its course. Millions of dollars have been invested, and thousands of jobs created as new grain elevators, flour mills, and oil terminals have been erected along the river's banks.

At Decatur, Alabama, on land where farmers once raised corn and cotton, ocean-going cargo vessels slipped down the ways into Wheeler Lake during the War and thence to their North Atlantic job. After the war, self-propelled barges were built there for use on the Rhine River in Europe, as well as barges for the inland waterways of the U.S.

And on these lakes are thousands of new pleasure craft of every kind—costly yachts, sailboats, homemade skiffs. Ten thousand miles of shoreline—more than the total of the seacoast line of the United States on the Atlantic, the Pacific, and the Gulf of Mexico—are available for the recreation of the people. Thousands of acres along the shore are devoted to public parks, operated by the states, by counties, and by cities. More than 225 boat docks serve the needs of fishermen from all parts of the United States.

There is far more fishing on the new lakes than there was on these same rivers before the dams were built—one hundred times more on the storage reservoirs and thirty times as intensive on the mainstream reservoirs. About half of the increase was due to dropping the traditional idea of a "closed season," and encouraging fishing any time of the year. Careful studies showed that not more than 10 per cent of the available fish "crop" is being harvested annually, hence a closed season was unnecessary. In 1952 sports fishermen alone are estimated to have taken some 8,000,000 pounds of fish from the streams, while commercial operations yielded nearly 2,000,000 pounds of fish and 10,000 tons of mussel shells.

Before the men of the Tennessee Valley built these dams, flooding was a yearly threat to every farm and industry, every town and village and railroad on the river's banks, a barrier to progress. Today there is security from that annual danger in the Tennessee Valley. When local protective works have been erected at Chattanooga this region will be completely safe, even against a flood bigger than anything in recorded history. A measure of protection resulting from the Tennessee's control extends even beyond this valley; for no longer will the Tennessee send her torrents at flood crest to add what might be fatal inches to top the levees and spread desolation on the lower Ohio and the Mississippi.

In others of the earth's thousand valleys people live under the shadow of fear that each year their river will bring upon them damage to their property, suffering, and death. Here the people are safe. In the winter of 1942 torrents came raging down this valley's two chief tributaries, in Tennessee and Virginia. Before the river was controlled this would have meant a severe flood; the machinery of vital war industries down the river at Chattanooga would have stopped, under several feet of water, with over a million dollars of direct damage resulting.

But in 1942 it was different. Orders went out from the TVA office of central control to every tributary dam. The message came flashing to the operator in the control room at Hiwassee Dam, deep in the mountains of North Carolina: "Hold back all the water of the Hiwassee River. Keep it out of the Tennessee." The operator pressed a button. Steel gates closed. The water of that tributary was held. To Cherokee Dam on the Holston went the message: "Keep back the flow of the Holston." To Chickamauga Dam just above the industrial danger spot at Chattanooga: "Release water to make room for the waters from above."

Day by day till the crisis was over the men at their control instruments at each dam in the system received their orders. The rate of water release from every tributary river was precisely controlled. The Tennessee was kept in hand. There was no destruction, no panic, no interruption of work. Most of the water, instead of wrecking the valley, actually produced a benefit in power, when later it was released through the turbines.

By 1945, two more large tributary and two more main Tennessee River reservoirs had been completed. January, 1946, brought water flows that without the river's new safeguards would have been a great and disastrous flood, the fifth largest ever to occur at Chattanooga. TVA reservoirs reduced the crest by more than ten feet. In the next two years, 1947 and 1948, the crests of potentially the sixth and seventh largest floods were similarly reduced; the saving in actual damage averted in Chattanooga alone in these three floods was more than $36 million.

Back of the orders from the water dispatcher to the men who operate the dams is an elaborate system of reporting rainfall and gauging the flow of streams so the height of waters can be predicted for days in advance. To the head of the TVA forecasting division, from all over the watershed, from every tributary stream, from three hundred stations, by teletype, telephone, and shortwave radio come reports of the river's "stages," i. e., its height. Here, for example, is one of the messages that came from H. S. Barker near Mendota, in Virginia, during the critical days of the 1942 flood:

River three feet eighty-four hundreths raining rainfall one seventeen hundredths inches.

That is, river stage was 3.84 feet; it was raining at the time; the rainfall during the past twenty-four hours was 1.17 inches.

Reports come in from hundreds of remote rain-gauge stations, telephoned in by a farmer's wife, a crossroad store merchant, a woodsman. From well-nigh inaccessible mountain streams ingenious TVA-made devices send in their reports by shortwave radio without human intervention. And all the reports are combined and interpreted by engineers, so that they know almost exactly how much water will be swelling the river the next day and the next. Yesterday's reports are checked with today's and revised tomorrow, and the best technical judgment is sent to the river control room: just how much water is being added to the river's flow in the French Broad, the Holston, the Clinch, the Hiwassee.

The operating orders go out, turning water off or on to meet the demands of the crisis along a watercourse from the headwaters of the Tennessee to the Gulf, almost as long as the Mississippi from its headwaters to New Orleans. The Tennessee River throughout its length is controlled, as water is retained at one dam, released at another. This valley has been made safe.

This is not true of other river valleys. Here, for example, is a press association dispatch of May 13, 1943:

Swollen creeks and rivers flooded more than one million acres of low-lying farmlands in six states Thursday, burying spring crops, blocking highways and taking at least seven lives.

High water left hundreds of farm families homeless as flood crests rolled downstream in Arkansas, Oklahoma, Kansas, Missouri, Indiana, and Illinois. . . .

As the river crest moved downstream Army engineers retreated before it, abandoning levee after levee as the hopelessness of combating the flood became apparent.

A few days later this summary appeared in the New York *Times* (May 27, 1943):

During May muddy waters have submerged 3,926,000 acres in Illinois, Missouri, Arkansas, Oklahoma, Kansas and Indiana, routed 160,000 persons and caused twenty-one deaths in the worst floods in the midlands since 1937, when the Ohio and Mississippi Valley disaster made more than 1,000,000 persons homeless and took 466 lives.

The story of one year's disaster after another in the floods of the Missouri Valley has become a familiar and sorry tale, culminating—though unhappily not necessarily ending—in the Missouri Valley floods of 1950 and 1951. Taken together these constitute a major national disaster; and for a country so advanced in engineering, soil technology, and management as ours, a national disgrace as well.

In the technically retarded or undeveloped parts of the world one comes to expect much the same kind of story of the devastation of man's works by floods. Here, for example, is a newspaper account from New Delhi, India, dated August 7, 1943:

Approximately 10,000 Indians were drowned in the past week by floodwaters of the Khari River which swept suddenly through nearly 100 villages. Nearly a sixth of the tiny British Province of Ajmer-Merwara was under water.

And in the fall of 1943 came that flood's horrible sequel: famine.

No major river in the world is so fully controlled as the Tennessee, no other river works so hard for the people, for the force that used to spend itself so violently is today turning giant waterwheels. The turbines and generators in the TVA powerhouses have transformed it into electric energy. And this is the river's greatest yield.

Chapter 3

EIGHTEEN BILLION GENII

THE dams and steam-electric plants the TVA has built have made this region the largest producer of power in the United States. During 1951 the integrated system produced about eighteen billion kilowatt hours of electric energy, nearly three fourths as much electricity as the utilities in the entire country produced when we entered World War I, and nearly one fourth the entire country's output in 1932.

Such figures as these are more than figures; they have deep human importance, for this must be remembered: the quantity of electrical energy in the hands of the people is a modern measure of the people's command over their resources and the best single measure of their productiveness, their opportunities for industrialization, their potentialities for the future. A kilowatt hour of electricity is a modern slave, working tirelessly for men. Each kilowatt hour is estimated to be the equivalent of ten hours of human energy; the valley's eighteen billion kilowatt hours can be thought of as 180 billion man hours applied to the resources of a single region! This is the way by which, in the Age of Electricity, human energies are multiplied.

In 1933 the per capita electricity production in the TVA area was about 50 per cent *less* than the per capita average for the United States; two decades later the figure has become about 25 per cent *more* than the United States average. Since TVA began operations, the amount of electricity produced, per person, increased more than 900 per cent, three times as fast as in the United States as a whole. In 1933 the estimated annual power produced per person in the Tennessee Valley area, as nearly as can be computed, was only 350

17

kilowatt hours; in 1951 this had increased more than ten times to 3,560 kilowatt hours, to be compared with the annual production per person of 2,830 kilowatt hours for the United States as a whole. In India the corresponding 1950 figure was less than 15 kilowatt hours. A high production of electricity per person of population is a requisite of a technical society.

Where does this valley's vast amount of electricity go? During World War II most of it went directly into war production. Electric power is the lifeblood of modern warfare. Take aluminum, for example. This valley's power has produced a large part of the aluminum for American aircraft—at one critical phase of the last war more than half—and aluminum is largely the product of electric power. During the war as much electricity went into one big bomber as the average household would consume in four hundred years.

But aluminum is only one example of the war use of power produced by TVA. The Oak Ridge plant of the Atomic Energy Commission was located in the valley by the Manhattan District largely because TVA could make available quickly an ample supply of low-cost power.

Up and down the valley were many smaller industrial plants, their furnaces heated, their motors turned by the controlled waters of the river. They processed metals, food, fibers, timber products, chemicals; produced boilers for ships, gas masks, and explosives. TVA's own chemical plants used power for the same military purpose: to make the ingredients of smoke screens, explosives, incendiary bombs, synthetic rubber.

With the end of the war the valley turned that rush of energy once again into the building of a region for peace. In the six postwar years (i.e., 1946 to 1951) the use of electricity in the homes and farms of the region increased from 914,000,000 kwh to 3,875,000,000 kwh, an increase of more than four times in six years.

With the advent of the cold war and later the hot war in Korea, the valley once again turned to producing for war as well as for peace. The Atomic Energy Commission, in particular, asked for more TVA power. For their plant at Oak Ridge, Tennessee, and for their new plant near Paducah, Kentucky, they have asked TVA to supply by 1956 about 25 billion kilowatt hours a year. This is equal to one twelfth of all the electricity sold by all utilities—public and private—during 1951 to all customers throughout the entire United States. TVA is preparing to meet an annual electric requirement load of 60 billion kilowatt hours by 1956, this in a region where 1½ billion were considered adequate less than twenty years previously.

The power which can be produced by any river is not inexhaustible. TVA has now reached the point where virtually all the power resources of the Tennessee River basin have been developed. Future growth of the region's power requirements will, of necessity be supplied from steam-generated power, utilizing coal, natural gas, and, a decade or two hence, the heat of the splitting atom.

In 1951, about 85 per cent of the power produced by TVA came from hydroelectric plants and 18 per cent from steam-electric plants. In December that year the generating capacity of the TVA system totaled 3,541,000 kilowatts, of which 2,872,000, or more than 80 per cent, was hydro capacity. So rapidly is this situation changing that in a few years the proportion of steam power will exceed that of water power. With the new generating capacity already authorized by the Congress the capacity of the TVA system will reach nearly 9,400,000 kilowatts by the end of 1955, more than 60 per cent of it in steam-electric plants.

The reason for this great expansion in steam plants is a simple one. The growth in the electricity needs of a people is not limited by a river's ability to produce hydroelectric power. Any other course would place a ceiling on the future growth of a region, a ceiling fixed by one particular source of electrical energy.

The power of the river spreads its way all over the land of the valley. Power has come to the farms of the region, 400,000 of them in seven states, about nine in ten. In 1933 there was electricity on only one Mississippi farm out of a hundred; in Georgia one out of thirty-six; in Tennessee and Alabama one in twenty-five.

Today, in parts of the valley, electrification of farm areas is almost complete; in others there is still some part of the task undone. But from here on, the main task of the farmers' co-operatives is to see that the farmer is enabled to *use* more and more electricity so as to increase his productivity and profit.

In tens of thousands of farmyards and farm homes you can see the change that power has already wrought. There are refrigerators and ranges in the kitchens. There is running water, too, and the water is carried by an electric pump instead of by the women, young and old, with the once familiar water buckets. There are hay driers in barns, freezing lockers in the crossroads stores. There are small motors to grind feed, cut the wood, turn a small lathe. Power is curing hams, cooling milk in the new dairies.

The farm people themselves are running this part of the electrification job, through a particular kind of TVA-inspired co-operative. That corporate device for getting electricity to farmers came into being at a meeting I attended back in 1934, in the rear of a furniture store in the small Mississippi town of Corinth. First there had been a public meeting and "speechifying" on the courthouse steps. Then, the "speechifying" over, a committee of businessmen of the town and leading farmers met with a TVA committee; the result was the birth of the Alcorn County Electric Cooperative, in which Corinth and her farm neighbors set out to electrify the whole county—and did. Such was the unpretentious beginning of farm electricity co-ops that under a national Rural Electrification Administration conceived by Senator Norris have since spread all over the country.

One has to attend the annual meeting of one of these co-operatives—there are now fifty of them distributing TVA power—to understand the change electricity has brought. The motors and appliances tell only a part of the story. I have been at such meetings where throughout a whole day as many as two thousand farmers and their wives and children discussed the financial and operating reports made to them by their superintendent and board of trustees, and later, while we ate a barbecue lunch, watched new uses of electricity demonstrated. Some of these enterprises are big: one now has 19,000 members, an investment of nearly seven and a half million dollars; five others have 15,000 members each, with investments of from five to six million dollars. During 1951 people served by the rural electric cooperatives in the TVA area, mostly farmers, used nearly as much electricity as the whole region, industrial use included, used in 1933.

But these membership "town meetings" are not simply business sessions. They have an emotional overtone, a spiritual meaning to people who were so long denied the benefits of modern energy and convenience which had become a commonplace to their city neighbors.

And you can follow the course of change that electricity has brought in the lives of townspeople, too, in the several hundred small communities, towns, and good-size cities in these seven states, where nearly a million and a quarter homes and places of business are served with power from their river by 146 independent and locally owned public and co-operative agencies, agencies which purchase the power at wholesale from the TVA.

What has gone on in the valley has never happened before in all the fabulous history of electricity. In 1933 the homes of this area which had electricity used it sparingly; a large percentage of the homes had none at all. The typical use was very limited—for lighting, perhaps also for an electric iron, a radio. In 1933 the 225,000 homes that had electricity used about 130,000,000 kwh; in 1951 in this same area the 1,065,000 homes that had electricity used 3,875,-000,000 kwh.

There are few regions of the world where the people make such wide use of power. In Chattanooga, for example, ninety-five out of every hundred wired homes now have electric refrigeration. Electric ranges are used in nearly three fourths of the homes in Nashville which have electricity. Among the more than one million homes served with TVA power it is estimated that 75,000 are heated entirely with electricity. Out of every four new homes being built, three are heated electrically.

The story is much the same whether in the larger cities or in small communities and rural areas. Take the record in the home use of electricity by the first dozen distributors of TVA power, the local public agencies, which, through systems they have themselves acquired, resell TVA power at the low rates agreed upon with TVA. When they started, in 1933 and 1934, the average use of electricity by their customers was 17 per cent below the national average. At the end of a two-year period the use of electricity had increased 146 per cent, 77 per cent above the nation's average household use, while the country as a whole was showing an increase of only 15 per cent.

This kind of increase was not just a flash in the pan. In 1934 the average household use throughout the entire area now served with

TVA power was about the same as for the nation as a whole; eighteen years later the homes in the valley had increased their average use more than six times while the other homes in the nation increased their use three times.

Another way of showing the effect of the change is in the increase in the number of homes and farms that are using electricity *for the first time*: from 225,000 in 1933 to 1,065,000 in 1951. This is an increase of 375 per cent. In this same period the increase for the nation was slightly less than 100 per cent.

The spread of the benefits of the river's power is not uniform in every community, of course, but the general result is much the same. The percentage increases in use of electricity in some of the communities are spectacular: in many instances from five to ten times. Of the ninety-five municipal distributors of TVA power, all but five exceed the national average in the use of electricity in the homes, which for 1951 stood at 2,004 kilowatt hours. The 1951 average for the TVA area was 3,747 kilowatt hours; by October 1952 it had climbed to more than 4,000 kilowatt hours. In the homes of seventy-six of these cities and towns the average use is 50 per cent greater than the national average. In fifty-one communities the average use is 100 per cent greater than the national average.

How can one account for this unprecedented change in the use of electricity in this valley? Why is the use so much greater than in other areas that have a greater income? The answer is to be found largely in a new way of thinking about electricity, best reflected in the principle of a low rate—with a resulting wide use of power. That principle was established in the very forms of the Act creating the TVA. Congress directed the TVA to see to it that this vast store of electric power should be widely used; the moral purpose behind the whole TVA Act, to benefit the greatest number of people, was thus written into an express mandate of law.

To effectuate the law's policy of a wide and extensive use of electricity it was necessary for the TVA Board, at the very outset, to break sharply with the ways of fixing electricity rates that with few exceptions had been followed in the electrical industry. The rates announced in September of 1933 were considered low, extraordinarily low, judged by then prevailing ideas. Those rates to the ultimate user were based on the principle that people wanted to use electricity not in a niggardly way, but generously and for many new uses. To reach that goal of wide use, rates had to be drastically cut, cut not *after* the use had grown, but as a way of making it grow. This, we were convinced, would be financially sound, for people would then use so much more electricity that the income of the distributors would rise proportionately. What had proved to be a good business principle for Henry Ford in the pricing of his first automobiles, what was good business in the mass production field generally, would be good business in electricity supply. It would, moreover, add to the strength and the richness of living of the people of the valley. The particular rates the locally owned distributors of TVA power were to charge their customers, as embodied in those early TVA schedules, were not designed, nor were they advanced, as an absolute standard of precisely what should be charged for electricity anywhere and everywhere in the country, with the implication that any company charging more than the TVA rate was therefore proved an extortionist. The country is far too diverse, conditions are far too varied, for any such oversimplification of the idea of a "yardstick." The example this valley has supplied is a yardstick in a much more important sense. It has been demonstrated here, to the hilt, to the benefit both of consumers and utilities, that drastic reductions in electric rates result in hitherto undreamed-of demands for more and more electricity in homes and on farms. That the yardstick, in this vital sense, has established its value and validity is no longer even challenged.

The experience of the private utilities in the area adjacent to the Tennessee Valley has shown this in an interesting way. A short time after TVA announced these low rates, the neighboring private utilities of the Southeast followed suit by making large reductions in their own rates. The immediate result was a spectacular increase in the use of electricity in the homes they served. The first year after the private companies adopted the principle of the TVA yardstick, five of the six companies in the entire United States with the greatest increase in electric growth were in the Southeast.

Following this rate reduction of 1934, these neighboring private companies immediately outdistanced the rest of the country in the sale of electric appliances. The Georgia Power Company, for example, twenty-third in size among the utilities of the country, sold more electric refrigerators the first year of that TVA-induced rate reduction than any other company in the country regardless of size, was first in the sale of electric water heaters, and second in the sale of electric ranges. Its neighbor company, the Tennessee Electric Power Company, thirtieth in size in the country, immediately following its rate reduction became first in the total number of electric ranges sold, second in the number of electric refrigerators, third in the number of electric water heaters. This company, with only 100,000 residential users, was actually selling more home electric appliances than companies in high-income states like New York and Illinois with many times the customers.

The TVA electric-rate yardstick has been the occasion for a great deal of controversy, and thousands of pages have been written on the subject. I do not intend in this book to add further to that output. The yardstick in its correct sense has served and continues to serve a public purpose. It led all over the country to a realistic re-examination of the financial feasibility of low rates. It established that rates far lower than were thought possible when TVA first announced its own rates in 1933 are sound and profitable for private utilities. In the Tennessee Valley the original Henry Ford-style electric rates have since declined even further because of large earnings experienced under them by the municipal and co-operative power distributors. As of 1952 some forty-seven distributors of TVA power now charge their customers rates in some instances 25 per cent below the original rates that caused such a furor in 1933. Rates not markedly higher than those announced by TVA in 1933 and vigorously denounced at that time as "impossible" are now being charged by not a few private utilities. They are returning a profit to the private companies, even in a period of higher costs. And the average residential rate for the country as a whole, which was 5.52 cents in 1933, was 2.81 cents in 1951, a decrease of 49 per cent below 1933 levels.

The average rate paid for electricity by all ultimate consumers in the country dropped only 2 per cent in the seven years from 1926 (the first year for which the statistics are reported) to 1933, the year TVA was created. In the seven years after the creation of TVA the average rate paid fell 23 per cent. By 1951 the average national reduction from 1933 was practically one third.

Now, of course, one cannot prove that without the TVA yard-stick demonstration of the business soundness of drastically lower electric rates, no such sharp revision of private utility rates would have occurred in the ensuing years. It would also be an act of dogmatism to overlook the fact that other forces than TVA were at work as well, or to give no weight to the countervailing fact that during those years of lowered prices for electricity there occurred an extreme inflation in the *costs* of producing and distributing electricity, an inflation affecting all producers and purveyors of electricity—private, public, and co-operative.

When all the various factors are considered, three simple facts emerge: (1) The drastic utility rate revisions *have* taken place. (2) The predicted spectacular expanded use of electricity *has* occurred. (3) Prior to the yardstick demonstration nothing comparable had ever happened.

The sharp controversy over this matter can now be left to historians and to those rugged souls who enjoy hanging on to old issues. As a reading of this book will show, the reduction in electric rates was only an incidental part of the TVA story; it is to a personal interpretation of the whole scope of the events in the Tennessee Valley that this book is directed.

Chapter 4

NEW LIFE FROM THE LAND

And he gave it for his opinion, that whoever could make two ears of corn, or two blades of grass, to grow upon a spot of ground where only one grew before, would deserve better of mankind, and do more essential service to his country, than the whole race of politicians put together.

—JONATHAN SWIFT,
Voyage to Brobdingnag

THE river now is changed. It does its work. But it is on the land that the people live. Millions of acres of the valley's land had lost its vitality. The people had to make it strong again and fruitful if they themselves were to be strong. For here in this valley more people depend for a living upon each acre of farm land than in any other area in America. The farms are typically small; the average less than seventy-seven acres, a third of the national average. Farm families are large; the birthrate the highest in the United States.

Many people living on impoverished land—that was once the picture. If the moral purpose of resource development—the greatest benefit to human beings—was to be achieved, TVA had to see to it that the land changed as well as the river.

And the land is changing. It is a slow job. Engineering a river with large-scale modern machinery and rebuilding soil that for generations has been losing its vitality are tasks of a different tempo. But you can see the difference everywhere. The gullies are being healed. The scars of erosion are on the mend, slowly but steadily. The many wounds yet to be healed are by their contrast eloquent evidence of what the work of restoration has accomplished. The cover of dark green, the pasture and deep meadow and upstanding fields of oats and rye, the marks of fertility and productiveness are on every hand. Matting and sloping, seeding and sodding, have given protection to eroded banks on scores of thousands of acres. Ditches to divert the water and little dams to check it, hundreds of thousands of them, help control the course of water on the land, hold it there till it can soak down and feed the roots of newly planted trees and grasses.

The farmers have built 128,000 miles of terraces on a million acres and more; their graceful design, following the contour, makes a new kind of landscape, one that led Jefferson, observing the effect upon the face of his own Monticello acres, to exclaim that in "point of beauty nothing can exceed" contour plowing with its "waving lines and rows winding along the face of the hills and valleys."

On 51,000 valley farms embracing a total area of 6,000,000 acres in the Tennessee Valley, farmers selected by their neighbors have carried on a demonstration of modern farming, sponsored by TVA and the valley's state agricultural colleges, built around a more scientific use by farmers of the almost magic mineral, phosphate, and other fertilizers, and the use of power and the machine. These farm families have been willing, sometimes at considerable individual economic risk, to undertake a changed way of farming. Quite aside from the effect on crop production this is a human fact of great importance.

These pioneers call themselves "test-demonstration farmers." They have their own county organizations, known generally as Farm Improvement Associations or by similar names. Much of the story of how these demonstrations function I shall tell in a later chapter. These are private farms, not public show places. There was a time when many of these demonstration farms were in about as severe straits as any in our land; now you can see the rich rewards that can come to those who through science and skill and learning from each other find the way to build their land and their region.

Farming throughout the valley has increased in yield and fruitfulness, but it is on the demonstration farms that you see the best of what this land is capable of and what farmers can do, with only small help from public expenditures. The best way to get the story of the results is from the records of the seven valley state extension services, the state agencies that in 1935 first agreed to carry out the actual program.

Out of the thousands of reports in the records of the state agricultural institutions here is one from a Tennessee county, a land of "thin soil" and struggling people. In 1939 the TVA co-operative demonstration program began; by 1942 the annual report stated:

The number of milk cows increased 70%, from 43 head in January 1939 to 73 in the fall of 1942 . . . The number of beef cattle and veal calves marketed annually from the community has doubled during the last three years . . . In addition, there has been a substantial increase in poultry and hog production for home use.

The county agent reported in 1948 that:

Twenty years ago corn yields averaged 27 bushels to the acre; now the average is 55. Pasture acreage in 1930 was 58,925; in 1935 it was 75,687; today the acreage is about the same but pasture quality is at least 300 per cent better. Milk production rose from 2,675,396 gallons in 1930 to 5,116,082 gallons in 1945; this year's estimate exceeds 6,000,000 gallons. Alfalfa acreage was 781 acres in 1930; this year it will approximate 5,000 acres; and seed dealers say they are selling this year three times more seed for winter cover crops than last year.

The director of the Virginia State Extension Service reported that farms that had been in the program 10 years or more by 1948 had achieved the following results.

The number of beef cows have increased 144 per cent while dairy cows are up 160 per cent . . . Total livestock numbers (animal units) have increased from 36.7 to 51.0 per farm, or 39 per cent. . . . Fertilizer purchases are up 354 per cent . . . Farm income is up 21 per cent. . . . The acres of corn decreased 14 per cent and the yield per acre increased from 37.6 bushels to 70.1 bushels, or 87 per cent. . . . Alfalfa acreage is more than double what it was, while the yield per acre increased 61 per cent. The acres of other hay increased 27 per cent.

A case study of typical test-demonstration farm in the Tennessee Valley area of Kentucky shows the progress that has been made in that state:

Through better fertilization and land use, corn yields increased from 30 bushels per acre in 1935 to 85 bushels in 1948 while tobacco yields increased from 1,600 to 2,000 pounds per acre during the same period. The pasture and feeding program changed from one utilizing mostly temporary pasture crops and all available roughage on the farm regardless of form to ladino and fescue pastures and largely alfalfa hay. The livestock enterprise in 1935 consisted of 15 beef cows kept annually and 10 to 15 purchased steers. In 1948 the farm was carrying 125 beef cattle, largely steers. For a five-month period in 1948, the farm carried one steer for every acre of pasture.

In Georgia the Dean and Director of the College of Agriculture, referring to a group of 31 test-demonstration farms that had been in the program for a period of fifteen years, reported:

The principal changes on these 31 farms have been a reduction in row crop acreage of over 20 per cent, and the increase of close growing crops by 140 per cent. Permanent pasture acreage is also up 34 per cent. A further important adjustment in land use on these farms has been an increase of summer and winter legumes three times over. The effects of the addition of minerals to these farms, together with the changes in systems of farm management, can perhaps best be measured in terms of yields per acre. Corn is the universal crop. The average yield on the 31 farms in 1935 was 18.7 bushels per acre, in 1948 it was 45.2 bushels, up over 142 per cent. And this has gone up even more in 1949 and 1950.

Greater production of feed, adjustments in crop acreage and enlarged pastures has made possible . . . greatly enlarged receipts from livestock and livestock products. . . . An item often overlooked is products used on the farm—these have increased in value from $114 per farm in 1935 to over $800 per farm at present.

There are hundreds of competent observers to testify that these changes in income have been translated into better living and protected resources.

This is one way agricultural experts measure how the people have changed the land. They will tell you how the grazing season has lengthened, how the land yields a more nutritious grass and a better grade of corn, how every acre supports more animals, how from every crop and every head of cattle, from every laborer on the farm, there is greater production and more food value in each unit produced.

They may tell you of the experience in Hamilton County, Tennessee, where a Negro farming community entered the demonstration program in August of 1940, on worn-out soil where corn yields ran only about ten bushels to the acre. In the fall of 1942, just two years after the experiment was started, the president of the group made this report:

The Community made 8 times as much hay in the fall of 1942 as was formerly made in a season. . . . Ten to 12 bushels of winter cover crop seed—crimson clover, vetch, oats and rye—were planted in the fall of 1942. . . .

The number of milk cows in the community has been increased from 8 to 35, work stock from 9 to 18, brood sows from none to 4, hens from 190 to over 600.

The stories of individual test-demonstration farmers and their achievements on their own farms constitute the rural Horatio Alger folklore of this valley. In almost every community one hears these accounts. I quote passages from an account in a well-known farm magazine, *The Progressive Farmer,* for October, 1951; it tells the story of Lum Cummings of Franklin County, Alabama:

"I went around rows with a little mule so long I just tried to find another way of making a living," said Lum Cummings of Franklin County, Ala.

This decision made more changes in the life of Lum Cummings and his family than any other he ever made. In 1937 he had an 80 acre farm with 26 acres in cotton, 16 acres in corn, and 17 acres in soybeans. Cotton was practically his only source of cash. . . . He just wasn't getting anywhere with the land use program he was following.

Then one day in 1937 his county agent, J. D. Wood, asked him if he would cooperate in testing some TVA fertilizer on pastures and other cover crops. He was willing to try, because he thought any change might be for the better. Mr. Wood helped Lum work out a program for sound use of fertilizer in growing clover-grass pastures, perennials and other cover crops. He started by clearing some swampland and improving 17 acres of pasture. The pasture was used by a small dairy herd. He also got his first purebred beef cattle.

After recounting the year-by-year changes and improvements made by Mr. Cummings since 1937, the author of the article, Mr. J. C. Lowery, an Extension Agronomist, quotes the demonstration farmer as saying that "the water comes off our farm clear. This is because we keep our soil in sod." Then follows this comment:

A man who started at the bottom now has one of the finest pastures in Alabama on upland not usually considered good pasture land. People from many states and foreign countries have traveled to visit this humble man and his family and see the miracles they have performed in pastures. . . . More than 5,000 people visited this farm last year. . . . The Cummings farm is now out of debt, from red ink to green grass.

To rebuild the soil and the farm life of the Tennessee Valley a detailed scientific survey of the quality of the various kinds of soils, probably the most intensive ever undertaken, has been going on in this region since 1933. And, as a result of soil surveys taken in a great many counties of the valley and of scientific analysis by the seven state universities on TVA's behalf, farmers can go to their county agricultural agent and learn whether their soil is Fullerton cherty silt loam or Maury silt loam or Hartselle fine sandy loam, or any one of the hundreds of types, each different from the others, each calling for different handling to get the maximum yield with the least injury to the basic resources. The soil can work for the people best when the people understand it.

The real pay-off of the test-demonstration program, as the name implies, is to be found in the extent to which it has helped stimulate the spread of better farm practices among other farmers who observe the results. The Alabama State Extension Service has reported some of the changes that have taken place on the farms in the Tennessee Valley portion of Alabama, an area of fourteen counties, between 1935 and 1951. In these Valley counties improved pastures have grown from 2,000 acres to nearly 350,000 acres; alfalfa, sericea, and kudzu acreages from 1,200 to 155,000; and winter legume crops from 60,000 to 308,000 acres. Until a few years ago, there were no winter grazing crops, but in 1951 there were 230,000 acres.

Livestock raising and dairying have increased greatly. During 1951 alone, the number of beef herds increased from 2,700 to 3,600 and the number of brood cows from 32,400 to 49,000.

In the whole valley, census figures show, the acreage of row crops has declined by 16 per cent since 1934, yet the actual production of these crops is greater than before. The acreage of hay and pasture has increased by 12 per cent (an acreage equal to the reduction in row crops), and the number of cattle, calves, and hogs has risen. Dairy production, at the time of the last census, was 50 per cent greater than it had been fifteen years before.

As the shifts and improvements in agricultural practices have taken place, the number of test demonstrations has, of course, decreased markedly, and the character of the program has changed. Thus in 1952 the test demonstrators pay a part or all of the cost of the fertilizers, rather than simply freight and handling charges as at first, in the days when it was difficult for many farmers to see why they should take the risks of using their farms for these experiments.

With the reduced number of farms in the program, the emphasis has shifted; thus there is concentration on closer observation and more intensive record keeping on the results obtained by TVA fertilizer use.

At the same time, the broad objectives of soil conservation and farm management improvement are being furthered by sale of TVA fertilizers through farmer co-operatives and commercial distributors for specified new and improved uses, which are agreed upon for each state by the land grant state colleges, agencies of the U. S. Department of Agriculture, the distributors, and TVA. Today, in 36 states, distributors are accompanying their sales of TVA fertilizers with educational programs designed to bring about better and more productive land use. TVA makes available only enough fertilizer to demonstrate improved fertilizer practices or farming systems recommended by the land grant colleges, but which are not as yet generally adopted by farmers. Thus TVA fertilizer materials, amounting to less than 2 per cent of the national supply, are strategically used to promote the basic educational objectives of soil conservation and to increase the demand for fertilizers manufactured by private concerns.

But the job of test demonstration—just another word for "learning" and "teaching," of course—extends beyond the crops and meadows and pastures, the farmhouse and the barn. It includes the woodland on the farm. Fifty-four per cent of this valley is wooded, and of these 14,000,000 wooded acres over 40 per cent belong to farmers.

The farmer is beginning to look at his woodlands as a producer of continuous wood crops, a relatively new idea to him. He is also planting new forests at the rate of about 20,000 acres a year. TVA nurseries since 1934 have produced over 234 million forest tree seedlings for the reforestation of eroded or otherwise non-productive land. Many of these tree plantations are now coming into production, yielding pulpwood from thinnings. As the trees grow larger other products, including saw timber, can be taken from these same stands. These plantations help to save the soil, to hold the water on the land. They raise the farmer's income and help relieve the pressure to rely for cash upon soil-costly corn and cotton.

The plentiful rainfall and long growing season in the valley push trees along at an incredible rate. In private woodland and forest, on thousands of acres of TVA reservoir land, the forests of the valley are coming back.

Farmers and landowners generally, singly and in associations, have attacked the forest fire problem, extending countywide fire protection to 9,600,000 acres in 92 counties, whereas in 1933 this was virtually nonexistent. In some seventy counties scientific methods of timber management and harvesting are being demonstrated. The industry built upon the woods, about 5,000 sawmills and other wood-using industries turning out products valued at over $200 million a year, is being shored up, its once crumbling foundation greatly strengthened. The brave new trees that you see everywhere are in the pattern of the slowly changing region.

The change is not only on the land but beneath it as well. The minerals of the earth must be made to work for the people. The Tennessee Valley has a great variety of these minerals—more than fifty. Some of them had never been put to much use, or the existence of the reserves little known, such as the extensive deposits of spodumene (source of lithium) in North Carolina's mountains or the white clays of Tennessee. The many kinds of minerals have been sought out by TVA, co-operating with state agencies, and their extent ascertained, in some cases by extensive drilling, so that businessmen have had a reliable basis for many new industrial activities all over the valley, based on converting these ores to commercial use at a profit. Some of these minerals were once of too low a grade to attract private industry. Now many of them, with improved technology and increased demand, as experimentation sponsored by TVA has shown, can be economically used. Kaolin, a kind of clay, for example, had been known in North Carolina since colonial days, but it seemed cheaper and easier to bring clays for high-grade china from abroad than to find a way in which our own deposits could be used. To develop a refining method which would make that kaolin useful for American potteries was an early project of TVA. It proved a success. The North Carolina deposits are now extensively developed for this purpose by several private concerns.

A process developed at Muscle Shoals by TVA engineers enables production of high-quality aluminum from clays abundant in Tennessee, Alabama, and Mississippi. It we are ever again faced with the submarine warfare in the Caribbean that sent to the bottom dozens of bauxite-carrying ships in our merchant fleet during World War II, such a process will be one of several similar ones ready to help in supplying our vastly expanded aluminum plants, and conserve our domestic bauxite supplies.

A process also has been developed for smelting clays in an electric furnace to make aluminum-silicon alloys that have a number of potential uses. The process is being put to use commercially. Another process was worked out for extracting magnesium from olivine found in the valley. This mineral was found useful, too, in making fertilizer by fusing it with rock phosphate, and this process has been used in the United States and abroad. TVA helped a group of private companies work out a method for making lightweight concrete aggregate from valley shales. Experiments such as these continue, on the basis of TVA state laboratory co-operation. In these developments are the signs of other changes yet to come.

Facts about the region are often just as potent tools of resource development as TVA's giant earth-movers, or the tilted terracing machines. There has been carried on in this region in the past two decades a gathering of facts about its resources and its institutions probably not equaled for thoroughness in any other American region.

Facts about the sanitary condition of the streams, facts about the financial structure of local government units and about the forests, about recreational possibilities, about present and future transportation arteries. Facts about the kinds of land, classified in many ways for many different purposes. Aerial photographs of every foot of the valley, maps of such detail and accuracy that TVA's mappers have been called upon by the military services to make similarly exact maps of many strategic war areas outside this region and outside the country. Facts about factory buildings not now in use, which might be converted by an enterprising businessman. Facts about how much soil was washed from a field planted in cotton, compared with that from one in pasture or in forest. Facts about the schools, hospitals, farm tenantry, about rainfall. Facts about men and skills available for industry. Facts about industrial and domestic water supply, freight rates.

Not facts for their own sake, to be encased in dull "reports." Live facts that live people use today or will need tomorrow to help them make their decisions about industrial location, farming, education, public health. The power of knowledge is also at work changing a valley, releasing the resources of the region to raise the income level of the people.

Chapter 5

THE PEOPLE'S DIVIDEND

THE story thus far as I have recounted it has been chiefly one of physical changes in the Tennessee Valley. But what has been the yield to the people—to those who live in the region, and to the people of the country as a whole?

First of all, the level of income of the valley's people has been rising since 1933 at a rate well above the national average. Between 1933-1951 the per capita income of the people who live in those counties that are part of this TVA region of the Southeast increased 477 per cent as compared to an increase of 330 per cent in the nation and 442 per cent in seven Southeastern states as a whole. The relatively more rapid economic growth in these counties is reflected in the growth of business and industry. Employees in private business and industry grew from 447,800 in 1933 to 919,-400 in 1950, an increase of almost a half a million, or 105 per cent for the valley, while the national increase was 88 per cent and the growth in the whole of the adjacent Southeast was 97 per cent. Meanwhile, income from business and industry increased by almost three billion, or 645 per cent, as compared to 598 per cent in the Southeast and 489 per cent in the nation.

All the available figures—and the evidence of one's eyes—affirm the fact of a steadily rising income level. But the Tennessee Valley is *still* a region of relatively low income, about three fifths of the United States average. What is heartening, however, is that in 1943, ten years ago, it was less than half the U. S. average, and twenty years ago 44 per cent.

The greatly increased contribution of the valley's people and their businesses toward the cost of the Federal government, through income taxes, is another index of the change since 1933.

In 1933, when their income was only $836 million (less than a billion dollars), valley people paid only about $3 million in individual federal income taxes. But in 1950, when their income had risen to $5.5 billion, they paid almost $300 million, so that the valley's share of the nation's tax load has doubled (from .86 per cent in 1933 to 1.71 per cent in 1951).[1]

Altogether the nation's gross investment of just over a billion dollars in TVA has amounted to about nine dollars per year for each of the six million valley people.

The dimension of these figures can be measured by comparison with the $5.5 billion yearly income of valley people—now almost $5 billion more than in 1933. The per capita income was $940 in 1951. This was $777 more than in 1933—or some 89 times the average yearly federal investment in TVA.

The annual income taxes paid into the federal treasury by valley people is about $300 million more than in 1933—or almost six times the yearly investment in TVA.

The effect of the region's development on the growth of private enterprise puts the spotlight where it belongs—on what the people have accomplished for themselves. The expansion of private business and industry is clearly the most substantial accomplishment of all in the valley in the last two decades. Although large amounts of public capital have been expended in the region itself, in point of fact two thirds of the TVA expenditures for material, equipment, and miscellaneous services were spent *outside* the valley. The valley's share of government work is on the lean side. Moreover the proportion of national and Southeastern Federal civil employees in the valley region has declined rather steadily since 1934. The result was that in 1950 the Byrd report on the Reduction of Nonessential Federal Expenditures showed that Federal employment per thousand total population in the valley region was only three quarters of the national and Southeastern ratios. Likewise, valley people draw less upon government sources of income. Income per capita from all government sources in the valley in 1951 was only

[1] But it should be noted that the lowering of the individual federal tax base increased the tax take more in low-income areas, such as this is, than in high-income states. Part of the tax increase is also due to change in tax laws.

three fourths the nation's average. Again, the Byrd Committee showed that between 1934-51 the Federal grants-in-aid to states amounted to $385 per person in the nation, but in Tennessee the average was only $367, or $18 below the national grants.

What has happened to the businesses of the people since the advent of TVA?

Farming as a business, as I have already indicated, is moving forward as the fruitfulness and stability of the land increase year by year. Farming has always been the number one private enterprise in the valley region; this continues to be true. But in view of the great and continuing rise of industry in the valley this may no longer be true in another decade.

What of the industrial progress of the region? Between 1933 and World War II the valley saw the addition or huge expansion of several large industries devoted to the basic materials of modern industry. Aluminum is one of these. The Aluminum Company of America was a pioneer industry in the region, building hydroelectric dams and factories years before the TVA was created; these were vastly expanded, partly as a consequence of co-operative business arrangements with the TVA. Phosphate chemical works—including those of Monsanto Chemical and Victor Chemical, two of the largest and finest such works in the country—were the first large industrial plants to be added after the advent of TVA.

The increase in heavy industry, well begun by 1940, was enormously accelerated by the coming of the war. In the first edition of this book, written during the war and, of course, before the atom bomb fell on Hiroshima, I said, referring to war-born expansion of industry: "For reasons of security little of this expansion can now be told. But when the full story of a once industrially laggard valley's part in production for war can be revealed, it will rank as one of the miracles of American enterprise, the kind of miracle that is marveled at when it occurs across the seas, rarely comprehended close at home."

Since that writing, the dramatic story of the secret atomic materials plant at Oak Ridge, Tennessee, has been told and retold. It was the time-tested ability of the TVA organization to meet "impossible" time schedules for added power supply, and within estimates of cost, that was a decisive element in locating the atomic plant—an insatiable eater of electric power—in this valley, together with other huge power-consuming plants making basic war materials. The further expansion of Oak Ridge since the end of the war, and the more recent establishment in the valley of "another Oak Ridge" near Paducah, Kentucky, are a logical extension of the original decisions.

It was chiefly the prodigious demand for electric power for the nation's atomic expansion program that compelled TVA to begin the erection of a series of coal-burning electric plants, with ultimate capacity greater than that of the entire Tennessee River's water power put together.

But industries related to national defense, huge as they are, constitute only part of the picture of this industrial expansion in the valley and the area served by locally managed distributors of TVA power. New plants for making synthetic fibers have been built by du Pont, American Enka, Monsanto, and American Viscose. Heavy industrial chemicals flow to all parts of the nation from plants recently built below Kentucky Dam by B. F. Goodrich, Pennsylvania Salt, and National Carbide. Monsanto and du Pont have also built other plants in the valley, as have the Quaker Oats Company and the National Carbon Company. The Shea Chemical Company is now pioneering in the more efficient use of the valley's phosphate resources.

The rise of heavy industries is matched by the establishment and expansion, both before the war and since, of a great variety of light industries. These have increased rapidly in number and diversity. In 1933 the number of manufacturing establishments operating in the valley was 2,400. By 1947 there were 5,900 and by 1950 the total number of manufacturing establishments had grown to 6,620, an increase over 1933 of 4,220, or 175 per cent, as compared with a national increase of 86 per cent.

The net increase of factories during the 1940's amounted to about 250 per year. These new and expanded industries, which are distributed widely throughout the valley region, have resulted in increased diversification of industrial activity and fuller utilization of valley resources than existed previously. And taken together, they represent an increase in the nation's productive capacity—new to the valley and new to the nation. Among the 3,000 names of new valley firms, only a handful have moved to the region from some other section of the country.

A similar type of growth pattern appears when one examines the figures on employment and payrolls in private manufacturing. By 1951 employees had increased 229,000 over 1933, or 135 per cent, compared to an increase in the nation of 120 per cent in that period. Meanwhile, valley private payrolls from manufacturing had increased by more than a billion dollars—from $127 million to $1,138 million. And as of 1951 the income derived by the valley from private business, construction industry, and mining was 61 per cent of the region's entire income, compared with 54 per cent in 1933.

There is the greatest diversity in the products of the 4,200 additional plants that have come into operation in the valley and TVA power service area since 1933. They range from the processing of frozen foods and the production of cheese to the manufacture of aircraft and sewing machines, mattresses, bottle washers, stoves, flour, inlaid wood, barrel heads and staves, electric water heaters, calculating machines, furniture, hats and shoes, pencils, carbon electrodes, textiles, boats, horse collars, ground mica, oxygen and acetylene, metal dies, ax handles, barites, and so on. The development of these industries provides an expanding market for raw materials which are being produced on the land, in the forest, and in the mines of the valley. Many new small commercial enterprises and industries are the immediate result of opportunities for profit provided by the chain of lakes that make the Tennessee River a new arc of beauty through the countryside, a major business development to which further reference is made later in this book.

The valley still has a long way to go. There are many factories yet to be built, in an area with such great potential wealth and with less than its economic share of the nation's industry and manufacturing. There are many new jobs to be created by the laboratories and businessmen out of the region's dormant resources. There are millions of acres yet to be restored to full productiveness. There are more trees to plant, houses, schools, roads, and hospitals to build. Many new skills have been learned—among farmers, industrial workers in the new factories, the tens of thousands of men and women who have added to their skills in the course of their work for the TVA—but lack of training is still a heavy handicap to be overcome. The task is barely begun—but the Tennessee Valley is certainly on its way.

Democracy is on the march in this valley. Not only because of the physical changes or the figures of increased income and economic activity. One's faith in this as a region with a great future is built most of all upon the great capacities and the spirit of the people. The notion that had been expressed that the region's problem, as one commentator put it, is one of "human salvage" completely missed the mark. As the passing years have proved, the human resources of this valley are its greatest asset and advantage. The people seized upon these modern tools of opportunity and raised up their own leadership. They have shown an ability to hold themselves to tough assignments with a singleness of purpose and a resourcefulness in doing much with little that will be difficult to match anywhere in the country.

This advent of opportunity has brought with it the rise of a confident, sure, chesty feeling. The evidence is everywhere. It was epitomized in an editorial in the Decatur, Alabama, *Daily*. The editor, a community leader, candidly related the doleful past of his home town, and contrasted it with the optimistic and fruitful present, for today Decatur is one of the most enterprising and promising small cities in the interior United States. "What happened?" he asked, and then he answered:

> We can write of great dams . . . of the building of home-grown industry and of electricity at last coming to the farms of thousands of farm people in the Valley. *Yet the significant advance has been made in the thinking of a people.* They are no longer afraid. *They have caught the vision of their own powers.* They can stand now and talk out in meeting and say that if industry doesn't come into the Valley from other sections, then we'll build our own industry. This they are doing today.

These changes were not wrought by TVA. In point of fact, the very essence of TVA's function in the undertaking, as I shall later indicate in detail, was at every hand to minimize what it was to do, and to encourage and stimulate the broadest possible *coalition* of all forces. Except upon the river itself, the chief role throughout has been that of private initiative, ideas, funds, and efforts, on farms and in factories. After that has come, in importance, state funds and state activities, local communities, clubs, schools, associations, co-operatives. Scores of other federal agencies co-operated—the Department of Agriculture through such agencies as the Rural Electrification Administration, the scientific research bureaus, the co-operative loan banks, and the Forest Service; the Public Health Service; the Army Corps of Engineers, which prior to 1933 had prepared a preliminary survey of the Tennessee River widely known as "House Document 328"; the Bureau of Reclamation, which prepared designs for early Norris and Wheeler dams, the Geological Survey, the Bureau of Mines, the Bureau of Fish and Wildlife Service, the National Park Service; the Geodetic Survey and the Weather Bureau—and so on; the list, if complete, would include most national agencies.

How much of the money of the people of the entire country has the TVA spent? What is there to show for that expenditure in useful capital assets? Is the TVA worth its cost, measured in benefits to the country?

It is at least as important that a public enterprise should produce benefits and values as great as or greater than their cost as it is when the undertaking is a private one. And, to those who are studying the feasibility of developments of a comparable character, the question of cost and the balancing of investment of materials and manpower against the yield the investment produces are considerations of the first consequence.

I shall not, of course, go into all the possible technical ramifications of TVA's financial affairs, since they are of little interest to the general reader. The facts are all readily available in TVA's financial statements,[2] in its annual reports to Congress, in thousands of pages of testimony before Congressional committees, and in technical books and writings on the subject. I shall here only sum-

[2] TVA, since 1938, "probably has the finest accounting system in the entire government and probably one of the best accounting systems in the entire world. . . . There is no private enterprise in this country that has any better." Testimony of T. Coleman Andrews, Commissioner of Internal Revenue, given at the time he was Director of the Corporation Audits Division, General Accounting Office. (See Hearings, House Subcommittee on Appropriations, 80th Cong., Part 1, Independent Offices Appropriation Bill for 1948, p. 36; 39-40.)

marize the basic facts and the considerations that may be useful in judging the significance of those facts.

In judging whether the country is currently getting its money's worth from these large expenditures, and whether the product of TVA's investment of the people's money has been worth the outlay, it must be remembered that much of the return, to the Tennessee Valley and the nation, is in benefits which cannot be exactly measured. It is only the investment in power facilities that yields the federal taxpayers a return in dollars in addition to other benefits. For power is the only major product of the TVA investment that is sold for dollars. Like most other expenditures of government throughout the nation, such as those for the development of agriculture, of forests and minerals and waterways and ocean ports, TVA's nonpower expenditures do not yield their return in dollars paid in as income to the federal treasury. That the return is not measurable in dollars does not mean that it is any less real.

The benefits of TVA's navigable channel are an example. These go to shippers, to industries using the channel, to consumers of grain, oil, gasoline, and so on. This is true, of course, not only on the Tennessee but also on the Ohio, the Illinois, the Missouri, all of the many rivers where billions of federal funds, contributed by taxpayers from all parts of the country, have been expended for a century and more. So it is not possible to record the same precise dollar measure of navigation benefits as it is with power. The value created by these expenditures does not appear on TVA's books as money income.

Likewise, the benefits of flood control produced by these dams extend all the way down the Mississippi River to the mouth of the Red. But since TVA is not paid for those benefits in dollars, the taxpayers' return cannot be measured in that way. And so it is with TVA's expenditures to produce phosphate plant food, and to demonstrate its use to control soil erosion not only in the Tennessee Valley but in Minnesota, Wisconsin, New York, Iowa, and many other states outside this region. So with forestry, industrial research, mapping.

The *cost* of such development work is recorded on *TVA's books, in the accounting terminology, as "net expense"; but the benefits appear on the balance sheet of the region and of the nation.* And, as with public improvement expenditures generally the country over, since the days of Henry Clay, it was anticipated that such expenditures would be repaid to the taxpayers not directly in dollars, but indirectly in benefits.

Turning now to TVA's expenditures and, first, the cost of developing the river: TVA's financial balance sheet as of June 30, 1952, shows that to provide a 650-mile navigable channel, flood protection, and power supply the TVA had a gross investment in completed plant of about $1,036,000,000. Of this amount approximately 68 per cent, or $702,000,000, represents the gross investment in power facilities. The river control works are substantially completed, although additional minor dams are planned for some of the tributary streams.

The wholesale rates for electric power, and therefore the revenues paid to TVA by the electric purchasers, include an allowance for depreciation that will recover the cost of depreciable property over its useful life. Subtracting the accumulated allowance for this purpose to date from the gross investment in power facilities leaves a net investment of $596,000,000.

The money for this net investment came from three sources— from funds appropriated by Congress, from bonds issued by TVA and sold to the U.S. Treasury, and from the net income of the power business. To avoid unduly complicating this statement, I shall treat the $596,000,000 as a single amount, representing the power investment upon which the American people are entitled to a return. What dividends for the people does this investment yield?

As to power, to arrive at an answer is relatively easy, since the power is sold and the revenues provide a dollar measurement.

In the fiscal year ended June 30, 1952, the sale of power yielded revenues to TVA in excess of $95,000,000. Operating expenses to produce that power, including over $3,000,000 of statutory tax payments and almost $14,000,000 in depreciation charges, left net operating revenue of $25,800,000. The average net power investment during the year was $555,000,000. Thus, in 1952, on the funds they had invested in TVA power facilities, the American people earned a return of 4.7 per cent.

In the whole period, from the beginning to the most recent reports, i.e., 1933 to 1952 inclusive, net operating revenue totaled

$215,000,000 and provided an average return of better than 4¼ per cent per annum on the power investment. During this period interest rates paid by the Federal Treasury on its borrowings—i.e., the cost of borrowed money to the government—were, on the average, in the order of 2 per cent. With minor exceptions Congress elected to provide TVA's power funds by appropriations. If, however, TVA had *borrowed* all its capital (including the portion represented by reinvested earnings) and paid interest on it at this average rate of 2 per cent, its total net operating revenue since 1933 would have covered such interest costs, plus a margin of over $100,000,000. The fact that Congress chose to advance most of TVA's power funds by appropriation rather than by authorizing TVA to issue interest-bearing bonds for its entire capital requirements does not in any way change the arithmetic respecting the return earned for the Treasury; *the margin over costs was earned*—which is the important thing. Whether it is called "return on the investment" or interest or some other terminology is secondary.

The total net income earned by the power system of TVA as of June 30, 1952, has actually been accumulated only since 1937, for between 1933 and 1937 the TVA was not a going power concern; the system was far from readiness; operations were beset by a multiplicity of lawsuits and injunctions which, while none were held to have merit in the courts of appeal, did prevent anything resembling a normal sale of the power produced by the river.

The size of the net income and the rate of return earned on the country's investment in power facilities indicate pretty clearly that the power asset of the valley is certainly worth its cost.

These calculations take into account only dollar returns to TVA, and none of the indirect benefits. But such benefits are many. Among them are the savings to consumers as a result of greatly reduced rates, savings which are calculated to total $58,000,000 per annum. Nor do the calculations of dollar return take account of the effects of low-cost power, used in unprecedented quantities in this region in such a way as to benefit business in other regions. Nor do the figures of return seek to measure the value to the country of the fact that it was largely because of power from this river that in 1943 America was able to build huge fleets of bombers to send over

Europe and the South Pacific, and to produce the atomic materials that ended the resistance of Japan.

By a provision in the Government Corporations Appropriation Act, 1948, the Congress required that TVA repay the U.S. Treasury investment in the TVA power system—represented at that time by appropriated funds and outstanding bonds totaling about $348,-000,000—within a period of forty years. Appropriated funds invested after 1948 were required to be repaid within forty years after the new power facilities they represented were placed in operation. Thus the Congress has defined the minimum amounts it believes should be taken from the business, leaving the remaining earnings to be reinvested in the system or paid into the Treasury at the discretion of the TVA Board of Directors.

Since a part of the TVA power investment is represented by reinvested revenues rather than appropriations, it is apparent that a return from power operations averaging something less than 2½ per cent annually will provide sufficient funds to meet the repayments required by Congress. In comparison, the average annual return on TVA's power investment over the entire period of its operations—1933 to 1952—has exceeded 4¼ per cent, nearly 2 per cent more than required for capital repayments. By the end of the fiscal year 1952, a total of $66,131,000 had been thus repaid to the U.S. Treasury from power revenues, and of this sum $42,500,000 had been repaid since passage of the 1948 Act. In the fiscal year beginning July 1, 1953, a sum of $25,288,000 is budgeted for cash payments to the Treasury and retirement of bonds.

There is an additional value that attaches to the power facilities of the river not to be overlooked in resource development. For the total investment of $1,036,000,000 in river development produces not only power, but also the benefits of navigation and flood control. *By combining these three functions in single structures* that serve all three purposes, so that costs common to all three may be shared, great economies are produced. Navigation and flood control benefits have thereby been secured at a lower cost. Similarly, because navigation and flood control are combined in the same structure with power, power is produced more cheaply than if the sole purpose of the structure were power.

Congress directed that TVA set down on its books what appeared to the Board to be the proper portions of the total investment attributable severally to power, to navigation, and to flood control. Of the total flood control, navigation, and power investment, approximately 68 per cent has been allocated to power, 15 per cent to navigation, and 17 per cent to flood control. These allocations have been made on the basis of elaborate technical studies.

The operational expense of providing navigation and flood control in the fiscal year 1952 was $4,932,000. This figure includes not only the costs of operation but also substantial charges for depreciation. From the beginning of the enterprise to the end of the fiscal year 1952, the total net cost of supplying navigation and flood control has been about $51,000,000.

What this expenditure has yielded in benefits I have summarized in a preceding chapter. Such benefits cannot be measured exactly in terms of dollars, of course, although some pretty close approximations of direct benefits can be made and compared with the costs. A saving of about eight million dollars annually already accrues to shippers using the channel, and traffic is still far from fully developed. In comparison, all the Federal costs of navigation on the river—TVA's costs, including depreciation; the costs of the U. S. Army Engineers who operate the locks; and the costs of the U. S. Coast Guard, which is responsible for channel marking and similar services it performs on all federal waters—amounted to $3,600,000. The difference of $4,400,000 between the direct shipper benefits and the federal costs is equal to a return of more than 3 per cent on the public investment in the Tennessee River navigation system.

With respect to flood control, estimates of the direct flood damage averted by operation of the TVA system from 1936, when Norris Dam was placed in operation, through 1952 amount to more than $51,000,000; whereas the cumulative costs, including depreciation, of providing flood control over the years have amounted to only a little more than $22,000,000.

The figure of $51,000,000, as a matter of fact, falls short of being fully inclusive. It does not include, for example, damage averted in the Birds Point-New Madrid floodway in southeastern Missouri during the January-February flood of 1950. The TVA system reduced the flood crest at Cairo, Illinois, by two feet, at a time when the

Army Corps of Engineers was preparing to open the "fuse-plug" levee and inundate the floodway. In view of the possibility that the floodway might have to be used, hundreds of people in this 200-square-mile area moved from their homes. Had it been necessary to use the floodway, the damage would have amounted to many millions of dollars.

Floods do not come every year, nor always in the same magnitude. However, conservative estimates of the average annual benefits of TVA flood control amount to more than $11,000,000 a year, over half of which is attributable to the lower Ohio and Mississippi River basins. In comparison, TVA's flood control costs in the last fiscal year were less than $2,500,000. The difference between these two sums—$8,500,000—represents a return of over 5 per cent on the TVA flood control investment.

There are in other valleys many dams built solely for the purpose of controlling floods. They were paid for and are maintained by the taxpayers of the whole country. There are scores of dams, locks, and other structures all up and down the Ohio, Mississippi, Missouri, and other rivers, built and maintained solely for the purpose of making those streams navigable. The total cost of building these navigation structures—running into the billions—was not paid by those who live in those valleys but by the people of the entire country, all of whom benefit by these investments.

But in the Tennessee Valley (and recently in other regions) a *single* dam *combines* in its design and structure the functions of a flood control dam, a navigation dam and locks, *and* the production of power. The fairness of charging part of the cost of such a combination dam to *each* of the separate functions of flood control, navigation, and power seems manifest. Yet there are still some critics of TVA's power program who year after year argue that TVA is "in the red," supporting the claim by the simple accounting device of charging the total investment of these combined-function dams *all to power*. It is on this basis that these opponents of TVA claim that TVA power is "subsidized by the taxpayers of the rest of the country."

But so long as dams for flood control and for navigation are paid for, in other valleys than the Tennessee, by the taxpayers of the country as a whole, it would be unjust and discriminatory not to follow the same principle in the TVA region. Of course when TVA builds a steam-electric plant, *wholly* devoted to power production, then of course that investment and expense should be and is charged 100 per cent to power. But to penalize the Tennessee Valley for adopting a more economical way of providing navigation and flood control than exists on the Ohio or Missouri, for example, is neither sensible nor just.

The real questions, I submit, are: (1) Is the public's over-all investment in TVA a good one, yielding returns—in dollars or in other ways—that justify the expenditures, in the interest of the whole country? (2) Do TVA's power facilities carry their costs and pay a return to the taxpayers?

Leaving the river and turning to the cost of fertilizer and munitions development, in the fiscal year ended June 30, 1952, this program resulted in a net income of $1,484,000. This includes not only the production of fertilizer but the administration of the demonstration farm activity in the Tennessee Valley and in other parts of the country. The expense of mapping, forestry, industrial, and all other kinds of research—in short, the entire development program, exclusive of fertilizer and agricultural development—totaled $2,201,000 for the year. These, too, are expenditures that do not yield a return in dollars, but they do yield a return in the building of a region and a nation. During the nineteen-year period the net expense of TVA's land restoration and all other development work has been $89,000,000; in addition $35,000,000 has been spent on fertilizer plants and equipment, including the phosphate plant at Muscle Shoals and the phosphate ore reserves, which are, of course, capital investments.

The total TVA capital expenditures for every purpose whatever to June 30, 1952, including work in progress as well as plant in service, were more than $1,300,000,000.

Are the expenditures for this entire development worth their cost to the country? There is, of course, no way of settling the question by statistical proof. You must look at the valley, appraise what the expenditure of these funds has done in increasing the productivity of the region and of the nation. You must look at the effect of the growing strength and new vitality of the valley on the total strength of the whole country in war and peace. One has to consider what it is worth to the country to provide opportunity to thousands of men and women in this valley—farmers, businessmen engaged in new enterprises, workers in new factories.

This is not a question that accountants or financial experts can answer for us. Whether the over-all results in this region are worth what they have cost is something the citizen must answer for himself as a matter not of arithmetic but of the highest public policy.

Chapter 6

A NEW WAY—AN OLD TASK

In order to master Nature we must first obey her.
—FRANCIS BACON

A NEW chapter in American public policy was written when Congress in May of 1933 passed the law creating the TVA. For the first time since the trees fell before the settlers' ax, America set out to command nature not by defying her, as in that wasteful past, but by understanding and acting upon her first law—the oneness of men and natural resources, the unity that binds together land, streams, forests, minerals, farming, industry, mankind.

This, of course, is not what the creation of TVA meant to most people who read in their newspapers of the action of Congress. For TVA was then ordinarily thought of simply as a "power" project, a venture in public ownership of hydro-electricity. And even today, in spite of its wide range of activities, it is as a "power" project that many people still regard the TVA. Why there has been this limited picture of the scope and purpose of the Authority is wholly understandable.

For fifteen years before TVA came into being Congressional and public debate centered largely on a single potential resource of the Tennessee River, hydro-electric power. For long years there had been determined efforts to dispose of the government dam and power plant at Muscle Shoals in Alabama, built with public funds for World War I, as if it were like any other of the flotsam left over from that war—the trucks and shoes and trench shovels—to be knocked down to the highest bidder. It was simply regarded as a power plant, either to be dealt with as such a plant in the hands of a private operator would be, or, if continued under public control, to be limited to the sale of generated power for distribution at a profit by private industry.

How those power facilities were to be used was the major question which attracted public discussion down the years. That question was settled by the passage of the Act creating TVA. But in the end it was not settled on the narrow issue of "public ownership" of power. The message of President Roosevelt urging approval of the Norris bill (which became a law with his signature on May 18, 1933) boldly proposed a new and fundamental change in the development of our country's resources. The words of the President's message were not only eloquent; there was in them a creativeness and an insight born of New York State's experience with the autonomous public corporation—the so-called "authority"—and in establishing regional planning as a political reality. That understanding was matured at his Georgia home, in long days of thinking of the problems of the South and its relation to the whole nation.

It is clear [the message read] that the Muscle Shoals development is but a small part of the potential public usefulness of the entire Tennessee River. Such use, if envisioned in its entirety, transcends mere power development: it enters the wide fields of flood control, soil erosion, afforestation, elimination from agricultural use of marginal lands, and distribution and diversification of industry. In short, this power development of war days leads logically to national planning for a complete river watershed involving many states and the future lives and welfare of millions. It touches and gives life to all forms of human concerns.

The President then suggested

legislation to create a Tennessee Valley Authority—a corporation clothed with the power of government but possessed of the flexibility and initiative of a private enterprise. It should be charged with the broadest duty of planning for the proper use, conservation, and development of the natural resources of the Tennessee River drainage basin and its adjoining territory for the general social and economic welfare of the Nation. This authority should also be clothed with the necessary power to carry these plans into effect. Its duty should be the rehabilitation of the Muscle Shoals development and the co-ordination of it with the wider plan.

Many hard lessons have taught us the human waste that results from lack of planning. Here and there a few wise cities and counties have

looked ahead and planned. But our Nation has "just grown." It is time
to extend planning to a wider field, in this instance comprehending in
one great project many States directly concerned with the basin of one
of our greatest rivers.

The TVA Act was nothing inadvertent or impromptu. It was rather
the deliberate and well-considered creation of a new national policy.
For the first time in the history of the nation, the resources of a river
were not only to be "envisioned in their entirety"; they were to be
developed *in that unity with which nature herself regards her resources*—the waters, the land, and the forests together, a "seamless
web"—just as Maitland saw "the unity of all history," of which one
strand cannot be touched without affecting every other strand for
good or ill.

Under this new policy, the opportunity of creating wealth for the
people from the resources of their valley was to be faced as a single
problem. To help integrate the many parts of that problem into a
unified whole was to be the responsibility of one agency. The development of the Tennessee Valley's resources was not to be dissected
into separate bits that would fit into the jurisdictional pigeon holes
into which the instrumentalities of government had by custom become divided. It was not conceded that at the hour of Creation the
Lord had divided and classified natural resources to conform to the
organization chart of the federal government. The particular and
limited concerns of private individuals or agencies in the development of this or that resource were to be fitted into the principle of
unity. What God had made one, man was to develop as one.

"Envisioned in its entirety" this river, like every river in the
world, had many potential assets. It could yield hydro-electric power
for the comfort of the people in their homes, could promote prosperity on their farms and foster the development of industry. But the
same river by the very same dams, if they were wisely designed,
could be made to provide a channel for navigation. The river could
also be made to provide fun for fishermen and fish for food, pleasure
from boating and swimming, a water supply for homes and factories.
But the river also presented an account of liabilities. It threatened
the welfare of the people by its recurrent floods; pollution from
industrial wastes and public sewage diminished its value as a source

of water supply and for recreation; its current carried to the sea the soil of the hills and fields to be lost there to men forever.

To a single agency, the TVA, the planning for the greatest sum total of these potentialities of the river for good and evil were entrusted. But the river was to be seen as part of the larger pattern of the region, one asset of the many that in nature are interwoven: the land, the minerals, the waters, the forests—and all of these as one —in their relation to the lives of the valley's people. It was the total benefit to all that was to be the common goal and the new agency's responsibility.

That is not the way public resource development had heretofore been undertaken in this country. Congress in creating TVA broke with the past. No single agency had in this way ever been assigned the unitary task of developing a river so as to release the total benefit from its waters for the people. Other rivers developed by private interests or public agencies serve to illustrate the contrast. On these rivers it is the common practice in public projects as well as private to build a single dam without first having fixed upon a general plan that will ultimately insure the full use of the whole river as a unit. There are dams built for the single purpose of power development. Such individual dams, in order to yield an immediate return in power, impair or destroy the river's full development of power at other sites, for they were not designed or built with the whole river thought of as it is in nature, a unit. These power dams are not built or operated to control floods, and do not provide a continuous navigable channel. The full usefulness of that river is lessened. Similarly, hundreds of millions of dollars in public funds have been expended for the single purpose of navigation on some of our rivers, but most of the dams constructed will not control the rivers' floods or create electric energy. They now stand as massive barriers against the erection of multi-purpose structures.

Over a long period of years hundreds of millions of dollars have been spent for levees to hold the waters back on the lower reaches of the Mississippi, the Ohio, and the Missouri, but at the headwaters there were no reservoir dams that could make local levee protection effective.

And through the long years there has been a continuing disregard of nature's truth: that in any valley of the world what happens on the *river* is largely determined by what happens on the *land*—by the kind of crops that farmers plant and harvest, by the type of machines they use, by the number of trees they cut down. The full benefits of stream and of soil cannot be realized by the people if the water and the land are not developed in harmony.

If the soil is exposed, unprotected from the rains by cover and by roots, the people will be poor and the river will be muddy, heavy with the best soil of the fields. And as a consequence each year the farmers will be forced more and more to use their land in ways that speed up this cycle of ruin, until the cover and then the top soil itself are wholly gone. When that day comes, as it has in the great reaches of China's sorrowful Yellow River Valley, or in once flourishing Mesopotamia, now gaunt and desolate, then the rains run off the land almost as rapidly as water runs from a pavement. Even a moderate rainfall forces the river from its banks, and every downpour brings disastrous floods, destroying crops and homes and bridges and highways, not only where the land is poor, but down the river's length, down in the areas where people are more prosperous, where the soil is still protected and factories have been built at the river's bend. Industries and railroads will be interrupted, farms flooded out, towns and villages destroyed, while heavy silt deposits fill the power reservoirs and stop up the channels of navigation.

It is otherwise where land is covered with sod or trees, and cultivated each season with the purpose of holding the rain where it falls. Such land literally serves as a water reservoir, a part of a system of flood control and river development, quite as directly as dams that stretch from bank to bank to hold the waters back. In many locations, after such proper land-use programs have been rather fully developed, the results should make it possible to reduce the magnitude and cost of engineering structures required for water control.

The farmers' new pastures and meadows themselves are reservoirs. If the changed farming practices now in use on many tens of thousands of Tennessee Valley farms were applied to all the agricultural area of our watershed (as some day I am confident they will be), the soil might absorb as much as a quarter of the customary 23-inch surface run-off of rain each year.

This is of course nothing new, nothing discovered by the TVA.

That a river could offer many benefits and a variety of hazards, that its improvement through engineering structures is inseparable from the development and use of the land of the watershed, has been recognized for many years by scientists and engineers. For over a generation a distinguished line of conservationists had seen this truth and written and spoken of it with great force; not the least among these were President Theodore Roosevelt and Gifford Pinchot. And as a matter of fact almost any farmer, standing in his barn door while he watches a torrential rain beat upon his land and fill his creek, could see that much. The point is that knowledge of this inseparability of land and streams has only once, here on this river, been carried into our national *action*. And though the force of example has compelled the formation of interagency committees in some river basins to carry on conversations about "co-ordination,"[1] it is still true that on every other watershed Congress continues to turn our rivers over to engineers of one agency to develop while farm experts of other bureaus or agencies concern themselves with the land. Thus far it is only in the Valley of the Tennessee that Congress has directed that these resources be dealt with as a whole, not separately.

The principles of unity whereby this valley has gone about the restoration of its land and the multiplication of the land's usefulness are, of course, the same as those that governed turning the river to man's account. The development of soil and its increased productivity are not simply problems of land, of farming, and of agricultural science, any more than the development of a river is only water control, dams, and engineering techniques. The restoration of land fertility, the healing of gullies, the reforestation of hillsides, these are no more ends in themselves than are flood control, navigation, and power. As the river is not separable from the land, so the land is

[1] In a spirited criticism of the Missouri Valley method of resource development, through a Missouri Basin Inter-Agency Committee on which sit representatives of a whole array of Washington-directed Federal agencies and representatives of the affected States, a Task Force of the Hoover Commission said: "The present system may also be criticized because there is no single administrative center in the region which can take leadership in pulling together the many segments for a comprehensive resources program for the entire basin. . . . They do not assure a basin-wide and active consciousness that *the basin is a unit for coordinated management* . . ." (My italics.)

inseparable from the forests and minerals, from the factories and shops, from the people making their living from their resources.

Here, too, the methods this valley has followed to achieve its purposes break sharply with those long prevailing. The methods differ because to think of resources as a unity compels the use of different ways. The idea of unity makes it inescapable that each man's farm must also be seen as one operating unit. The farm, too, is a "seamless web."

To the farmer on his land the problems do not fit into neat cubicles labeled "forestry" or "soil chemistry" or "mechanical engineering," nor to him is soil erosion or holding water on the land separate from the whole business of making a living on the land. And so in the way TVA goes about its responsibilities there are no "jurisdictional" lines, no excluding of the chemical engineer, say, because this is a "farm" problem, or of the businessman or the inventor because soil erosion is an "agricultural problem," or of a county or state expert because agriculture is a "national" question. The invention by this valley's technicians of a new kind of machine and the decision of a businessman to produce and market it may be almost as relevant to land restoration as check dams in the gullies, if it thereby enables the farmer to make a living by raising soil-conserving crops. The invention of a portable thresher, or a furrow seeder, designed to overcome specific economic obstacles in the farmer's path toward land conservation, are just as real factors in land restoration as the terracing of the slopes.

Because they sinned against the unity of nature, because they developed some one resource without regard to its relation to every other resource in the life of man, ancient civilizations have fallen into decay and lie buried in oblivion. Everywhere in the world the trail of unbalanced resource development is marked by poverty, where prosperity seemed assured; by ugliness and desolation, with towns now dying that once were thriving; by land that once supported gracious living now eroded and bare, and over wide areas the chill of death to the ambitions of the enterprising young and to the security of the mature.

How industry came to Ducktown in the mountains of eastern Tennessee a generation ago is one such story. Copper ore was discovered; mining began; a smeltery was built. One of the resources of this remote region was being developed; it meant new jobs, income to supplement farming and forestry. But the developers had only copper in their plans. The magnificent hardwood forests to a distance of seven miles were cut and burned as fuel for the smelter's roasting ovens. The sulphur fumes from the stacks destroyed the thin cover that remained; not only the trees but every sign of living vegetation was killed and the soil became poison to life.

The dead land, shorn of its cover of grass and trees was torn mercilessly by the rains; and the once lovely and fruitful earth was cut into deep gullies that widened into desolate canyons twenty and more feet deep. No one can look upon this horror as it still is today without a shudder. Silt, swept from unprotected slopes, filled the streams and destroyed fish life. The water was robbed of its value for men, for animals, and for industry, while farther down the stream a reservoir was filling with silt. One of Ducktown's resources, copper, had been developed. But all its other resources had been destroyed in the process. The people and their institutions suffered in the end.

All this desolation caused as much pain to the officials of the copper company as it did to the lovers of nature. For balanced resource development is not, as the naïve appear to believe, a simple moral tale of "bad men" versus "good men." It is much more than that. In fact, in this case, the early operators came to see the point better than most people, for they had to pay cash in damages for some of this destruction, after long and bitter lawsuits by the injured landowners.

The fumes from Ducktown's copper smelteries are harmless now. Indeed, in the hands of a successor company a new technical process that makes the fumes harmless yields a by-product—sulphuric acid —now more valuable than the copper itself. The copper company itself is co-operating actively with the TVA in an extensive reforestation program on the area the fumes destroyed. What it has already cost and what it ultimately will cost, in manpower, materials, and the dollars of taxpayers, because copper was developed rather than the resources of Ducktown as a unity, has never been calculated. But the bill will be high.

This case seems to be extreme only because the accounting came quickly and was so clearly evident to the eye. It often takes some time before the balance shows that more is being subtracted than added from the assets of a region. But there is no escape from the arithmetic. The fall in the "water table," the sub-surface level of water, threatens industry's water supply in the Ohio Valley. The forest areas of northern Wisconsin and Michigan are dotted with towns that are dying and people who are stranded and poor. Lumber was "developed" from the wealth of the forests; there was prosperity for a time. But farming and fish and game were destroyed, and eventually the forests. Now in some regions there is next to nothing to support the towns, the highways and the schools and human beings. Unless the benefit of the people is the purpose, and the principle of the unified development of resources is the method, the harvest in the end is only such bitter fruits as these.

The "played-out" farmlands of the South, now in the process of rebuilding, were "mined" to grow a single crop of cotton: they are one more illustration of the remorseless arithmetic of nature. Here once lovely manor houses stand seedy and deserted because their foundation, the soil, has been exhausted, romantic monuments to a national tragedy of waste. And the great towers of Manhattan and Chicago, the modern business streets of Omaha on the prairies, all rest on the same foundations as the old plantation manor—the land, the waters, the minerals, and the forests. We are all in this together, cities and countryside.

There is no security or safety for us anywhere if nature's resources are exhausted. This day of machines and increasing populations multiplies our jeopardy. For this we must remember: Unless nature's laws of restoration are observed, modern technology can compress a once gradual process of resource exhaustion into the quick cycle of a generation or two.

The effect of large supplies of low-cost electricity upon industrialization illustrates the modern hazard. For electricity is not freed of these dangers simply because it is publicly owned, as some single-track enthusiasts would appear to imply. Electric power from the Tennessee River has had a great deal to do with the very considerable expansion of industry in this valley in the past two decades. Indeed, it is a *sine qua non* of heavy industry, whether in India, in Arkansas, or in the Balkans. It was with electricity that the transformation of rural Russia into an industrial and military giant began.

Electricity can bring great benefit to a people. But it may bring disaster. For the stimulation of industrial development by large supplies of electricity, unless the principles of unity govern, can hasten the destruction of natural resources and bring closer the day of decline.

Electric power, like the products of other resources, can be used as part of a balanced and unified program of development. Electricity is the most humane and the most efficient form of energy. It is mobility itself: It can be brought to people; people need not be brought to the source of energy. Electricity symbolizes the multiplication of human energies through science. But benefit, lasting and secure, will result only if the potentialities of power are seen as a whole, utilized not as ends in themselves but to aid in sustaining and restoring resources; this book will contain illustrations of that kind of development in the wake of power that serves the conservation of resources.

For when a people or a region rely almost exclusively for their living upon the extraction of raw materials—the cutting of lumber, the growing of wheat, the mining of coal or iron—and depend little upon the processing, by manufacture, of those raw materials, these natural resources are put under a severe drain to support a growing population. The income which comes to a region from cutting trees or growing cotton and bringing them to a point of transportation is only a small fraction of the income, the "value added," when those trees have been processed into paper or the cotton into overalls. If a region depends—as most "colonial" regions do—almost entirely upon the income from cutting the lumber or growing the cotton, and hardly at all upon making the paper, the textiles, the furniture, or any of the other articles manufactured from the raw resources, then the pressure to "mine" the fertility of the soil, to devastate rather than harvest the forests for lumber, to deplete the oil fields by wasteful, inefficient competition, becomes very great indeed.

That pressure to deplete resources can be lessened by the growth of the industries which electric power encourages. But if the industry is only exploitative, if it does not *sustain* the productivity of the resources upon which all of us depend, industry can exhaust a region and hurt its people's chances of security and happiness. The "how" of industrial development, like the "how" of developing a river or the land or the forests, is the all-important point.

Great energies are now being released in the development of many parts of the world. But unless a new way of thinking and acting wins support, this period of "development" may duplicate for every continent and every region the stories of modern Ducktown and of ancient Mesopotamia.

Good will is not enough, nor speeches nor noble intentions. There are those in abundance. There are principles and policies to develop and to observe if people are to benefit and democratic institutions are to flourish. The unity of nature's resources must not be disregarded, or the purpose for which such developments are undertaken will be betrayed as it has been betrayed before: by the way the job is done.

Chapter 7

A SEAMLESS WEB:
The Unity of Land and Water and Men

IT WAS the methods of the past which the Act creating TVA
deliberately repudiated. For in this major characteristic—the
unified approach—TVA was a definite break with government tradition. There was, however, nothing particularly novel about the individual public tasks entrusted for execution to this new agency. There
were long-established American precedents for government activity
in flood control and navigation, in forestry and agriculture, and in research. Public power systems were by no means an innovation. The
new thing about the TVA was that one agency was entrusted with
responsibility for them all, and that no one activity could be considered as an end in itself. Constructing dams or rebuilding soil, whatever the activity, it had to be treated as an inseparable part of a
general program to promote the well-being of all the men and
women of the region, whether they worked in offices, in factories,
or in the crossroads stores, in kitchen or in the fields.

The jurisdiction of the TVA cut across existing lines of federal
bureaus and departments. A single agency, instead of half a dozen,
was to design and build the dams, buy the land, construct transmission lines, and market the power the river produced. One agency
was to "envision in its entirety" the potentialities of the whole river
system, for navigation, for power, for flood control, and for recreation. The contrast between such an administrative scheme for the
Tennessee River and the plans on other rivers is illustrated by a
contrasting instance, where one set of men designed a dam, another
agency "supervised" the private contractors who actually built it, a

third group of men then took over the operation and maintenance of one part of the dam, still a fourth group another part, a fifth disposes of one share of the output—each acting under separate direction and policies, with the power of decision for the several parts of the task centered in different departments in distant Washington.

Each TVA dam is a project of several purposes. TVA's engineers have designed it not only to give navigation depth to the river and the greatest possible protection from floods, but to assure every other benefit, of which power production is only one. And every dam is part of a system for the whole river, from headwaters to mouth. The location, the size, the operation of each dam is determined in relation to all the others, so that the total potential value of the entire river may be realized.

It makes a great difference in the way a job is done when responsibility is as broad as that of the TVA, when the welfare of the region is the direct objective, when the construction of a dam or a series of them is seen as only one means to that end. Each task must be carried out in such a way as to contribute to that total result, to salvage every possible benefit. With this range of responsibility in mind, the Board of the TVA decided at the beginning to build the dams by "force account"—that is, that the TVA should directly select, hire, train, and supervise the workmen and be responsible for the policies governing wages and conditions of work. The almost universal federal practice is otherwise. Government construction projects are generally "let out to contract"—that is, a contractor agrees to do the job, to buy the materials, select and pay the employees, and turn over a finished job for a price. With a few exceptions, for work of a special and temporary nature, such as tunnel building or the raising of a bridge, every man who has worked on these Tennessee Valley projects has been employed directly by his government. All were recruited and employed by the TVA.

Building the dams has been not only a matter of digging foundations and placing concrete so that the river might be controlled. It has also afforded an opportunity to the men of the region to learn new skills, skills that have proved invaluable for private industry as it has developed in the South. As a result of TVA's apprentice training, sharecroppers have become skilled craftsmen and tenant farmers have learned to be mechanics. In this way the TVA has helped to add to the reservoir of trained workmen, white and Negro, who are ready to help process the raw materials of the area.

For the same reason the job of providing adequate housing for the workers at dams built at isolated points was undertaken by the TVA itself. Creative engineers, architects, and builders spent several years developing various types of low-cost housing—demountable houses, for example, houses that could be set up on one building site and then moved on to another, always with the widest general use for the region in mind. The influence of these standards of housing, by the contagion of example, upon the private housing development throughout the valley is not difficult to detect even by the casual visitor, and the designs of prefabricated, demountable, and more conventional low-cost housing that have come out of this effort have been made available and are being used by private builders over the country.

It is not for "moral" reasons or a patronizing kind of benevolence that TVA construction villages are not "wide open," as is so generally the custom on public and private dam-building jobs alike. It springs from the driving force of the broad purpose of regional development, from the obligation laid on the TVA to encourage the greatest use of every opportunity to benefit from participation in this job of building the region. Because of these villages TVA was once described by a visiting satirist as the "Little Lord Fauntleroy of the construction industry." What induced this remark was probably not so much watching construction workers playing ping-pong in the Community Building as it was observing crane operators spending their evenings studying blueprint reading, or seeing men climb out of a bulldozer's seat to go and read books from the library—for such a library has been made available to every construction location, however remote in the hills.

These practices are not costly even in money. For when provisions for good food and a decent place for rest and recreation are made— assumed requirements on every TVA construction job—the stage is well set for the more important conditions of an efficient job: union organizations if the men want them, the procedures of collective bargaining, and joint committees to deal with problems of project efficiency. The unit costs of TVA construction have been low compared with private and public undertakings the country over. TVA came within about 3 per cent of keeping within its cost estimates even though many of the major projects were built in wartime when costs were rising rapidly. The jobs have been done with unusual speed. Thus, from the day the Douglas Dam—a major structure on a fractious stream—was authorized by Congress until it was built and producing power took thirteen months, a world's record.

Accidents have been kept to a minimum. In 1941 TVA won thirteen first, second, or third places in the annual rankings of the National Safety Council on accident frequency or severity on large construction projects. During 1952, Awards of Honor, the highest given by the Council for the best safety performance, were awarded to TVA's Johnsonville Steam Plant and the Department of Chemical Engineering, operating huge chemical plants.

The accident rate, the unit costs, and the records in keeping schedules are recognized measures of efficiency on such construction jobs. Responsibilities undertaken and methods developed not merely to build dams, but to build a region by seizing every opportunity that the unified way of looking at things suggests—this it is that has contributed to the efficiency with which each single enterprise has been accomplished. And when this is the way of doing the job, the by-product benefits persist long after the crews have been disbanded and the camps dismantled. It has been TVA's purpose, by devices which I shall later describe, to weave the housing programs, the library service, and the public health facilities available to construction workers into the fabric of the adjacent community institutions, where they have remained ever since, as locally supported services, long after the workers departed.

Added responsibilities result when no single job can be considered an end in itself. For TVA this meant that we could not ignore the dislocations of men's lives which the building of such structures inevitably caused. When the swinging buckets have poured concrete in the final open "block," and the great steel gates are closed, the river's flow is stopped. What about the hundreds of farm families upon whose acres the waters will soon be creeping; what of the communities and churches and schools affected? Under the single-purpose scheme of development, private and public alike, the answer traditionally has been: "The landowners have been paid a fair price for their land, the town has been compensated for the streets that have been inundated and for the access road that is deep below the waters. That discharges our obligation. Our job was to build a dam; that job is done. We are pulling out."

The TVA could not close the gates of the dam, pay off the landowners and townspeople, and call it a day. That would not do because Congress had directed that the resources of the region—human energies included—were to be seen as a whole, and the development of a river was only a single part of the total job of regional building.

And so, when a dam on the TVA system is still under construction and long before the waters have risen, trained men and women of the vicinage—largely local extension service workers—are on their way into the countryside. They examine farms that may be for sale, so that families moved from the reservoir may have disinterested and expert advice, if they ask for it, on values and locations. The expert counsel of technicians and neighbor farmers is available to those who must move; that change provides a chance for the farmer to improve his agricultural practices. Thousands of families have obtained such guidance on a great variety of matters: simple architectural plans for a new house or the remodeling of an old one on the new location, or for the building of a poultry shed; information about the electric co-operative line near by, or about a Farm Improvement Association.

The records of this "family readjustment" were carefully kept for twenty reservoir areas, 14,725 farm families. The general conclusions are of some interest. Almost no farmer took cash for his land and promptly yielded to the blandishments of a "gold stock" salesman. Detailed reports, based on about half the families removed from one area, indicate that approximately 70 per cent of the farm families expressed themselves as better or equally well satisfied in their new locations. The new methods of farming they have followed have shown how a better living could be made from the uplands than older methods had provided on the river-bottom farms from which they had moved.

Farms and crops are facts. But so are human emotions, and they too must be a part of the reckoning if the idea of unity is to be realized. Take the case of burying grounds, for example. A cemetery has no economic or engineering importance. But to the families whose forebears were buried there it is often a precious symbol, a symbol rich in meaning. The personal distress it would cause to have a grave submerged under 200 feet of water—this is a serious human fact. To ignore that reality would be to accept technical "progress" as cold, hard, untouched by any understanding or concern for the emotions of men. TVA moved thousands of such graves and hundreds of cemeteries to locations selected by the families or church communities. But this physical job was not enough; it was done in a way that would express respect for the feelings of those to whom these graves meant so much, though after the lapse of many years they were often quite empty. This is a detail in a huge undertaking. But I am confident that attention to this and other similar details affecting the sensibilities of men, has had much to do with the confidence in the TVA's technical leadership and in its technicians that one finds today so firmly fixed in the minds of many people in this valley.

Because of the breadth of the underlying purpose, towns were not simply paid money damages for streets that would be inundated by the waters of the reservoirs and thereupon marked off the list of "headaches." What happened in the little city of Guntersville in northern Alabama is an instance. The backwaters of Guntersville Dam would cover a number of streets in the business section of this cotton-farmer trading center. A considerable readjustment of the streets and business life of the community was inevitable. It was not easy for the city to face the change, but, long before the waters rose, TVA planning technicians were consulting with the city and state officials. Out of this consultation came a Guntersville City Planning Commission, and later a city zoning ordinance (the first in that part of the state), subdivision controls, and a major street plan. The deep waterfront at the city's center made Guntersville a port through which today large tonnages of freight pass. Under the town's own plan, the industrial uses of the waterfront are separated from the recreational uses, and this city, extending in a long peninsula into the broad blue waters of Guntersville Lake, is today one of the most attractive small cities in the whole South, with its population increased more than 50 per cent. What at first seemed a calamity was turned into an opportunity, and a community sense of direction has resulted that continues to bear fruit.

Chapter 8

THE COMMON PURPOSE

IN ADMINISTERING a project of such broad scope there are of course difficulties quite aside from the multiplicity of responsibilities. Not the least of these arose within the TVA when the experts who made up its staff began to work together. Technical men are rarely trained, in the schools and universities, to see the problems of the people as a whole, as the TVA was obliged to do. It will, I think, be useful to describe how TVA, by concentrating upon a *common purpose* has tried to surmount these barriers to unified development, barriers that loom in the minds of men, and particularly of those technical specialists and experts whose collaboration is essential.

The work upon which TVA first embarked called inevitably for men of many different kinds of professional and technical skills: geologists, agronomists, foresters, chemists, architects, experts in public health, wild life, and fish culture, librarians, wood technicians, specialists in recreation and in refractories, accountants, lawyers, and so on. Such an undertaking, and indeed any modern technical enterprise, requires or in any event has resulted in a high degree of specialization of function.

The terms engineer or biologist or agronomist or chemist are today classifications too general to be of much meaning. In dealing with the resource of the land, for example, foresters represent one of a dozen special fields of skill whose services are required. But forestry, itself a specialization, is divided among a considerable number of even stricter specialists—tree crop experts, nursery technicians, cutting experts, and so on. And so it is with almost every one of the major fields of knowledge upon which an administrator must depend for even the basic steps of such a great change. TVA for example once had on its staff a dendrologist, a man who had spent most of his adult life as an expert in the reading of tree rings. By the examination of the rings of ancient trees he was able to throw some useful light on rainfall cycles and extreme floods far beyond the humanly recorded data on these matters. This expert saw the whole world in tree rings, almost literally. The degree of special function is not always so refined as that, but it is extreme in such a modern undertaking as TVA. The scope of TVA's effort was no less broad than the full sweep of nature and of technology; such *specialization* of function threatened the very fundamental change in point of view toward *unity* that the TVA was intended to effect.

It was clear, therefore, that we could not hope to deal with resources as a unity through modern science (itself the product of specialization) unless we could establish a basis for the unification of these highly specialized skills upon which the enterprise wholly depended. The problem of collaboration among men of highly special responsibilities is a general one, of course, and by no means peculiar to the TVA. In the steps which we in this valley have taken toward working it out, there is a clue to the ways in which in other fields, too, these spiritually disintegrating forces can be overcome.

The unification of the various technical skills was a central part of the task in the TVA, as indeed it is a central problem in modern life. The skills are not self-co-ordinating. In the selection of TVA's technical staff the importance of the expert's need for a broad view was seen. The breadth of TVA's undertaking itself made it imperative that a search be made for the kind of experts who preferred to work as a part of a unified program. But even at best it is not easy for each specialist to appraise the relative importance of his own task as part of the whole picture, or its importance as compared with the tasks in some other technical branch. In fact, the desperate part of the problem, as many people have observed, is the realization of how rarely these different groups of specialists seem to care about anything beyond their own specialties.

This is not to say that specialists are narrow human beings. It is understandable that concentration and preoccupation with a particular phase of a problem breeds impatience with anything not directly in the line of vision. The more conscientious and excited the specialist is about soil chemistry, metallurgy, fish and wild life, or statistical methods, the more likely he is to see all else as an adjunct.

It is an ironic fact that the very technical skills which are ostensibly employed to further the progress of men, by the intensity of their specialization, so often create disunity rather than order and imperil the whole success of their common objective. Resources cannot be developed in unity until each technologist has learned to subordinate his expertness to the common purpose, has come to see the region and its problems "in its entirety."

The ways in which this diversity of special interests appeared in TVA's actual experience will illuminate the problem. Take the questions that arise when a dam is built and the waters of a huge man-made lake will soon cover tens of thousands of acres of farms, as well as cemeteries, schools, highways, parts of or even entire towns. First of all the Board of the TVA has to decide just how much land is to be purchased. From the engineers comes a map showing just where the water will extend when the dam has been closed. The land that will be under water must, of course, be purchased. There is no debate about that. But what additional land along the new shoreline should also be purchased?

The TVA's agricultural experts urge that no more land be taken than is actually to be covered by the waters. Farm land, they argue, is land on which to grow crops; all of it is needed. At once, however, the expert on public recreation is heard from; *he* urges strongly the purchase of a wide "protective strip" along the entire shoreline, which is often several hundreds of miles long. That land, he says, ought to be forever reserved for its scenic beauty, to be used for public parks and playgrounds and to prevent the growing up of private developments that may mar the beauty of the land and lead to speculative profits for a few on what should be a public benefit for all. To the agriculture expert this is nonsense; his point of view in turn is entirely unpalatable to the recreation planner.

The malaria-control expert has still another opinion; he may want dikes built to keep the impounded waters out of low, flat areas, to reduce the opportunities for the mosquito to breed, even though this requires extensive investment in earthworks and plumbing equipment. In selected areas he may prefer that no one should live within a mile of the shore, so that infection may not be carried from one man to another by malaria mosquitoes. He may even insist that such an area be completely evacuated between the hours of sunset and sunrise, which is when the malaria mosquito is active. The highway engineer may have still another special attitude. He will urge, for example, that great peninsulas be purchased in their entirety and the farm families moved to other locations—this for the sake of avoiding the considerable expense of providing access highways to take the place of roads that will be flooded when the water rises.

The power expert, on the other hand, urges the most limited possible purchases of land, so that the dollar investment which his electric revenues must cover will remain at a minimum. The expert in navigation likewise will press his specialized interest; his claims to the purchases of areas to be reserved for terminal and harbor facilities or marineways may conflict with claims for the use of that same land for recreation or farming or malaria prevention. Sometimes the problem is even further complicated, as by the archaeologist, intent upon the removal or preservation of prehistoric remains in the reservoir area, or by the expert in public revenue, concerned with the adverse effect on the finances of a local government unit when certain tracts, by reason of their purchase by the government, are removed from the local tax base.

These experts, needless to say, had no pecuniary interest impelling them to insist on their various views; in that sense they were disinterested. Many of them had come to TVA because they wanted just such an opportunity to be part of a task broader than their own special fields. Where such an atmosphere of disinterest, in a pecuniary sense, does not exist, the pressure toward "special solutions" is sometimes even further intensified.

It was apparent to us, in the case I have described, that, at first look, at least one or more of the interests were in conflict. Differences of this kind could not be intelligently settled merely by compromise between the various technicians' views, a variation of the trader's "splitting the difference." But they had to be settled; a decision had to be made. Relative dollar cost was only one factor to be considered. The final question was always this: looking at the situation as a whole, and not merely at the professional or technical standards of any one or several of the specialized interests, what course of action would yield the best results *as judged by the common purpose*, the goal of the whole undertaking—the well-being of the people of the region? The TVA experts and the Board of Directors on these occasions came together to learn from one another and merge the various special judgments into decisions of broad public purpose. The decisions made in many such reservoir cases are certainly not beyond question for their wisdom, but this at least is clear: they are products of a new kind of thinking. The problem was studied as a single problem.

With time, the barbed-wire fences began to come down within the TVA, the fences between the fields of special knowledge put up to keep one specialist out of the other fellow's domain and keep him in his own, barriers so characteristic of present-day science, of education, of engineering, even of theology. The TVA experts, themselves convinced of the value of combining their special judgments into a unified conclusion, soon developed workable methods of teamwork. It began to be taken more and more for granted (although "backsliding" was, of course, not unknown) that expertness is not an end in itself, and that each skill is only one part of the unity of knowledge necessary to do the job of developing and conserving resources.

The common moral purpose of benefit to the people, by dint of observation and participation, came to be as real to the experts as some highly technical procedure had always been. They welcomed the chance to broaden their view of their own special fields and to relate them to other areas of knowledge.

TVA's engineers, who have developed new chemical fertilizers, have no tendency today to perfect a product in the laboratory as an end in itself. They know the story of farming and the practices of farming; they are, in fact, often in the fields near by, where their products are used by farmers. Delegations of farmers frequently visit the TVA's chemical laboratories and experimental plants. And farmers and agricultural experts have learned that the most important aid to soil rebuilding may be a device invented by the industrial engineer and marketed by a businessman. Nowadays there are fewer conflicts between experts to be settled by the Board of Directors. To most questions the specialists themselves apply the touchstone and reach a joint recommendation. An incident will illustrate my point.

When water has been backed up behind a great dam, the resulting lake offers opportunity for the malaria mosquito to breed. It increases the hazard of spreading the disease in this valley region where it is endemic. To minimize this danger and if possible to drive malaria entirely out of the valley is plainly, of course, part of the obligation of TVA, for the disease is a drain on its human resources —the South loses a substantial part of its working time to the malaria mosquito. An extensive program to this end was set up, under the direction of leading malariologists, and today malaria has been virtually wiped out; annual surveys now show an incidence of a small fraction of 1 per cent, compared with 30 per cent in some areas in pre-TVA days.

The malaria mosquito (*Anopheles quadrimaculatus*) deposits its larvae in the shallow water along the lake's edge. One of several methods of killing these larvae is suddenly to open the gates of the dam, and thereby quickly drop the level of the lake, leaving the larvae stranded on the shore where they will die in a day or two. But unfortunately dropping the level of the lake thus suddenly may waste an enormous amount of power that could be produced if the water were slowly fed through the waterwheels at the dam in the usual manner. The power expert objects quite naturally to "pouring a quarter million dollars worth of power down the river" as the level of the lake is suddenly dropped, by spilling water over the crest or through sluices, unused.

At the particular time I have in mind—the spring of 1942—power was desperately needed for war industries, while abnormally low rainfall had brought the river to unseasonably low levels. Unhappily it was also the season of the year that is most critical in the life cycle of the *Anopheles*, with conditions almost perfect for the larvae, and the consequences could have been grave. The situation was sufficiently important for the matter to come to the Board for consideration. But the whole case was submitted to us by only one expert, who stated that he was authorized to present the malaria as well as the power aspects of the problem. This was real progress in collaboration through the impelling centripetal force of a common unifying purpose. The malaria expert volunteered to make a day-by-day rather than a less frequent check of field conditions, a serious added burden to the members of his staff. As a consequence, however, the staff was in a position to take instant advantage of any change in the rate of mosquito breeding. Day-by-day decisions based on emergency reporting and collaboration between malaria experts, power operators, and water control engineers dissolved the crisis. The drastic draw-down of lake levels that a more arbitrary "specialist" attitude would have called for was avoided.

The crisis was met in stride; malarial hazards did not spread; little power was wasted. It was evident that the malariologists were intent also upon saving power if it could be done without risk to human life and health; they exercised their ingenuity toward that end. The power experts were likewise more interested in saving life and health than dollars, but they wanted decisions in this crisis to be based upon day-by-day facts to be sure the consequences of choice were real. I could not help recalling the early days of the Authority, with every expert fighting for his own special point of view, sometimes politely and sometimes vigorously, rarely trusting and sometimes even a little contemptuous of the specialities of other men.

I have dwelt upon the effect of the principle of unity upon the minds of technical men within the working staff of the TVA, for after all it is only through the minds and skills of men that resources can be developed, and those skills are, in these times, largely technical.

Here the men who design and build the dams, who operate the power systems, who build the terminals and roads, are working together, literally and with a conscious purpose. Their physical proximity helps. The public health physician and the many kinds of specialists are in daily touch with one another as a matter of course. They work under a single management. That helps to unify their efforts and their thinking. There would be no excuse here for such results of specialization and single-purpose thinking as Lewis Mumford refers to in *The Culture of Cities*: ". . . the paper engineer —this is an actual case," he writes, "designs an irrigation project with admirable skill in hydraulics, only to discover, after the water works have been built, that the soil is unfit for cultivation."[1] In the TVA the experts in soil are too close to the engineers for that to happen; their judgments are built into the original decisions.

A fundamental change in resource development then must begin at the beginning, *in the minds of men*, in the way men think and, so thinking, act. Because a few men began to think differently about resources a new statute was enacted, a new kind of institution, the Tennessee Valley Authority, came into being, and the thinking was on its way to an ever-widening circle—to experts, officials, and the people as a whole. For this way of thinking cannot be confined to the technical task force within the TVA. The unified development of resources must become the *common purpose*, as nearly as possible, of all the people and all the agencies of the entire valley.

This is a people's job. All the human forces and energies of the valley are essential to it. And what is true of this one region is, I deeply believe, equally true of regions and people everywhere. It is just as important that a farmer upon his uplands should see this unity, as that the TVA's agricultural experts should see it. The job cannot be done unless the individual farmer, "standing at ease with nature," as Whitman said, sees his farm, his community—"the little watershed"—and the larger region all as parts of a single whole. It is quite as essential that the businessman in this valley should envision the river and the farms and the minerals and forests in their entirety as that they should so appear to the engineering forces of TVA. For a program of resource development is effective only when it is in the hands and minds of the people. The foundation of this conviction I shall seek to establish, in succeeding chapters, by calling upon the ways of this valley as supporting proof.

There is a grand cycle in nature. The lines of those majestic swinging arcs are nowhere more clearly seen than by following the course of electric power in the Tennessee Valley's way of life. Water falls upon a mountain slope six thousand feet above the level of the river's mouth. It percolates through the roots and the sub-surface channels, flows in a thousand tiny veins, until it comes together in one stream, then in another, and at last reaches a TVA lake where

[1] (Harcourt, Brace & Co., 1938) p. 375.

it is stored behind a dam. Down a huge steel tube it falls, turning a water wheel. Here the water's energy is transformed into electricity, and then, moving onward toward the sea, it continues on its course, through ten such lakes, over ten such water wheels. Each time, electric energy is created. That electricity, carried perhaps two hundred miles in a flash of time, heats to incredible temperatures a furnace that transforms inert phosphate ore into a chemical. That phosphatic chemical, put upon his land by a farmer, stirs new life in the land, induces the growth of pastures that capture the inexhaustible power of the sun. Those pastures, born of the energy of phosphate and electricity, feed the energies of animals and men, hold the soil, free the streams of silt, store up water in the soil. Slowly the water returns into the great man-made reservoirs, from which more electricity is generated as more water from the restored land flows on its endless course.

Such a cycle is restorative, not exhausting. It gives life as it sustains life. The principle of unity has been obeyed, the circle has been closed. The yield is not the old sad tale of spoliation and poverty, but that of nature and science and man in the bounty of harmony.

Chapter 9

DEMOCRACY AT THE GRASS ROOTS:
For the People and by the People

It is not the earth, it is not America who is so great,
It is I who am great or to be great, it is You up there, or any one,
It is to walk rapidly through civilizations, governments, theories,
Through poems, pageants, shows, to form individuals.

Underneath all, individuals, I swear nothing is good to me now
that ignores individuals. . .

—WALT WHITMAN

PEOPLE are the most important fact in resource development. Not only is the welfare and happiness of individuals its true purpose, but they are the means by which that development is accomplished; their genius, their energies and spirit are the instruments; it is not only "for the people" but "by the people."

The purpose of resource development must be more than the mere physical welfare of the greatest number of human beings. It is true that we cannot be starving and cold and still be happy. But an abundance of food, the satisfaction of elementary physical needs alone, is not enough. A man wants to feel that he is important. He wants to be able not only to express his opinion freely, but to know that it carries some weight; to know that there are some things that he decides, or has a part in deciding, and that he is a needed and useful part of something far bigger than he is.

This hankering to be an *individual* is probably greater today than ever before. Huge factories, assembly lines, mysterious mechanisms, standardization—these underline the smallness of the individual, because they are so fatally impersonal. If the intensive development of resources, the central fact in the immediate future of the world,

77

could be made personal to the life of most men; if they could see themselves, because it was true, as actual participants in that development in their own communities, on their own land, at their own jobs and businesses—there would be an opportunity for this kind of individual satisfaction, and there would be something to tie to. Men would not only have more things; they would be stronger and happier men.

Resource development need not be held fast by those de-humanizing forces of modern life that whittle down the importance of the individual. Surely it should be freed of their grip, for they are the very negation of democracy. ". . . nothing is good to me now that ignores individuals."

It is the unique strength of democratic methods that they do provide a way of stimulating and releasing the individual resourcefulness and inventiveness, the pride of workmanship, the creative genius of human beings whatever their station or function, and however large the enterprise of which they are a part. A world of science and great machines is still a world of men; our modern task is more difficult, but the opportunity for democratic methods is greater even than in the days of the ax and the hand loom.

A method of organizing the modern task of resource development that not only will be based upon the principle of unity but can draw in the average man and make him a part of the great job of our time, in the day-to-day work in the fields and factories and the offices of business, will tap riches of human talent that are beyond the reach of any highly centralized, dictatorial, and impersonal system of development based upon remote control in the hands of a business, a technical, or a political elite.

It is just such widespread and intimate participation of the people in the development of their valley that has gone on in the Tennessee Valley.

The spiritual yield of democratic methods, a renewed sense that the individual counts, would be justification enough. But there is yet another reason, a practical one, for seeking at every turn to bring people actively into the task of building a region's resources; there is, I think, really no other way in which the job can be done. The task of harmonizing and from time to time adjusting the intricate, detailed maze of pieces that make up the unified development of resources in a world of technology is something that I do not believe can be done effectively from some remote government or business headquarters.

The people must be in on that job. In the long run the very necessities of management make it mandatory. Efficiency, in the barest operating sense, requires it. There is nothing in my experience more heartening than this: that devices of management which give a lift to the human spirit turn out so often to be the most "efficient" methods. No code of laws or regulations can possibly be detailed enough to direct the precise course of resource development. No blueprints or plans can ever be comprehensive enough, or sufficiently flexible, as a matter of management, for so ever-changing an enterprise. It is the people or nothing.

From the outset of the TVA undertaking it has been evident to me, as to many others, that a valley development envisioned in its entirety could become a reality if and only if the people of the region did much of the planning, and participated in most of the decisions. To a considerable degree this is what is happening. Each year, almost each month, one can see the participation of the people, as a fundamental practice, grow more vigorous, and, although it suffers occasional setbacks, it has become part of the thinking and the mechanics of the development of the Tennessee Valley.

In this and the next several chapters I shall illustrate how TVA undertook its job of region-building at the grass roots, and how regional decentralization is at work in almost every side of the valley's life—among farmers, workmen, businessmen, local officials, and in TVA's relations with state and local governments. In telling how these ideas have been put in practice, I have chosen to begin with the story of how TVA has applied grass-roots democracy to the job of rebuilding the land.

The farmers—there are now about three hundred thousand farms in the watershed of the Tennessee River, with 1,340,000 people living on them—had long seen that their lands were in trouble. They knew, almost all of them, what they wanted. They knew that what was needed was to increase the productivity of their lands, to heal the gullies, to keep water on the land, and to prevent the soil from washing away. Like almost everyone else they were reluctant to change their habits of doing things. They wanted to have a say-so about changes, they had to be "shown"; but when their confidence had been earned they were enthusiastic, and they were generous of spirit.

The farm experts, both in the Department of Agriculture's scientific bureaus in Washington and in the state agencies of the Tennessee Valley, had known most of the technical answers to the *separate* problems of soils, of fertilizer, of terracing, and had known them for a good many years. They were competent in their special fields, and devoted to their work. Nevertheless farm income in the valley as in the whole Southeast continued at a low ebb; in some counties the average cash income for a farm *family* was less than $150 a year. Soil losses were appalling. Farm tenantry increased. Changes in farming favored by the technicians, away from cotton and corn, for example, did occur, but the pace was so slow that the direction on the whole continued downward. Entire rural counties, the towns included, were without a single telephone, a mile of farm electric line, a public library, a newspaper, a hospital, a single public health officer.

The technical knowledge of farming problems in the agricultural agencies, state and federal, was extensive, but it was largely generalized. It was not based on the needs of a particular farm or farming community. When this knowledge did reach the farmer, through reports of scientific results on experimental plots, in pamphlets, or by word of mouth through one of many agencies, it was usually a succession of separate bits of knowledge, and it was often remote from the farmer's individual problems. He was likely to be confused by the multiplicity of "remedies" and the more than a score of different governmental agencies with which he must deal on agricultural problems.

What was needed was not alone more technical information, but that *on the farm itself* there should be a unification of all the available knowledge and skills. The technical knowledge of all kinds available at the various state university agricultural experiment farms had somehow to be moved to thousands of valley farms, actual farms. What happened on a splendidly equipped experimental station farm or laboratory was one thing; what would happen on a man's farm under practical farm conditions was quite another. The laboratory had to be taken to the farm; the whole farm as a business was the farmer's problem.

Furthermore, as TVA saw it, and as the agricultural colleges were quick to confirm, the individual farmer was the only one who could *apply* all this available expertness. He must therefore become the center of the scheme of education in new methods. We did not want a method of restoring soil whereby the farmer would be ordered; he would learn *by doing*, on his own place; his neighbors would learn by watching him and adapting what "worked out." Nor did we want a mere false front, using the outward form of voluntary and educational methods to disguise actual coercion, or "uplift," or narrow political purposes.

After some searching the method that was worked out, with state, local, and federal agencies as co-operating parties, centered about "whole farm demonstrations" on tens of thousands of dirt farms. The results in physical terms I have already summarized. On the land of these demonstration farmers two ideas met and were combined in action: the idea of unity of resources, and the democratic idea that much of the planning and execution of resource development must be localized, must be in the hands of the people directly affected.

These thousands of typical working farms are the schoolrooms of the valley. Here farmers, their wives and children, with their neighbors learn and demonstrate the unity of resources, learn and demonstrate the principles of grass-roots democracy. Here there is brought to them the fruits of the technical man's skills. In each of the valley's counties one or more Farm Improvement Associations were formed. These associations were organized by the farmers and operated entirely by boards of trustees elected by them.

Many of these organizations soon went into private business as farmer co-operatives. As such they branched out into ownership and use of terracing equipment, distribution of agricultural limestone, marketing of farm crops, operation of such enterprises as fertilizer plants and feed mills, and similar activities related to their interests as farmers. By 1949, six federated farmers' co-operatives and ten unaffiliated county organizations served all but 10 of the 125 valley counties. The federated co-operatives did a $7,000,000 business in sale of fertilizer, seed, and other farm supplies. County organizations, both federated and independent, covered 115 counties and did about $14,000,000 worth of business.

The test-demonstration farm program of the Tennessee Valley began, back in 1935, in this way: The farmers in a community, called together by their county agricultural agent, selected several of their own number who were willing to have their farms serve as a "demonstration" for the rest. Later on it became apparent to farmers and technicians that all the farms in a community usually constituted a more useful unit for demonstration than one farm or a scattered few. As a consequence what were called "area demonstrations" were set up by the farmers' associations. Some counties contained twenty such community-wide demonstrations, with as many as eighty families in such a single "little valley."[1]

The hub about which these demonstrations started was the mineral *phosphate*. (In some of a thousand other valleys over the earth differently situated, the use of water for irrigation, say, or electric power might be that hub.) The technicians in the state institutions had long known that most of the valley land was deficient in phosphate. More than a generation ago the pioneer conservationist Charles Van Hise had said that the depletion of soil phosphates "is the most crucial, the most important, and the most far-reaching problem with reference to the future of the nation." This the technicians had long known. But the drain had gone on, at unabated pace. My associate on the first TVA Board, the late Dr. Harcourt A. Morgan, a leading agricultural scientist, knew more about the almost magic effect of adding this mineral to "poor" soils than any man in America. But he knew, too, and patiently taught that what was necessary was not merely adding phosphate to the soil but a change in the entire management of individual farms, including the addition of lime and other fertilizer materials. In that change phosphate could be a fulcrum for other needed adjustments, a central vantage

[1] At the height of this activity, during 1946-47, there were 628 such area demonstrations under way, embracing a total of 28,048 individual farms with a total of 2,679,127 acres. Since that time the numbers of farms included in this program (which had largely served its underlying educational purpose) has been sharply curtailed, in 1952 the number being about 2,400 farms, in 21 states. The present emphasis is upon intensive observation of a limited number of demonstrations on special problems, the introduction of new plant nutrient materials, better use of fertilizer materials, etc. See the TVA *Annual Report* for 1952, p. 55 *et seq*. See also *Annual Report* for 1950, p. 50 *et seq*.

point from which to see and to learn the lesson of the seamless web.

Between the expert and the farm was a crucial gap which the methods of the past left unfilled. What TVA has done is to help the state extension services throw a bridge across that gap.

Furthermore TVA brought together and concentrated upon the solution of the problems of these typical farms technical and scientific forces of every kind, and not just those usually deemed "agricultural." The inventor, the engineer, the transportation expert, and the businessman have all had a hand in the work of farm adjustment. As important as any of these "outsiders" were the chemical engineers. The adequate use of phosphate in the past had in part been impeded by its cost to the farmer. A group of TVA chemical technicians, aided by every other source of expertness in Washington and the Tennessee Valley, was set to work in 1933 to point the way for industry to reduce the cost by producing this fertilizer in *highly concentrated form*, thereby making large savings on transportation and bagging costs.

The huge munitions plant at Muscle Shoals, inherited by TVA from World War I, became the center of technical research of this kind. By 1935 a wholly new electric-furnace phosphate process had gone through the pilot plant stage and was technically proven.

TVA subsequently constructed a plant capable of producing 200,000 tons annually of concentrated superphosphate, containing 45-48 per cent of plant nutrient, a material previously made only in relatively small amounts by a so-called "wet" process and used mostly in low analysis "mixed" fertilizers. With this material, made by the new electric furnace process, moving out to the test-demonstration farms, TVA chemical engineers went on to new fields. A process also based on the electric furnace was developed for producing calcium metaphosphate, a material having 63 per cent of phosphate plant nutrient—the highest concentration ever developed for a commercial fertilizer. After long pilot plant tests, a plant was built with a capacity of 40,000 tons annually. Another relatively simple process promising considerable economies was developed to produce fused tricalcium phosphate, containing 28 per cent plant nutrient (40 per cent more than ordinary superphosphate), by removing fluorine from phosphate rock in a shaft furnace. A commercial-size plant capable of producing 40,000 tons a year was built;

there the final problems of large scale production are being worked out, while the material is being tested on the region's farms.

More recent developments have included pilot plant development of four processes for producing nitric phosphates, containing both phosphate and nitrogen and permitting addition of potash to produce a "complete" fertilizer. In the pilot plant stage in 1953 was a process for producing diammonium phosphate, containing 54 per cent phosphate and 21 per cent nitrogen. Limited pilot plant work had also been done on a process for producing a highly concentrated material from phosphorus, air, and ammonia. Laboratory experiments had produced a small quantity of the material containing 82 per cent phosphate and 17 per cent nitrogen.

The state agricultural agencies and TVA, working together, showed that phosphate fertilizer applied to the land, in combination with ground limestone (a cheap and plentiful rock) and properly supplemented, if needed, with potash and in some cases minor elements, would enable clover and other legumes to grow where before the soil would not sustain them. These legume plants, such as clover, bear on their roots tiny nodules, rich in another element, nitrogen, drawn by the tiny bacteria in the nodules from the inexhaustible supply in the air. Phosphate and lime, through legumes, might thus add nitrogen, giving the farmer one pattern for the sustaining of his land's fertility.

A soil badly deficient in these basic elements is dead, sterile. A soil rich in these elements could, with planning and with "know-how" in the farmer's hands, be made part of the valley-wide scheme to conserve the soil and the streams, and thereby to strengthen the people.

Here were new, modern technical tools: a concentrated mineral phosphate, and the experts' generalized knowledge of what science could do to help increase the productiveness of land. But it was the people on the farms who must use these tools. And to use them effectively meant that the individual farmer must plan ahead, adjust and readjust the management of his entire farm, as a plant manager must plan and readjust his whole operation to a radical new machine. It meant that in that planning he needed technical counsel, as the problems arose. He ought to have the advice of the ablest farmers in his neighborhood. Before he could "realize" on these new tools he would have to surmount all manner of barriers, physical and economic. And, finally, if the community and national interest were to be served by this technical advance, the farmer on his land must learn the truth of unity in resource development: that his farm was not only a field or two, woodland, a pasture and a house and barn, but a unit; that likewise the land and water, forests and minerals, power and industry were all inseparable parts of his own work and life; that on that farm he is part of the cycle of nature.

There, on that land, the farmer would see how science affected his own daily life. In this way the chemical plant at Muscle Shoals, the great turbines at Pickwick Landing Dam, the laboratories of the state universities, in short, the world of science, would come to have meaning to the man who after all was their "boss." Science, if brought thus close to him, would enable the average man (on a farm or in the town) to learn what it is that technology makes feasible, for him, what, in short, are his *alternatives*; without that knowledge what reality is there in the free man's democratic right to choose?

The benefits of such grass-roots thinking are almost as great for the scientist as for the layman. Technology is never final. What the farmers themselves observe, in the actual use of a soil mineral on their land, is of great value in laboratory research to open new doors to ever new discoveries. And this has actually occurred at TVA's Muscle Shoals plants and laboratories where not only businessmen but also farmers have stood at the elbow of chemical engineers while they designed new equipment for new products adapted to the farmers' actual observed needs. Keeping open a living channel of communication *between the layman and the technician*, a needed stimulus to science, invention, and industry, is another yield of grass-roots methods.

To return to the functioning of the demonstration farm. Once selected, the first step was to map and inventory this farm schoolroom. These maps and inventories were not "documents," built up by questionnaires from a distance, nor were they "professional." They were made by the farmer and the committee of his neighbors. Then the farmer, the technicians, and the county agent and his demonstration assistant, "talk over" that map. They walk over the place, map and inventory in hand, often several times, still talking it over. A new management plan for the farm is the result, reduced to writing. In return for the use of his farm as a schoolroom and for his promise to keep detailed records so that others may profit by his experience, the demonstrator, at reduced cost, is supplied with TVA concentrated phosphates. He agrees with his neighbors to use these minerals on crops that will further the building of the soil and store more water in it, and not otherwise. For all the other adjustments he must pay his own way: the needed lime, terracing, cattle for the pasture that takes the place of the cotton field, and fencing for that pasture; the sheds and barns and necessary machinery; and the necessary fertilizers over and above those supplied by TVA. Most of these farmers had depended for their cash upon the row crops: cotton, corn, tobacco. They embarked upon a change that would rebuild the soil. Most of them had little if any working capital. What they put in, out of often meager resources, was "venture capital," and many of them, too, risked the loss of their source of cash income to carry the family through the winter. But they tried it voluntarily, more than 50,000 of them in the Tennessee Valley alone, and succeeded.

Most demonstration farmers have increased their capital resources, many have increased their income in cash received or in a rising family living standard; at the same time they have conserved and revitalized their soil. This is important because this method, being voluntary with no powers of enforcement in anyone, depended upon hitching together the farmer's self-interest and the general public interest in the basic resource of the soil. The individual made himself one with the common purpose which the TVA idea holds for all individuals, the development of the resources upon which all stand. Self-interest here has served that public interest.

For a time such new ways of doing things were viewed with some suspicion. All kinds of rumors spread through the countryside. One story was that, once a farmer put this TVA phosphate on his land, the land would thenceforth belong to the "gov'ment." But when on one side of a line fence there grew little but worthless sedge grass, and on the other the field was heavy with crimson clover and alfalfa, a change in attitude and interest took place. The demonstration farms became places to visit, to study, to emulate. The greatest effect in spreading new farming practices has been among those who have never been selected as demonstrators at all.

Hundreds of farmers, non-demonstrators, would spend a day going from one of these farm schoolrooms to another.

A report from Virginia shows that large proportions of the "students" went home and adopted some or all the changes on their own farms. When I worked in the TVA I used to attend such all-day meetings where scores of farmers gathered in the fields, earnestly observing, asking questions, arguing, prodding the "experts" for an answer to this difficulty or the "why" of this or that.

Thomas Jefferson, also a Virginia farmer, saw that education is the foundation of a democratic nation; what was true in the eighteenth century is doubly true when technology of a hundred kinds must be at the hand of every citizen. At these meetings one man steps up and tells his experience; then another adds his story. One man's planning is compared with another's. The "lessons" learned are taken back to be tested at home.

At one meeting in northern Alabama, for example, three hundred farmers from eight different counties gathered on the Aaron Fleming farm in a single day's meeting. As a result of what they saw at this one session alone 150,000 acres of the land of non-demonstrators were affected; 10,000 Alabama acres were for the first time put under a protective cover of legumes against the washing of winter rains; and so on with other changes—restoring and saving soil, storing water on the land, increasing by 30 to 100 per cent the efficiency in production of once almost exhausted American soil, providing new business in the neighboring towns and cities, and in manufacturing centers far away.

First of course the farmer thought about his own land, his own family, then about his neighborhood. He began to work with his neighbors. First they concerned themselves with farming, then community forest-fire protection, then the school, the community's health problems, the church. Thus what begins as "soil building" or "better farming," by the inevitable force of unity of resources and men, soon "touches and gives life to all forms of human concerns," to use language of President Roosevelt's original message concerning the TVA.

Farmers began working together, concentrating their efforts upon a matter far more important than any one man but in which each individual was deemed an essential part. The single farm demonstration developed into area demonstrations, these into county-wide associations, with trustees elected from all parts of the county. From phosphate and lime other common interests grew, such as livestock and its improvement, since without cattle and sheep no farmer could utilize the forage of his pastures and meadows.

What about refrigerating some of the meat produced on these pastures? The technical men were called upon, a simple matter since they were close at hand. Agricultural engineers worked out an answer: a walk-in locker refrigerator that would accommodate a dozen families. This cooler was so simple that any community carpenter could build it at a low total cost; at that time their financial resources would not permit the more elaborate apparatus commercially available. One was set up for a demonstration at White Pine community. It worked, was practical, became accepted, was adopted, on their own, by many communities. Hundreds of thousands of pounds of meat were stored in them. Income increased. The diet of thousands of farmers was improved, not merely by preaching about the need but by setting the experts and businessmen to work figuring out a *workable alternative* by which the people could make their choice of better diet a reality. And a market for standard freezers, available through private industry, had been established; with their greater income, farmers could afford them.

In much the same way a number of other technical answers which the valley's experts have devised have been tested by groups and organizations of farmers acting together: portable irrigation, a simple low-cost electric barn hay drier, new farm uses for small electric motors, a portable thresher, quick-freezing, and so on. Each of these technical efforts to make it possible for a farmer to afford doing what he wanted to do, i.e., farm so that his soil would be conserved, was tried out on actual farms by a group of farmers studying the "contraption" together, making suggestions together, and later often ordering one of the appliances from a commercial source for their own community use.

Buying feed or fencing, and selling eggs or berries or cattle, by individual farmers quite naturally gave way in many counties to group purchasing and marketing through the same association which administered the demonstrations. Today, through this natural evolution, the Farm Improvement Association has become more and more a medium for initiating many other projects for building rural life.

The habit of working together, properly nurtured, spreads quickly. The area test demonstrations provided the nucleus for a vigorous rural community betterment movement. The heart of the test demonstration, as the University of Tennessee explained in a recent pamphlet, was "inclusion of both the farm and the home, all activities and enterprises, into a farm-home unit improvement demonstration." When a number of neighbors in a small area found themselves embarking together upon these "whole-farm" enterprises, talking and comparing notes, the next step came easily—planning and working on projects for the improvement of the community generally.

In 1944, a spark was provided when Knoxville business and civic groups got together with the University of Tennessee and TVA to sponsor an East Tennessee Community Improvement Contest. Within five years, the idea had spread over the entire state, involving 650 communities and 250,000 rural Tennesseans. The contests, sponsored by business and civic groups in the cities, brought town and country closer together in understanding. The idea spilled over state lines into Georgia, Virginia, North Carolina, Kentucky, Alabama, and several other states. Hiwassee College, a training school for rural ministers of the Methodist Church, developed a seminar for training of church workers in the field of rural community life—social, economic, and spiritual.

"It is impossible to enumerate the number of school and church buildings and grounds that have been improved, conveniences and furnishings bought for homes, school lunch programs assisted, acres of land terraced or fertilized, water systems installed, homes painted, grounds improved; the improvement of livestock, pastures, and crop yields because of better methods and practices," the University reported.

A number of communities have started health programs, with clinics for children, and some have built and equipped community hospitals. County councils of community clubs have been formed to handle problems too big for individual groups. Community buildings have been built as social centers, and educational tours to other states and the national capital sponsored.

All of the area test-demonstrations have been discontinued as the number of test-demonstration farms has been reduced, but the spirit of co-operative enterprise which they initially engendered remains and grows.

In the Tennessee Valley the effect of working together, building a fertile soil, and finding ways to protect it and keep it strong is not merely a matter of men's livelihood. Revitalizing the soil has done things to the people and their institutions quite as much as to the land. Schools have been painted, lighted, or rebuilt, church and community activities stimulated; the effect is felt in a score of people's activities which they share in common. Only cynics will find this surprising. To those with faith in humankind it is natural enough that when men adopt a common purpose so deep and broad as that of working with nature to build a region's resources there ensue inevitable consequences to the spirit of men. These indeed may be the most important result of all.

Similar consequences in the rural life of this valley have followed upon another fruit of technology: electricity. Here again farmers worked together, organizing their own electric co-operatives, sometimes against the opposition of private agencies. Electricity became a fulcrum, as did phosphate, for many changes. Electricity induced changes in farm management practices; soil conservation was encouraged. The portable electric motor, the refrigerator, electric cooling of milk, meant increased farm income, so the farmer could afford to buy more phosphate at the store, bid in more cattle at the auction, put in more grass, winter grain, and legumes, less corn and cotton.

And, as in the case of the technical lever of phosphate, electricity's part in furthering unified development of resources through human understanding went far beyond the business of making a living. The coming of electricity has had an important effect upon standards in rural schools, for example. Similarly in farm homes. When an electric range or refrigerator comes into a farm kitchen the effect is always much the same: the kitchen gets a coat of paint, is furbished up; not long after, the rest of the house spruces up; a new room is built on, pride begins to remake the place—pride supported by the added income that comes from "smart" use of electricity for farm purposes. You can follow the trail of new electric lines in many sections by observing the houses that have been thus tidied up.

When the principles of grass-roots democracy are followed, electricity, like soil minerals, provides men with a stimulus in their own lives, as well as an opportunity to work together with others toward a purpose bigger than any individual. By that act of joint effort, of citizen participation, the individual's essential freedom is strengthened and his satisfactions increased.

A common purpose furthered by grass-roots methods not only draws neighbors together in a community, then in a county and a group of counties; as time goes on the whole region, from one end to another, has felt the effect. The North Carolina farmers in the high mountains of Watauga or Jackson counties are brought closer to the Virginians and to the Alabama and western Kentucky farmers of the red clay flatlands. A common purpose is making this one valley.

Nor is this cohesive effect confined even to the Tennessee Valley. In twenty-three nonvalley states outside the valley, seventeen of them outside the South, similar demonstration farms using TVA phosphate, numbering over 9,000, have been organized by the farmers and the institutions of those states and operated along similar lines, though on a less extensive scale. Their effects continue, evidence of genuinely democratic methods.

I recall when two busloads of farmers from the great dairy state of Wisconsin came to the valley "to see for ourselves." Something had gone wrong with their own lands. They spent days walking over Tennessee and Alabama demonstration farms. Today, in Wisconsin, TVA phosphate has been used in the same kind of demonstrations in fifty-three counties of that state.[2] For me one of the pleasantest experiences of my years with TVA was the sight of a Wisconsin farmer sitting on an automobile running board with an Alabama cotton farmer, both completely absorbed, talking over together their experiences with their land. Their grandfathers may have fought against each other at Shiloh. These citizens, however,

[2] One of the great stories of Midwestern farm community life grew out of such a visit, the story of the Little Trappe Farm Improvement Association, as recorded by the University of Wisconsin Extension Service in *Circular 385*, July, 1949.

would never think of Alabama and Wisconsin in the same way again. Not even the visits to the valley of hundreds of earnest "learners" from Mexico, China, Brazil, Australia, and a dozen other foreign lands has more meaning than the meeting of those two men on that Alabama farm.

Chapter 10

THE RELEASE OF HUMAN ENERGIES

THE story of TVA at the grass roots is not merely a story of soil conservation. It is an account of how through a modern expression of ancient democratic principles human energies have been released in furtherance of a common purpose.

The human energies that can build a region and make people's lives richer in the doing are not confined to any one kind or group of men. There is, essentially, no difference in this respect between farm people and industrial workers, businessmen, librarians, ministers, doctors. All who live in the valley are needed in varying degrees, in this task of resource development.

The individual satisfactions that come to a man from actively participating in such a basic undertaking are great whatever his calling. Working on one's own farm or upon a TVA dam affords such an opportunity, and so do public or private industrial research and development, or furthering the use of the new TVA-made lakes as a transportation resource. The principles of democracy remain throughout the same; every plan and action must meet the test of the question: Does this activity in furtherance of unified development employ *methods that bring in the people*, that give the people themselves, in this fundamental task, the fullest opportunity for the release of the great reservoir of human talents and energies?

Take, for example, the construction workers who actually built the TVA structures one sees up and down the valley. Those men have played an active and a major part in the whole task of region-building. The particular TVA methods which brought about this result, although of course quite different from working at the grass roots with farmers, are the same in principle; those methods meet the test I have just stated.

In pouring concrete so that the huge Douglas Dam could be built on a world-record schedule, in tending the glow of the giant electric furnaces at Muscle Shoals, or in stringing aluminum and copper wires along the line of march of transmission towers, TVA workers know, and show they know, that in thus working for their valley they are working for themselves; they build for themselves. Cheaper electricity is worth their labor; development of the valley's resources means more of the right kind of private industry—a better chance for their skills and the skills of their sons.

Since 1933 the TVA has carried on its construction work as a direct employer of tens of thousands of workers. Nearly 200,000 different individual workers have done their stint in the TVA. Most of them have come from the Tennessee Valley. Thousands of craftsmen—carpenters, machinists, electrical workers, equipment operators, "cat" drivers, steam fitters, to mention but a few of all the skills required in such a construction job—have had a vital part in building a man-made control and plan into the flow of the river.

Many of these men have more than once wiped their tools at the completion of one dam and a few days later laid them out again miles away or over the mountain where the next dam was going in. Some have seen their sons "learn the trade" as apprentices, and seen them take their places as full-fledged certified journeymen in the course of TVA construction. Some have seen their boys go up as foremen in their own trade. Each knows the youngster can handle the job because the apprenticeship he served was measured step by step with requirements for skill defined and taught by the proven journeymen themselves, supervised and administered jointly by their unions and the TVA management. These men and their labor organizations—nearly all of TVA's construction and operating employees are members of unions—have for years had a formal agreement with the TVA covering hours of work, wages, working conditions, the adjustment of grievances by orderly procedures, and the like. More recently professional and clerical workers have had a similar agreement with TVA. The workers' recognition of the part they play in the unified development of the valley was written into the opening words of the initial agreement in this language: "The *public interest in an undertaking such as TVA always being paramount . . ."*

How well labor has served the public interest, the valley's interest, as their own through the rigors and rewards of building dams, of keeping the power lines hot and the phosphate moving to the land, is written in the fastest schedules ever met for major dam building anywhere, in low costs, and in the quality of the jobs they have completed. Labor's rank and file and their chosen leaders have made TVA's business their business and hence the valley's interest their interest.

Management in the TVA takes but small credit for enlisting the active participation of organized labor in the job of harnessing the river. It was labor, almost from the beginning of the project, that saw in the TVA an opportunity to prove that the worker of the South is worthy of his hire, that he can master new skills, that good wage standards and working conditions arrived at among free men through the process of conference and collective bargaining are democracy's key to superior management, low costs, and quality workmanship. There have been false notes and setbacks occasionally, of course. In the first year or so of TVA there were those who saw in the job at the dam nothing more than a chance to get a "government job." Among the supervisors and labor representatives a handful of aspiring tough guys thought, mistakenly, that here was an opportunity to muscle in with their special brand of local racketeering. But the vast majority looked at it quite differently.

The way the very first workers were selected had something to do with the way things worked out in later years. In 1933 the TVA held written examinations in 179 counties in seven states as a method of finding the few thousand recruits needed to build Norris Dam, the first of the chain. For the man whose mental processes were inclined to freeze when he had pencil and paper before him, a part of the examination was in pictures—for we were seeking mechanical aptitude and general intelligence. Thus, on a given day, some 38,000 of the original 60,000 applicants for jobs went to the school or courthouse of their county seat and did business with the TVA for the first time. It was an act of faith. No one had ever done such a thing before in selecting construction workers. But to thousands of men grimly eager to work after years of the depression, and accustomed to seeking a government job only through political obeisance or influence, the Workmen's Examination apparently seemed worth a try; maybe it meant a fair break on their merits.

TVA kept faith with them. And so well did the system work (as the carefully kept figures of statistical correlation between the examination results and subsequent job performance show) that the TVA Workmen's Examination was repeated in modified form every few years. It became a repetitive symbol of TVA as an "efficient job" and no need for "pull" to get on.

Men came from the mountains; their hill farms were left for their kinfolk to tend. From the cities down the river came the veterans of the building and metal trades. Coal miners in the Cumberland Plateau country took the examination. They had long been idle from the stalemate of a strike that left them in mining towns the operators had finally deserted. Many of them were later called to TVA work. After a few months at Norris Dam anyone could see that this was not an ordinary construction force. These TVA workers, on the job and in their union meetings, in specific ways made it known they had a stake in what the success of TVA could mean for labor and what it could accomplish for their region. The workers said they wanted training courses, for there would be other dams. Norris Dam was the beginning—if TVA made a good record there would be more dams and a valley-wide power system. They said they wanted to know more about cheaper electricity; and what was TVA going to do with the idle nitrate plants at Muscle Shoals?

The workers went about the job in a way that showed there was something big at stake. Visitors who talked with the men at work told us they could sense this underlying purpose among the men of TVA. Numerous incidents that came to light in hearings to consider job grievances revealed a deep loyalty to the expressed broad purposes of TVA. Frequently those very grievances were aired because the men believed that the public purposes of the whole project were being violated by supervisors or others; they wanted something done about it.

Other dams followed Norris, and at Wheeler Dam, at Pickwick, Guntersville, Chickamauga, Hiwassee, Kentucky, Watts Bar, Cherokee, Douglas, Fontana, and the others, the tone and tempo of the work was much the same. It persists to this day, though the men are more casual about it in 1953 than in 1933. That is easy to understand. They are a smoothly functioning organization. They know what they can do.

Nor have organized labor's interest and partnership in the development of the valley been confined to their TVA pay check. The leaders of labor who have worked alongside TVA's management have seen the scope of the TVA's efforts to uncover and try to remove the barriers standing in the way of the valley's—and hence their own—chance of a better living. Many of them know from bitter personal experience of the wasting farm land, of floods that devastate factories, jobs, and homes. TVA they saw as a way to rid the valley of these forces that held them back.

Around the wage conference table the intensity of this faith in the valley and labor's desire to help to build its future were repeated again and again down the years. Once a year union officials, flanked by delegates from each of the major jobs, meet with management to work out adjustments in wages, working rules, and supplements to their basic agreements with TVA. On these occasions and in frequent joint meetings on other subjects there is ever-increasing evidence that the TVA to them is more than a place to work. They show this too in the formal briefs presented by the Tennessee Valley Trades and Labor Council, through which the fifteen building and metal trade unions representing some 14,000 employees present to management their facts, arguments, and ideas. They show it in the long-range studies of joint problems made by the panel which represents white-collar employees.

You hear expressions of the same attitude of being in on the job of building the valley in the numerous joint union-management committees that do the grinding detail work of the wage and salary conferences, or the joint committee on apprenticeship training. You see this sense of participation in the sixty local joint union-management co-operative committees which promote better ways of doing the job and better understanding of the TVA program. In this machinery devised and formalized by joint agreement and experience is *a steady process of citizen self-education*: a learning in this way of the economics of this valley and the problems of *all* of its people, not of its industrial workers alone. As the men leave TVA jobs for

private employment, many carry with them not only new skills but
broader understanding.

The leaders of organized labor, as they participate in the affairs
of the TVA, inject a strong note of realism into problems to be faced
for the region's future progress. From the information they gain in
their working partnership with the TVA they, like the demonstration farmer, carry the lessons of TVA into the daily stream of life
and affairs throughout the valley. These leaders, the members of
the Tennessee Valley Trades and Labor Council and of the panel
representing white-collar employees, are active, responsible citizens
in their own communities. One, for example, was a member of the
postwar planning committee of a large valley city. The problems of
the industrial future of his community, as puzzled over by that committee, may well represent the problem of the valley in miniature.
Another member of the Valley Council was president of the State
Federation of Labor in his state, active in various public advisory
committees and commissions dealing with education, industrial development, and the conservation and use of resources. The facts
and alternatives facing the region as a whole which emerge from
the discussions of labor and management in the TVA are enriched
by the wealth of experience of these labor leaders; in turn the
knowledge about the valley as a whole—its potentialities and the
barriers to progress—which comes from the TVA staff in these
joint conferences is bound to find its way into the deliberations and
decisions in which labor leaders participate outside their activities
directly associated with TVA.

The process of self-education on the part of both labor and management in the TVA has its effect in another way. TVA is required
by law to pay its trade and labor employees the "rate of wages prevailing for similar work in the vicinity." The same standard has
recently been accepted, by agreement, for professional and clerical
employees. Labor and management currently carry on factual field
surveys; the facts so ascertained form the basis for wage negotiations once each year—to reach agreement as to what the prevailing
rates are for the whole area in which TVA operates. In reaching
agreement on this complex question two sharp alternatives are ever
present: should wages be established on each TVA project to
correspond to the rates "prevailing" in that particular locality; or

should rates be adopted which will be uniform throughout the region on all TVA projects?

There is in this issue a myriad of conflicting interests within the ranks of labor itself—locality versus region, locality versus locality. But the give and take of discussion in the first wage negotiation and since has established a policy of viewing *the region* as the "vicinity." Labor as a whole obviously gains something in supporting this policy. But it also loses something in specific communities, because the TVA prevailing rate, while not the lowest, is not the highest or even a mathematically perfect average. And in such a process the participants on both sides of the table have learned to test the interpretation of the facts and the wisdom of their judgments by this measure: what is the answer that will best serve the *whole region*, promote the efficiency of the TVA, encourage labor standards that will aid the development of the region as a whole.

In mid-September of 1943 the Board of Directors and staff of the TVA held an all-day session with the Executive Committee of the Valley Trades and Labor Council. Not, however, to consider wages and hours; these were not dealt with at all. What was discussed in detail were problems of after-the-war demobilization; the intricacies of the freight rate differentials between the Southeast and other interior regions of the country and the East; the future fertilizer and land program of the valley.

These are not "labor" issues. They are problems of common interest to labor as to businessmen and to farmers, and because all three groups have a rising concern for the development of their valley the wise handling of these problems constitutes a bond between farmers, businessmen, and labor.

The workers of the Tennessee Valley do not need to be urged to apply their labors and pledge their faith to the rebuilding of the region, for this simple reason: *they want to live here.* Many of them have lived for varying periods in the industrial cities of the North, the East, and, more lately, the West. They have been in the "big money." Frequently in the past there has been no other choice but to stay away after such a periodic migration out of the South. But they see that a change has taken place in the valley. They want to live here, do their work here—these men, bred to the ridges, to the slopes and open lands of a beautiful valley, and to the ties of long established kinship in their communities and in their cities. And a man's wish to be in one place and not another must be respected as a basic fact in any democratic planning.

The methods of TVA, working at the grass roots, apply to businessmen as well as to farmers and to labor. The changes in this valley have been due, to an important extent of course, to businessmen. Although many at first were suspicious of TVA, or saw it only as a power producer or a form of "politics," by the end of the first decade most businessmen accepted as their own the TVA idea of region-building quite as wholeheartedly and understandingly as have farmers and industrial workers.

What is most encouraging to me is the unmistakable evidence that many businessmen have come to think in terms of the unity that seems to me so essential: unity of all resources, and unity in developing them as between farmers and businessmen. And they are becoming articulate about it, able in informal ways to express the "lessons" we are all learning in the now mature experiment in democracy that is the TVA. For example, a half-page newspaper advertisement of the Alabama Dairy Products Corporation provides an unpretentious but genuine illustration of what I have in mind. This business was set up in the small city of Decatur, Alabama, by local capital and local management to build and operate a cheese factory, the first in all northern Alabama. The ad begins in large letters:

THE CHEESE PLANT
IS A
CHILD
OF THE PEOPLE AND
TVA . . .

TVA brought new hope to the farmers who were struggling with the washed, worn-out lands. The Authority's wide erosion control plan combined with an intensive soil rehabilitation program resulted in richer farming lands.

Then electricity came to the farm, lighting the way to a wide diversification program. This electric power was to aid the farmer to expand into branches other than the production of one major crop.

Following expert advice the farmer now began to build a fine dairy herd. Steadily it developed to the size which demanded a ready market for the product.

Here is where the cheese plant began . . .

The primary purpose of the cheese plant, established in 1940, was to provide a market for milk and thus to encourage the improvement of agriculture through dairying; those who backed the enterprise financially were warned that they might "kiss their money goodby." They were agreeably surprised. The cheese factory did a good job and it prospered, giving the investors an excellent return.

Nevertheless, it was felt that still more promotional work was needed to develop the dairy industry in the area, and the enterprise was too small to finance the job. So a few years later, in 1948, the company leased its plant and its milk supply rights to the Carnation Milk Company, which had a much broader base of resources with which to assist the farmers of the area in their production efforts. The cheese plant went out of operation, except as a receiving station, but the job of encouraging the spread and improvement of dairying went on and milk production in the Decatur area has continued to increase.

And there was an interesting aftermath. Over across the state line, the people of Cedartown, Georgia, heard about the Decatur cheese factory and proceeded to investigate. As a result, the president of the Alabama Dairy Products Corporation was called to Cedartown to set up and operate a new cheese plant there, thus helping to build up the dairy industry in that area.

Businessmen and business enterprise have come to understand to a remarkable degree the principles of interrelation upon which, under the TVA idea, everything depends. An instance is that of a large manufacturer producing paper from wood pulp. In this operation immense quantities of water are used, drawn from one of the mountain tributaries of the Tennessee. The company was put to considerable expense in processing the 45,000,000 gallons of water it used each day to remove the silt that drained into it, borne from the farm lands of the watershed.

Near this plant was a farm "area" demonstration. The company's officials began to observe that the water flowing to the streams from these phosphate-using farm lands contained less silt than before, because of the improved crop cover over their slopes, and that the flow of water was more nearly equalized. If the farmers on the watersheds from which the company obtained its own supply of water could adopt the methods used on these area demonstration farms, it might so reduce the silt in the water as to cut down these expensive desilting operations. Therefore these businessmen offered financial assistance to set up other farm area demonstrations; they became members of the Haywood County Mutual Soil Conservation and Land Use Association. I attended a meeting held on several farms of the associations of the area, with a membership of six hundred farm families. Standing under the hot August sun, taking an active part, examining a field of clover or bluegrass pasture with the farmers, was one of the company's officers.

The "sights" of businessmen had widened. But so had the understanding of farmers grown, as a result of their new associate from business. They learned how important their farming practices might be to an industry where many of their sons and neighbors are earning their living.

To strengthen the opportunity for a particular kind of businessmen to make a profit is sometimes the best way to induce their enterprise to add its part to the unity of resource development. The valley's development of a new pressure cooker for obtaining oil from the seed of the cotton plant, is an illustration.

There are in the South hundreds of mills for the extraction of oil from cottonseed. Their purchases of cottonseed from the gins, and the methods of marketing the cottonseed meal left over after the oil is pressed out, exert an influence on cotton agriculture and on the fortunes of all who depend upon cotton for a livelihood. Despite the present shift away from cotton production, cotton continues to be a southern staple, and is bound to be such for many years to come. Here again is the seamless web, for soil fertility in parts of the South is in a measure dependent on the success of the cottonseed oil industry. If the meal left over after the oil is pressed from the cottonseed could be fed to livestock in the South, as much as 80 per cent of the fertilizing value of the meal would be returned to the soil rather than continuously drained from the soil by export. And export has long been the general rule. If the operators of cottonseed oil mills in the Southeast made money, so that the meal could be produced locally and consumed locally, the whole region would benefit. Soil fertility in this case depends in part upon businessmen.

A farm family watches as the linemen from their locally owned cooperative prepare to get electricity into their home.

(*This photograph and those on the following pages are reproduced through the courtesy of the Tennessee Valley Authority.*)

A tow carrying a million and a half gallons of gasoline arriving at its terminal at Knoxville, 630 miles from the Tennessee's confluence with the Ohio near Paducah, Ky.

A vacation resort—one of many operated by private concerns or local government, visited by millions of recreation-seekers.

The task of re-building the land is far from complete.
(Note: this is a close-up of badly eroded gully)

A Kentucky farm boy displays his own reforestation project, to heal the gullies and to produce a cash crop of loblolly pine.

Views of TVA's huge Johnsonville, Tenn., steam-electric plant,
units of a Valley-wide chain that make TVA one of the country's largest consumers of coal.

A North Alabama farmer and his son prepare to experiment with TVA concentrated phosphate fertilizer, and see if it will bring new life to the land.

A new "hired hand"—a portable electric motor. Electrified farms have increased from 3 out of 100 in 1933 to 90 out of 100 in 1953.

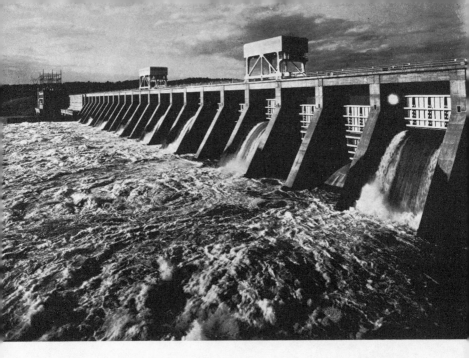

The Tennessee under man's control: releasing water through spillways at Pickwick Landing Dam, to provide storage capacity against the time of flood waters.

Fontana Dam, capable of storing more than a million acre-feet of water in the North Carolina mountains, to control spring floods hundreds of miles away, and in the dry season to increase power output through 10 dams downstream.

The new Valley's permanent grasslands—one consequence of TVA fertilizer research and demonstration program.

A new type of TVA electric furnace, for the smelting of phosphate; resulting technical improvements are made use of by the fertilizer industry.

Part of a fleet of seventy pleasure craft making the 630-mile cruise through the length of the "Great Lakes of the South."

Game fish are so plentiful on the Valley's new lakes that the states have imposed no closed seasons.

The businessmen in the cotton oil industry have had a hard time. Hundreds of the small mills operated for years at a very low rate of return, just hanging on. Before TVA the equipment used in the extraction of cottonseed oil had not been improved for over forty years.

The valley's technicians in the TVA and the University of Tennessee, and businessmen represented by two of the cotton oil industry's associations, after several years of work invented a cottonseed pressure cooking device, a radical improvement in the technical processes of this business. The invention was by a public agency; the machinery was made, under license, by several well-known machinery plants. By aiding business to secure a better margin of profit, this machine gave an added opportunity to aid soil fertility and thereby the regions' over-all development.

Wood-using industries furnish another instance of businessmen turning to public technical agencies that work at the grass roots. The men in this important business have learned that they can turn to the Authority's area-wide inventory of forest resources to learn the location, kind, and quantities of timber stumpage, prices, stocks on hand, and other factors affecting profitable production.

Bowater Southern Paper Corporation, for example, recently requested information concerning possible sites in the Tennessee Valley for a $50,000,000 newsprint plant, data on the necessary power, water for processing and for disposing of plant wastes without exorbitant costs, coal, labor supply, etc. Most important of all, of course, was a continuous supply of pine timber. At first it appeared that the plant would not be built, for on the basis of the highly generalized information such as is developed for the country as a whole it appeared that the adjacent area might not be able to provide the timber. However, TVA's detailed studies showed that the area could supply enough pulpwood for the plant initially, and with good management the forests could grow a continuous supply. On this basis the Bowater Corporation, in 1952, secured its financing and commenced construction of its plant on the banks of the Hiwassee River, near its confluence with the Tennessee.

Besides assisting a private concern, TVA thus was able to contribute also to the improved management and use of the region's forest resource. While growing about half its requirements, the corporation will purchase the remainder from forest and woodland owners. This will provide a market for pine thinnings, thus encouraging reforestation and better forest management.

These businessmen put reliance upon this counsel because, for one thing, it showed an understanding that businessmen must make a profit. And yet from the point of view of the region's resources the recommendation was sound. A good market was developed for a species of timber hitherto regarded as undesirable. The development of the valley's resources was helped. Another group of businessmen was drawn into the task of unified development.

But of course the effort to draw businessmen into the task of unified development is no more uniformly successful than would be the case with any other group. The development of traffic on the Tennessee River illustrates how businessmen have become part of that aspect of the valley's changing life. It also serves to illustrate some of the difficulties that lie in the path of grass-roots democracy, and how essential is patience in working out sound rather than merely "quick" solutions.

America's inland waterways have been used extensively only by a relatively few large shippers of such commodities as coal, oil, sand and gravel, and wheat. This traditional and important kind of traffic alone would not aid greatly in developing the whole valley, and particularly its manufacturing opportunities. What is specially needed is the smaller shipper, who could not use a whole tow of barges or even a whole barge—the shipper of manufactured or partly processed articles, such as baking soda, cotton textiles, fertilizer, flour, radios, furniture.

How could this objective be reached? One way to promote shipping on the river would be for the TVA itself to promote and develop such traffic. This would mean sending a corps of TVA traffic experts directly to prospective shippers to solicit business for the river. That method was rejected, for the grassroots principle dictated another course, and the one that was followed. If businessmen would accept the function and responsibility of promoting the use of the river, dealing directly with prospective shippers, this would draw into the development of this regional resource a whole new group of private citizens, and give them the compensation of direct participation in their region's building.

A number of businessmen who had understood for many years

how the river would further their own interests were encouraged to take the leadership. A private organization, the Tennessee Valley Waterway Conference, was formed. This association and TVA technical experts developed plans for a series of terminals physically tying the railroads and truck highways into the waterways—the first system of public-use terminals on any of our inland waterways. These would open the river to the smaller shipper who could not afford to erect his own terminal. TVA secured an appropriation from Congress for the construction of these facilities.

Thus it was the businessmen of the Tennessee Valley who became the most active participants in developing commercial use of the new navigable channel. In studying whether this or that article was suitable for river movement, wide fields of education were opened. Businessmen came to discuss many matters with TVA's staff—not only its navigation experts, but inevitably industrial, railroad, agricultural, chemical, and other specialists. It was soon clear that more than transportation rates and savings were involved in the use of the river.

The river became a kind of schoolroom, too, like the demonstration farm, this time principally for businessmen, a schoolroom in the unity of resource development. Minerals and forests and the products of the farm were seen in specific cases to be inter-related closely with industry and transportation. The reservoir system, like phosphate and power, became a stimulus to a new kind of thinking, and that thinking bred new factories, new industrial ideas, and the further release of creative human energies. The pride and satisfaction which the business leaders in the Waterway Conference derived from thus performing a public service was not the least important result.

This story, I have said, also illustrates one of the difficulties of TVA's methods—and there are many. In Knoxville, Tennessee, one of the largest of the river communities, local business leadership seemed apathetic. Yet it was important to the whole region that a terminal be built and used at this point. There was a considerable temptation for TVA not to wait for community initiative to develop, but to go ahead on its own, developing the traffic which we were sure would be available. But it was our judgment that this method would prove far less effective than citizen participation.

Unless the businessmen of the community would assume responsibility for traffic development we doubted whether there would be traffic through the terminal sufficient to justify the use of the critical materials (this was during World War II) required in its construction. We decided, therefore, that the construction of a terminal at this one point should be deferred indefinitely. This action created considerable indignation against the TVA in some quarters in Knoxville.

The businessmen, however, saw the point at once. They organized a committee, and called meetings of manufacturers and other prospective shippers. At the first of these meetings one of the local committee members, a banker, summed up the situation by this comment, as quoted in the press: "I don't believe but one thing was responsible for the apparent apathy—we looked on it like Christmas. Santa Claus was coming. There wasn't anything to do but hang up our stocking and we wouldn't do that until the night before Christmas." The services of the president of the Waterway Conference, a resident of another city, were requested and gladly given. TVA's staff assistance was, of course, made available and fully used, on a host of technical questions. The report of this citizen committee showed that a volume of prospective traffic had been found and developed by the committee clearly beyond anything TVA's own staff could have produced.

It would have been simpler and easier, and would have involved less unpleasant recrimination, if TVA had accepted the role of a bureaucratic Santa Claus. But the results, simply in terms of economic effect alone, would have been less effective. Democratic methods are not only right in human terms; they are the most "efficient."

This Knoxville terminal has since been built, as have similar ones at Chattanooga and at Decatur and Guntersville, Alabama. From the outset, it was TVA's purpose to turn these public use water terminals over to private business, or to some non-federal association representing shipping and industrial interests, for operation. Early in 1952, private concerns began operating all four of the terminals under license-lease agreements with options to purchase, and the new operators immediately commenced active work to develop new business. Another public use terminal went into operation at Sheffield, Alabama. These are in addition to the 30 terminals which private industry has built along the river since 1933.

Democratic methods are often slow. They sometimes require a willingness to wait. Sometimes they strike a stone wall of inaction, where other methods would seem to yield quick results. But the benefits of such "action" by nursemaid or dictatorial practices are usually temporary, and often more apparent than real.

Chapter 11

THE DECISIONS OF BUSINESSMEN

THE decisions of businessmen have never been so important as today. The way businessmen think and act in respect to the resources upon which we all depend, the way in which they use the modern skills of experts, in short the breadth of their statesmanship, will determine the future of our resources and thereby the fate of many millions of human beings.

The fate of private industry as we have known it may be at stake as well. Eloquent orators and the message of full-page advertising extol the advantages of private industry in vain if industry loses the confidence of the people. And that confidence will almost surely be forfeit if in the coming decades the people believe the results of industrialization are bad when they think there is a way that they could be good.

One has only to live in a valley that is still relatively undeveloped industrially to realize how great is this gamble of the future. Looking upon the magnificence of this natural beauty you cannot fail to reflect upon what an ugly, wasteful mess industrialization brought to many other once lovely and livable countrysides—on the Monongahela and the Tyne, the Delaware and the Ohio.

With the eyes of industry now upon this valley (as they are indeed upon many valleys the world over) planning a further considerable industrial expansion, there is an opportunity to plan and to build so that resources will endure, natural beauty be spared despoliation. Here there is a chance to see to it that human well-being in city and town will not, through lack of ingenuity and foresight, be needlessly sacrificed. Is the only choice one between pastoral poverty and industrial slums? Can private industry utilize these resources, at a profit, and yet sustain their vigor and longevity? Can business and the common weal both be served? To be able to make an affirmative reply is a matter of the greatest moment.

In the Tennessee Valley the answers may turn to some extent upon how successful the TVA is in its efforts to weld a union of the public interest and the private interests of businessmen. TVA appears to be uncovering and developing in this valley principles and practices for effecting a jointure of public interests with private, by methods that are voluntary and noncoercive. The actual experience is unpretentious as measured by the scope of the problem, but it is definitely encouraging and of not a little significance for industry and the people of the country generally. Although touched on in preceding chapters, some aspects deserve more precise discussion.

What the TVA, in specific ways, has sought to do can be simply stated: to accept an obligation to harmonize the private interest in earning a return from natural resources, with the dominant public interest in their unified and fruitful development. The method— and this is the distinctive part of the experiment—is to try to bring to bear at the grass roots the skills of public experts and administrators not for negative regulation but *to make affirmative action in the public interest both feasible and appealing to private industry*. By public interest I mean the interest of people—individual human beings—not "the people" in their institutional roles as wage earners or investors or voters or consumers. "Underneath all, individuals," men and women and children.

These technical skills can be most effective in promoting the people's welfare when they function close to the conflicts between private and public interest at the time they occur and before they become hardened and confused by the dogmas that flourish under absentee and over-centralized administration. Herein lies the reason for such productive results as have been thus far obtained, and the not unfavorable prospects for the future. The real tests of the method still lie ahead, perhaps a full generation or more; this I fully realize.

To process the raw resources of nature is a major job of private industry. For industry to be able to do the job, consumers must pay to industry for that task all of its costs, including a chance for adequate profit. Those resources, however, are the total of the people's physical substance, so if they are wasted, or spent with no thought of the future, we, as a people, are insolvent and stranded. A civilization is only strong and long-lived to the degree that it shows skill in sustaining the life and productivity of its resources. From this law of history there is no escape by the chanting of catch-phrases. These are bedrock realities.

Good, prudent management of resources by industry is a matter of national life and death. But it cannot rest upon industry's good intentions alone. Private industries are rarely either in a position (this is often overlooked), on their own, to see specifically what is needed to protect the basic public interest in resources, or able, as an industry, to take action that will protect that interest. And yet when from time to time it fails to do so we all "cuss out" industry, often in a fine frenzy of self-righteousness. As a remedy legal punishment is imposed. A recently added remedy has been to impose some form of regulation, almost invariably static and negative. This is usually a judgment based on hindsight; it assumes that industry knew how to protect the general public interest and, knowing, deliberately failed to use its knowledge.

An industry may well have the keenest desire to maintain the people's resource solvency and their long-term interest; but what it may *want* to do and what it feels *able* to do as a private industry are often quite different things. The two interests often clash, or appear to do so. It is to this task of harmonizing such conflicts that TVA's efforts have been directed.

An important illustration is the TVA's extensive program of phosphatic fertilizer research, production, and demonstration. I have already related how the continual and alarming decline of phosphate in American lands led TVA, at its Muscle Shoals laboratories, to develop an electric furnace process for making fertilizers. That process produced fertilizers highly concentrated in terms of what technicians call "plant nutrient." But rock phosphate—the raw material—is exhaustible, and when exhausted is irreplaceable. With this electric furnace not only high-grade ore deposits but also the sometimes wasted low grades could be drawn upon. This was in the long-time interest of our phosphate reserves, of the land, of the production of nutritious food, and hence of the vigor and permanence of our civilization.

The TVA was hopeful that private industry would adopt these technical improvements. Thereby lower grade ores would be utilized; higher concentrations would reduce transport and other costs of getting fertilizer to the land. We envisaged, as a consequence, expanding farmer demand, and a resulting large increase in private production and distribution. Thus the then woefully limited use of phosphate on the land could be multiplied and both the private and the public interest could be served.

The fertilizer industry, however, with some exceptions, was not convinced. Its position in 1934, at the beginning of TVA's work, was substantially this: However desirable it might be for the land and for the husbanding of ore reserves to produce concentrated phosphate, with admitted savings in cost, farmers simply would not use it. "In the past we have tried to get them to buy 'high-analysis' (i.e., concentrated) fertilizer," the industry said quite reasonably, "but they don't want it; what they want is the mixed and low-analysis fertilizer. And what the customer wants, we must supply."

TVA obtained the best technical advice in the country, from the federal Department of Agriculture, the state agricultural institutions, and private consultants. It concluded that by actual test, demonstration, and proved results, farmers would themselves be persuaded to make wide use of these concentrated phosphates.

The story of the successful valleywide (later nationwide) educational program to test and demonstrate to farmers the value of concentrated phosphate fertilizers I have already outlined. Following upon these demonstrations in twenty-eight states and the nationwide program of the Agricultural Adjustment Administration, the sale of concentrated fertilizer produced and distributed by private industry rose sharply.

In 1934 the country's phosphate industry produced 2,984,375 tons of ordinary superphosphate and 69,552 tons of concentrated superphosphate. Seven years later, in 1941, this had increased to 5,055,737 tons of ordinary superphosphate and 317,990 tons of concentrated superphosphate, while in 1951 the production reached 9,432,283 tons of ordinary superphosphate and 717,237 tons of concentrated superphosphate.

Fertilizer consumption in the valley states was 64 per cent more in 1941 than in 1934. By 1951 it was 197 per cent more than in 1934. And whereas production of ordinary superphosphate had about trebled in the period, production of the concentrated superphosphate had multiplied more than ten times.

In the counties of the Tennessee Valley the rate of increase in use of phosphatic fertilizer, purchased by the farmer with his own funds from regular channels, was 500 per cent greater than in the country as a whole. Heretofore no such increases as these had ever taken place in the production and sale of this private industry's product.

Commercial fertilizer sales, in the fifteen valley counties of Alabama where TVA-concentrate farm demonstrations were conducted, increased from 103,100 tons in 1935 to 332,300 tons in 1951, an increase of 222 per cent; during the same period commercial fertilizer sales in the rest of the state increased only 139 per cent. In the fifteen valley counties of North Carolina commercial fertilizer sales increased 203 per cent from 1935 to 1947, while in the rest of the state the increase during the same period was only 68 per cent.

A report from a Virginia state agency makes the following statement:

In the beginning, only the demonstrators used phosphate, that supplied by the Tennessee Valley Authority. Then, as their results were observed, other farmers began to buy phosphate from dealers. . . . One concern, which has six affiliated stores in the valley area, sold 60 per cent more superphosphate during the 1937-40 period than during the preceding four years.

As such results from these demonstrations came in, the manufacturers of fertilizer ingredients, for the most part, became actively interested in the TVA's work. TVA's policy was (and continues to be) to make its technicians available to industry for counsel. Electric furnaces were installed by private concerns, with the benefit of TVA designs. The flow of results secured the approval, too, of the national and state farmers' co-operative associations that sell fertilizers. But opposition came, with a few encouraging exceptions, from the makers and distributors of low-analysis "mixed" fertilizers. The use by farmers of concentrates—high-analysis material—calls for changes in the present costly methods of *distribution*. This may account for the opposition by fertilizer "mixers" and thousands of middlemen. But in public the arguments are largely in the familiar abstract phrases: "government in business," "invasion of the field of free enterprise." Neither farm organizations, Congress, nor the progressive private producers of concentrated phosphatic fertilizers have ever been much impressed by the distributors' reasons for opposing TVA's program.

The TVA chemical engineering laboratories and production facilities at Muscle Shoals have been relied upon more and more by private manufacturing companies as the years have passed. The story is one of successful government-industry relations in the public interest. In the fiscal year 1952, for example, more than 750 chemical engineers, chemists, and other technicial people came to Muscle Shoals to study new and improved processes, equipment, and products which have been developed there. All of the producers of elemental phosphorus in the country, and virtually all the manufacturers of phosphate, have had technical assistance from the TVA between 1933 and 1950. During that period the phosphorus production capacity had increased to 145,000 tons (seven times that of 1933); estimates of capacity for 1952 were double the capacity of 1950.

One of the early objectives of TVA research was to develop methods for using lower grade phosphate ores. One purpose was to encourage the development of the large deposits in the West, constituting perhaps three quarters of the U.S. known reserves. Such development started in 1949, when Westvaco Chemical Division of Food Machinery and Chemical Corporation began to build electric furnaces in Idaho, to be followed by Victor Chemical, Monsanto Chemical, and others.

Illustrative of the role of TVA with respect to private industry is the story of dicalcium phosphate, a material used as a supplement to cattle feed. TVA built and operated a plant for the production of this material during World War II, when imports of bone meal from Australia and South America for cattle feed supplements were cut off. Since the process offered scant opportunity for further research, TVA discontinued operations in 1950 and offered complete data on both process and markets to private enterprise.

Several firms, including the Hoosac Valley Lime Company in Massachusetts, began to use the process. In 1952, Shea Chemical Company, a new subsidiary of the Hoosac Valley Lime Company, constructed a new plant, including an electric furnace installation, in central Tennessee, calling upon TVA for technical advice and the loan of engineering drawings.

TVA's policy of technical service to private industry in the fertilizer field, to farmers and their co-operatives, has become fully established. In 1951 a formal working agreement was reached with the trade association of the industry. The National Fertilizer Association employed a representative to keep in touch with the industry, TVA, and other government agencies, and commenced issuing a monthly bulletin to keep the fertilizer industry currently informed on technological developments by TVA and others. TVA's nitric phosphate processes were featured in four of the first five issues. In 1952, the National Fertilizer Association, at its annual meeting, proposed that TVA include in its research program some of the projects suggested by the Association's subcommittee on chemical processing and manufacturing.

The extensive recreational use of TVA's reservoirs provides a further illustration of how public interest in a natural resource—the use of these beautiful man-made lakes for recreation—and the private interest of businessmen in developing profitable enterprise can be harmonized.

In addition to their primary purposes of a navigable channel, flood control, and power, the lakes behind these dams now form the basis for a major private industry representing almost $27,500,-000 of private investment in recreational facilities and equipment, and the mainstay of a tourist and vacation business in the valley estimated to gross over $400,000,000 a year and steadily growing. Nothing quite like this has occurred anywhere in America, on such a scale.

Prior to TVA the recreational potentialities of reservoirs were considered of little or no consequence in the traditional methods of Federal river development in this country. Nor at the beginning of TVA were these money-making possibilities of recreation on the lakes apparent to private business in the valley. In order to stimulate this business development with all its public benefits, TVA set up a few "demonstration" park areas such as the one at Norris Dam; these have been seen by millions of people. The demonstrations established that recreation— fishing and boating in particular—was entirely consistent with the primary purposes for which the reservoirs were created, and that the raising and lowering of the lake's water levels for flood control, navigation, power, and malaria control did not interfere markedly with such recreational use. Standards and costs of construction and operation of docks, cottages, and village services were developed during this demonstration period.

Most important, the demonstrations gradually established in the minds of businessmen that here was a form of enterprise that with good management could be made financially attractive. As a consequence the public benefits of these lakes now extends to an ever-increasing number of that two thirds of the American population who live less than 500 miles from the Valley's lakes. During 1951 there were an estimated 24 million person-day visits to the TVA lakes and dams.

By 1950 TVA had disposed of all of its demonstrations. Every recreation operation along the 10,000-odd miles of lake shoreline is now being run either by the states or counties or by private business. The TVA's experts in recreational and land planning and development, the management experts, and the business community have thus succeeded in bringing together the public interest in a natural resource and the private interest of businessmen in a profit.

A comprehensive and unique contract between the TVA and the Aluminum Company of America, whose point of view is generally different from that of the TVA, provides still another illustration of harmonizing public and private interest in resources.

The Aluminum Company of America has long owned several dams at the headwaters of the Little Tennessee River, a tributary of the Tennessee. Those dams, lying above the many dams of the TVA, if operated as part of the TVA system of dams, would result in greater public benefits both in power and flood control than if they continued to operate independently. The purpose of the years of study and negotiations that resulted in the contract was to find a way whereby the maximum public usefulness of the river's water resource could be secured without reducing the power available to the company from its dams or increasing its costs. Under the contract, signed in 1941, the Aluminum Company agreed to turn over to the TVA, indefinitely, the right to direct just how Alcoa's dams should function, that is, when water should be stored from hour to hour, and when released through power turbines or sluice gates. The contract's effect (without any change in Alcoa's title to its property) is to unify the control of water of the entire watershed, and thereby increase the public benefits accruing not only in power but also in flood control and navigation. The added power benefits created by the arrangements are divided between the parties to the contract by a formula which both sides believe advantageous. A strategic power site, long owned by the company, was also turned over to TVA, and upon it Fontana Dam in the high mountains of North Carolina was built.

The Aluminum Company of America and TVA are organizations widely apart in their purposes. And yet by keeping their attention on the physical facts—that the river could be made more productive if Alcoa's private dams and TVA's public ones were operated as a unit—agreement was reached in a complex situation. By avoiding the conventional abstractions and clichés that often mark discussions where public and private interests and philosophies appear to conflict, it was here possible to promote both private benefit and the people's interest.

There is still another kind of clash, or *apparent clash*, between private interests and the public as a whole. I refer to that between industry and the people as consumers of industry's products. And just as we have generally taken it for granted, that industry is *able* to determine what is the best use of resources, similarly we have uncritically assumed that each individual industry or business is always in a position to determine what are the actual needs of the consumers of its products.

There is prevalent an idea, often mistaken, that the needs of consumers will be met by industry quite automatically. It is true that in a real sense customers in our highly competitive country hold a kind of daily plebiscite. If sales fall off, that does tend to prove that the particular product or service does not fulfill the public's needs; if sales rise, that establishes that they do. Such a referendum is supplemented, of course, by customer advertising, and by many devices that induce people to "vote right" on a product.

The theory, generally quite sound, from time to time breaks down badly. A case in point is the way in which phosphate supply has failed by a wide margin to keep up with the needs of the land and of the farmers' willingness to buy more of the concentrate product if it were available. Then too we sometimes see that the customer has no way of knowing what kind or variety of products *could* be produced, and therefore that he is forced to state his wants only in the terms of his ignorance of what he could get if he had a real choice (not unlike a "free" election where one may vote as he pleases so long as it is for the one candidate who is "eligible"). Or we learn that monopoly keeps a new enterpriser from supplying essential needs, or that the customer is misled or "high-pressured." The remedies usually applied are sporadic and protracted antitrust or fair trade proceedings or negative regulation, the everlasting "don't do it again."

Most manufacturers are thoroughly competent on their own to produce almost any kind of industrial product and to judge of market needs. Not all of them, by any means, however, are in a position to ascertain the best use of resources as judged by the over-all public interest, and some do not get so close to actual consumer needs in special cases as even the promotion of their own interests as manufacturers would make desirable. Thus the ablest agricultural machinery concern did not create a thresher for grain farming in this Appalachian Mountain country, for example, because, in part, their technicians had no intimate knowledge, or "feel," for the special farming conditions and no confidence that there was a profit to be made from such a product.

Because TVA's engineers were closer to the problems and had such knowledge and confidence, they were able some years ago to design a successful portable thresher for use under the conditions of this valley. About 80 per cent of the farmers in this mountainous area, as of 1947, have forty acres of tillable land. To haul the conventional large thresher to these scattered and small fields over rough hill roads was impractical and expensive. The small threshers on the market proved unsuitable. The new design proved practical in extensive tests, and is being produced and sold by a private concern.

Through all the examples I have been reciting runs the theme and purpose of bringing into union two vital concerns: the compelling necessity that our natural resources be made sustaining and permanently productive for everyone's welfare, and the business necessities of private industry.

Chapter 12

EXPERTS AND THE PEOPLE

THE TVA's collaboration with business and industry is based upon the use of technical skills in the public interest, the skills of public and private experts.

Such a conception of public-private collaboration sometimes meets with a cool, not to say hostile, reception. This will almost invariably occur where a particular industry clings to the traditional idea that "co-operation between business and government" means that the function of public agencies is to accept and bless all of industry's existing policies even if thereby natural resources are misused. That is not the reaction of a responsible fellow worker, but of a yes-man.

Around such a mistaken notion of "co-operation" a whole philosophy and practice in business and government has grown. It has, for example, led trade associations and industries into the ambiguous practice of taking a public official directly out of government service and making him their government "contact" man in order that the relations with government will be "friendly." This idea of co-operation has likewise led to the deliberate practice of buttering susceptible public officials—both the senile and the young—plying them with flattery, using elaborate publicity build-ups that describe them as "statesmen," and in other ways feeding the personal vanity and ambition of men in government.

In the short run this has had occasional success with men in the public service who are unable to distinguish between deference to themselves and deference to the responsibility that, temporarily, has been entrusted to them. But on the whole this practice—and all the other expressions of this variety of co-operation—has made suckers of particular businessmen willing to pay for the dubious advantages of such relations; and when the inevitable smelly incidents come into the open, all business is hurt. To the public this is a betrayal of their interests. It is an invitation to the demagogue, the political baiter of business. It creates a political issue out of what is often simply a problem calling for the practical use of technical knowledge.

Some of the methods of the liberalism of 1904, now embraced too by many conservatives, for example the idea that government has only one role, that of an impartial referee pulling contestants out of clinches and calling fouls, are wholly inadequate today. Government is not exclusively an umpire, nor is it a combatant. The technical services of the government have a *job* to do—for business, for labor, for consumers, for the sustained productivity of all of us.

I have discussed cases of conflicts, apparent or real, between the interests of private industry and the interest of the public, and how the TVA tries to bring those into a productive unity. Of course there are clashes which as of any given moment cannot be harmonized. The private interest must then be subordinated. But the area of conflicts that appear irreconcilable *can be reduced* to an extent not yet fully realized. Under modern conditions this will call for increased reliance upon the technician in industry and government rather than upon the "front man," including under technician the business manager and the administrator. And it is a job that can best be done close to the problem itself, where men are able to get beneath prejudices, dogmas, and broad generalizations, down to the facts themselves, the working facts.

It is here that TVA, decentralized from any Washington department or bureau, has had such an advantage in its efforts, so largely successful, to eliminate or harmonize many conflicts which from a distance had always been assumed impossible of solution except by "fighting it out." For unless clashes of interest are examined on the spot, at the time they occur, by technicians who have a knack of getting at the facts and a deep desire to suggest practical alternatives, the conflict can soon become a deep issue, encrusted in prejudices, fed by ignorance or indifference to the facts, the subject of slogans and "crusades."

The experts, using the term in its broad, modern sense, have a

central role to play not only in the development of harmony between private interests and the public interest, but in every facet
of modern living. *The people and the experts:* the relation between
them is of the greatest importance in the development of the new
democracy. For the people are now helpless without the experts—
the technicians and managers. This goes for all of us. Not only for
the major industrial executive, the investment banker, or the huge
manufacturer of electric appliances, but for the farmer's wife, too,
working in her poultry yard, the operator of a small planing mill in
a remote town, the tobacco grower, the truck gardener and the
dairyman, the coal mine operator, the little and big merchant, the
county health official—wherever there are men engaged in growing
or mining or transporting or processing or distributing goods, or
maintaining government services.

One of the tasks of the administrator or executive in public or
private affairs who is committed to democratic principles is to devise
ways of bringing modern science and technical skills to the hand
of the layman. And this it is that TVA's work at the grass roots seeks
to bring about. If the technical knowledge can be made to serve the
individual in the daily decisions of his life, if it can be made to
serve the common purpose of improving opportunity for human
beings, that is an achievement of democracy in modern form and
application.

This will require some drastic changes in the prevailing relations
between experts and the people, both in industry and in government.

First of all, the experts and the people must be brought together.
The technicians should live where the people they serve live. There
are important exceptions, in highly specialized fields, but they do
not affect the principle. An expert ought not to be remote from the
problems the people face, and, although physical proximity will not
guarantee closeness to the people, it will encourage it, whereas
physical remoteness in distance definitely encourages, if it does
not actually insure, remoteness in spirit and understanding, particularly in our country of vast area and great diversity in regional customs and natural conditions.

Keeping the experts and the people apart is not ordinarily due
to the personal preference of the technical men. It is usually the result of a deliberate policy on the part of the executives, both in

government and in private undertakings. When the technicians and the people live together, away from the central seat of power, by that very fact the power of knowledge and of decision is diffused. To some executives this in itself damns the idea, though the condemnation is usually wrapped in a jargon of administrative or business "principles."

The experts who live with the people should be the ablest men, not the weakest—not those left over after the needs of national conferences at headquarters in Washington or New York are cared for. The people's willingness to follow technical leadership—business and public alike—has already been impaired because so often the experts sent to the field from central headquarters are in responsibility little more than errand boys.

Bringing the technician physically face to face with the people's needs where they occur, in short, I regard as fundamental. This is what Congress made possible by setting up the TVA on a decentralized regional basis, a point I shall elaborate later.

Not only should the experts be brought to the people, but the different kinds of experts, working in special fields that are *related* in their effect upon the people, should live together and work together. Laymen cannot be expected to put together or understand the separate bits of a technical solution of their problems as they are worked out, separately, by specialized experts. And, unless specialists are required by appropriate managerial methods to live together and work together, they will not *unify their conclusions* so that they will make sense to the laymen who must put the results to use in their lives.

Technicians are more competent experts in their special fields when they live and work in the midst of lay problems. The education of the technician by the people themselves is only second in importance to the education of the laymen by the technician. Neither is possible at a distance in an atmosphere of remoteness, formal reports, memoranda, and the other trappings of absentee government and business.

Technicians will not be so likely to lose themselves in their work, hence will not be most effective, unless they can see that their talents are part of a whole task that appeals to them as important. Whether in private business or public service a man's conviction that he is performing an important service for others, that he is part of something far more important than himself, is a measure to him of the importance of that job. It is this, I think, that accounts in considerable part for the continued enthusiasm of the TVA technical staff long after the newness of the undertaking has passed, a spirit that has been observed and remarked upon by a long succession of visitors from other parts of the country and the world. The notion is naïve that only by the incentive of pay or profit do men "keep on their toes" and do their best work.

People generally, I have found, place great importance upon the development of resources for human well-being, especially if they are vividly made part of that effort. What they think of the importance of the expert's part in that job is mightily persuasive, to the expert, of the importance of his own task. And that to a considerable degree determines not only his personal satisfaction in it, but his effectiveness.

The experts who live with the people's problems are better able to learn of the people's aspirations, what it is that the people want and what they would want if they had available a knowledge of the alternatives from which they could make a choice. The people will not trust the experts and give them their confidence until they are persuaded that technicians in business as well as in government service are not setting up their own standards of what is "good for people." If technicians, by living with people, come to understand what the people want rather than what the experts want, then people will more and more repose confidence in them and their counsel, protect them from partisan and political attacks, and even help them further their specialized professional and scientific interests.

And the physical presence of the expert, the fact that he has elected to live with the people and their problems, to share their physical and social circumstances, will be accepted by laymen as one kind of proof of the sincere devotion of the expert to the improvement of the everyday living of the people, rather than to his own specialized interests and concerns. The technician, whether he be a forester, a social welfare worker, a manager, a financial or farm or mineral expert, has no more excuse to pursue his expertness simply for the pleasure its refinements give him or to increase his own or his profession's repute, than a physician at the bedside or a general in the field would be justified in following a particular course for comparable reasons of a personal or professional character.

Technicians must learn that explaining "why" to the people is generally as important (in the terms in which I am speaking) as "what" is done. To induce the action of laymen, which is the only way resource development is possible, "why" is almost always the key. Experts and managers at central business or government headquarters, isolated and remote, tend to become impatient of making explanations to the people. From impatience it is a short step to a feeling of superiority, and then to irresponsibility or dictation. And irresponsibility or dictation to the people, whether by experts or politicians or business managers or public administrators, is a denial of democracy.

Chapter 13

GOVERNMENT IN THE OPEN AIR

THE unified development of resources requires the broadest coalition of effort. This is a job not only for all the people, but for all of the people's institutions. The purpose is national, but the task is one that calls for a partnership of *every* agency of government, state and local as well as federal, that can further the common purpose. Therefore the grass-roots policy of drawing in private organizations and individuals—such as those of farmers, workers, and businessmen, discussed in preceding chapters—has in like manner been applied by TVA, a *federal* organization, so that the governmental agencies of *local* communities and of the *states* of the Tennessee Valley have become TVA's active and responsible partners.[1]

Decentralizing the administration of government functions that are clearly national has been carried so far in this valley that it is literally true (I can think of no exceptions) that, whenever there is a state or a local institution which can perform part of the task that has been assigned by law to the TVA, TVA has sought to have that non-federal agency do it. This way of getting results is an exacting test of managerial skill in defining functions clearly and in securing a union of effort. Purely legalistic argumentation about "states' rights" or "federal supremacy" have largely faded into irrelevance.

[1] President Eisenhower, in his State of the Union Message of February 2, 1953, said: "The best natural resources program for America will not result from exclusive dependence on Federal bureaucracy. It will involve a partnership of the states and local communities, private citizens and the Federal Government, all working together. This combined effort will advance the development of the great river valleys of our nation and the power that they can generate."

There is therefore nothing in this region's experience to support the genuine fears or the partisan outcry of the thirties predicting that to set up a federal regional agency would mean the undermining and ultimate destruction of state government and local communities. The contrary has been the case. It is indisputable from the record that because of the decentralized methods by which TVA is able to carry out its federal responsibilities, state government is far stronger and more vital in the Tennessee Valley today than it was in 1933 and has more functions to perform. Governors and private citizens alike have often attested to this fact. Similarly, since 1933, when TVA began, local community government and functions have become more vigorous. I have heard of no other place in the United States where as a consequence of a federal activity these things can be said with equal basis in performance.

In developing extensive and close relations with state and local agencies TVA has not "discovered" a new principle. A number of other federal agencies have been making progress in this direction over a period of years. The TVA's demonstration of local-state-federal collaboration strengthens the hand of the many federal and state administrators and legislators who have been working to a similar purpose, against obstacles of indifference, hostility, and the inherent difficulties of the problem.

The device for effecting this widespread partnership relation with local and state government in the Tennessee Valley has been the written contract. There are now hundreds of such formal contracts between the TVA and every manner of public institution in the valley, ranging all the way from county library boards to state universities and the highway, conservation and state planning commissions.

These contracts are more than a definition of legal obligations. They constitute, too, expressed agreements on common purposes, often defined in broad terms. The discussions, arguments, and resolution of conflicting ideas and policies that precede final agreement serve a purpose almost as important, perhaps more important, than the contract itself. And as from time to time problems arise that are not covered by the contract (which, of course, is often the case) or if either agency is ready to add a new step in the relationship, a review of the broad purposes as well as the specific terms of the contract provides an occasion of great educational value. Instead of abstract talk about "co-operation" between local and federal agencies, the device of the contract encourages consideration of specific issues under existing conditions, but within the broad framework of the common purpose of strengthening the region. The bilateral contract, TVA experience has shown, is a device that lends itself to the needs of a relationship which to be most effective must recognize that it ought to be constantly changing and dynamic.

It is through such joint undertakings that many of the achievements I have pointed to as evidence of the great change have been accomplished. The scope of these partnership arrangements has been as broad and their content as richly varied as the valley's life itself: investigation of mica or manganese deposits; field tests of crop-bearing trees; development of a county recreational park for Negroes; work toward a specific cure for malaria; establishment of woodland wildlife refuges; forest-fire protection; housing; stream pollution and industrial water supply problems; preservation of archaeological materials; industrial research in flax processing; highway location; development of a small dairy milk cooler, a trailer threshing machine, and many other similar farming devices— hundreds of joint enterprises, great and small. There are few agencies in these states of the Tennessee Valley that are not in this way a part of this national enterprise, as a result of deliberate policy.

Most of the activities thus carried on under these contracts by a community or state agency *could have been done by the TVA alone*, if the matter were viewed as a narrow issue of TVA's "prerogatives" or "jurisdiction" under its charter from Congress. But dynamic decentralization is not concerned with the abstract issue of whether the national government under the Constitution has a superior "right" in a particular field from which it may exclude state and local action. TVA is charged with a broad national responsibility. Its function is that of leadership, stimulus, guidance: planning in the broadest democratic sense.

In calling upon a state or local agency to share responsibility instead of setting up a TVA organization to do a specific job alone, and in negotiating the contracts upon which such joint efforts rest, we have deliberately tried to "start something" that local forces might later carry on, on their own. In case after case this is just what has happened as the years have gone by, in forestry, in minerals research, in recreational development, and so on. TVA tried from the very beginning to place each new activity into the stream of the region's life, in the hands of local agencies to be continued when the initial federal support is curtailed or withdrawn. Grassroots methods, decentralization as here applied, are therefore not simply the making of "grants-in-aid" to state or local bodies, and the "matching of federal funds" technique.

Let me take the growth of libraries as an example. The Authority wanted to provide library service for its thousands of employees building the Watts Bar Dam. But we did not want to set up an independent library that would be closed and disappear once the dam was built. So TVA contracted with the Tennessee Division of Libraries and the City Library Board of Knoxville, to provide this service at an expense to TVA that did not exceed what direct TVA library service would have cost. These two agencies knew the people of the localities, knew whom to turn to for local leadership. This contract then became the nucleus for the development of local interest in library service. Regional library service grew naturally out of this beginning. As TVA construction work moved up the river to other dams in counties near by, more and more local agencies and leaders joined, all contributing funds raised by local town councils or county governments, until the library project had expanded into thirteen counties of east Tennessee. In only one of these counties had there ever before been adequate public facilities for the reading of books. Mobile library units were going through the area, reaching TVA construction workers at their homes, and also, under the terms of the contract, non-employees living in the remote regions.

By the autumn of 1942 the Watts Bar Dam was nearly completed. TVA's contributions of funds would therefore soon be terminated. Now came the real test of the methods that had been inaugurated. Had the roots sunk in deeply enough to sustain and continue what was now under way? A meeting was called to see what could be done to keep the regional library system operating. A dozen women and a half dozen men attended, representing the library boards of eleven out of thirteen of the counties, and one by

one they rose to tell of their experience. Mrs. Willis Shadow of
Meigs County began the discussion:

We have 6,000 people in Meigs County, and no railroad, no telephones,
and no newspapers. The bookmobile and the grapevine are the only
means of communication. If we lose the library bookmobile, how will
we know what is going on in the world? What chance have we to
improve standards of health or living except through reading? Talk
about country people not reading! In Meigs County we read 4,000 books
a month. There is not a family in the county that the library doesn't
touch.

Many of these board members had been reluctant a year or two
before to ask their county officers for a few hundred dollars' contribution to the regional library. Yet before the meeting adjourned
they had all agreed to ask the State Legislature for an annual appropriation of $25,000. They organized a legislative committee and
mobilized state-wide support. And on February 9, 1943, the Governor of Tennessee signed a measure setting up an east Tennessee
regional library office, with an initial state appropriation of $20,000.

Three years had intervened between the beginning of the library
program in the Watts Bar area and the state appropriation for the
larger unit. In January, 1940, 263,000 people were practically destitute of books. Three years later these twelve counties, previously
with none, now had 52,000 library books; the books were being
distributed from two hundred locations covering the most remote
limits of the area. Twenty-two thousand persons were registered as
borrowers. In January, 1943, they read 250,000 books.

The State Commissioner of Education, in a newspaper interview,
expressed the opinion that this appropriation was the first step
toward a statewide system of libraries. He was prophetic. Two
years later, another group of Tennessee counties in another reservoir
area faced a similar problem in the prospective termination of a
TVA contract for library service. Again citizen interest was aroused,
and in 1945 the state legislature allotted $75,000 for the biennium
for regional library service. For the 1951-52 biennium, the State of
Tennessee appropriated $190,000. By this time the idea had spread
so that there was regional library service in 63 counties with a
population of over 1,500,000. The library service, which began with

2,000 books at Watts Bar Dam construction village, at TVA expense, today at *state* expense provides over 375,000 books with an annual circulation of over 1,500,000. There are 69 branch libraries, serviced by 12 bookmobiles and 19 professional librarians.

One day in the spring of 1950, I was visiting the development work in the valley of the River Rhône—referred to as "the TVA of France." One of my French hosts, a farmer, said he had only one question he wished to ask. It was this: "And how is it now with the lady and the little libraries?"

It took me some time to realize that he was inquiring about Mrs. Shadow, about whom he had read in the French translation of the first edition of this book. The ensuing conversation confirmed what I have observed over and over again: it is the relatively modest but very concrete demonstrations of the workings of grass-roots democracy that impress themselves upon people generally, more so than the more grandiose piling up of statistics or the description of large but less comprehensible undertakings.

This Tennessee development is not unique. Up to the present time every library program for TVA employees that has been entrusted to local agencies for administration has grown into a permanent service when the Authority has withdrawn. Regional library systems covering three counties of northern Alabama and three counties of western North Carolina grew out of construction periods at the Guntersville and Hiwassee dams. It appears evident that out of these co-operative efforts between the TVA and institutions at the grass roots a useful and practical type of library organization has come into the Tennessee Valley states.

In the same way and by similar devices the maintenance of public parks by local agencies has been expanded. When the TVA began its work, there was little provision for outdoor public recreation in the whole valley. There was no state park system in Tennessee, no county had provided for park areas, neither Tennessee nor Alabama had a state department of conservation. Today both these states have very active departments of conservation. There is an excellent system of state and county parks.

Where there had been not a single state park in the Tennessee Valley in 1933, there are twelve along the margins of TVA reservoirs in 1953, operated by four different states. There are eighteen county parks and twenty-two municipal parks along the reservoirs. Thus the scenic and recreational resources of the region are being developed under state and local leadership.

This began in 1934 when TVA developed several demonstration parks, to which I have previously referred, on land that lay on the margins of its reservoirs. The multitude of people in the valley who visited these demonstration parks approved the idea, and were ready to support efforts to further state and county park developments. In this general public interest there was a basis either for expansion of TVA parks or of parks managed by state and local agencies. The latter way was the course chosen.

Today the TVA no longer operates any parks; the demonstrations have served their purpose and the states are now carrying on the job on their own initiative and with their own funds.

In Tennessee TVA assisted in the drafting of state legislation creating a state Conservation Department. A state park system was begun. Continued under successive state administrations ever since and well supported at the state's sole expense, Tennessee now has one of the best state park systems in the Southeast. A comprehensive agreement has been entered into between TVA and the State Department of Conservation, under which active collaboration is carried on in the development of scenic resources. TVA, as the owner of strips of land of great natural beauty bordering the new lakes, has leased a great deal of this land to the state and to county and municipal commissions, at a nominal rental but under conditions that insure that the land will be used for public access and recreational uses and not inconsistently with the primary national functions for which it was originally purchased by TVA.

The TVA's program of industrial research in new methods of utilizing the valley's resources is a further illustration of the way agreement between the federal government and the states are used to advance this national program. Instead of setting up entirely new facilities and personnel, this work, wherever possible, has been carried on in partnership with a state university engineering or agricultural research department. Time and again in a project initiated by the TVA or jointly by TVA and some state institution, TVA's financial and other contributions diminish or terminate while the state agency's increase or the project is taken over entirely. As a result of grass-roots methods the state's technical services are strengthened and stimulated, and at the same time TVA's national obligations are met, and at the lowest cost to the federal treasury.

This policy of a federal agency "working itself out of a job" has been conscious and deliberate from the very beginning. It continues as TVA enters upon its third decade. The results, in concrete, specific cases, represent one of the major achievements of TVA, in my opinion, as an experiment in the decentralization of the federal government. How this policy has actually worked to date was summarized recently by the Chairman of the TVA Board, Gordon R. Clapp, in testimony before an appropriation subcommittee of the House of Representatives. In view of the current importance of this technique of decentralization, and the clarity and concreteness of Mr. Clapp's statement, I have reproduced substantial excerpts from it as Appendix B.

In the farm program the device of contracts with state and local agencies was followed from the very beginning, and has been carried out consistently through every step of the work. Written agreements providing for small-scale testing of TVA's new phosphatic fertilizer were first executed with the state agricultural experiment stations of the land-grant colleges of the valley. And, when the product was ready to be demonstrated in actual farming operations, the county agent was the man selected to assume general managerial responsibility for demonstration operations in the field, with the aid of an assistant to concentrate on demonstration supervision, the latter's compensation covered by TVA funds. The county agent is a local official, but he also represents and is partly compensated by the State Extension Service and the federal Department of Agriculture. An extensive Memorandum of Understanding was entered into between the TVA, the seven State Extension Services, and the Department of Agriculture, covering the new joint activities broadly and yet with considerable precision.

At the time this program was begun in 1934, many Tennessee Valley counties had failed to appropriate funds for their share of the county agent work, and so were without agents at all. A few months after the TVA program was under way, however, all but one of the counties in the valley had provided for full-time agents. In one county, for reasons of local politics, an appropriation for an agent was refused by the county government. A group of citizens raised the necessary funds by voluntary contributions so that the inauguration of the program need not be delayed until such time as the county politicians could be retired from office or induced to change their mind. A year later the county itself provided the funds. Today the number of state and local farm extension workers in the Tennessee Valley is the highest it has ever been; although the total central staff of TVA devoted to counsel and supervision of this joint enterprise work was never large—thirty-eight in the beginning days of 1935—and never larger than one hundred at the peak.

Yet with this relatively small federal staff a completely new pro gram of soil rehabilitation and land use has been supervised; new concentrations and combinations of plant nutrients have revitalized the soil, new machinery and new techniques have raised the farmer's income; his self-interest and the nation's welfare have been joined. State and county institutions have been strengthened in the process. In this valley the muscles of local and state government are stronger. They are stronger because they are used.

The most far-reaching instance of a grass-roots partnership between local agencies and the TVA is afforded by the valley's power system. The largest integrated power producer in the world, it presents the picture of a joint enterprise of the federal government and hundreds of local communities in seven states, and the reliance for power of more than five million people. These communities range from small farming centers and mountain villages to a major city of a third of a million people.

Centralized large-scale production combined with decentralized local responsibility: this formula may prove of considerable importance in a number of other fields of business and of domestic and international governmental affairs.

Electricity, like the land, touches the everyday lives of people, directly and intimately. What TVA has done in decentralizing the distribution service of this vital necessity of modern life may throw light not only upon public administration but also on how grass-roots methods may provide an opportunity for large business enterprises to decentralize without sacrifice of the obvious advantages of bigness.[2]

Nowhere is the fear of bigness for bigness' sake and distrust of

[2] See Lilienthal, *Big Business: A New Era* (New York: Harper & Brothers, 1953), pp. 151 *et seq.*

control from a far-off place better exemplified. People want not only government but also such essential services as electricity as close to them as possible.

A degree of centralization in a power system produces certain economies which cannot be effected in any other way. For some years I have been convinced, however, that a substantial measure of decentralized administration can be achieved with distinct social gains and without impairing the efficiency of the service. The power program of the Tennessee Valley constitutes the first large-scale demonstration by which the country can judge. Power generation and transmission require great size and technical and physical integration to achieve economies. In the valley those responsibilities requiring bigness alone are centralized: the powerhouses and high-tension transmission network are operated directly by the TVA itself.

But the same principles of economy through bigness and centralization do not apply necessarily to the retail distribution of this "bulk electricity." And in the valley system the ownership and management of the *distribution* systems are decentralized. The decision to enter into a contract for wholesale power supply with TVA, and thereby to participate in the region-wide power program, was made community by community, after public discussion, council meetings, referenda. Responsibility for those municipal and co-operative systems which deliver the power directly to the consumers who live in the cities, on the farms, and in the villages is lodged with managers and trustees selected locally.

From the power plants on the river TVA is supplying power at wholesale to one hundred and forty-six separate and independent distribution systems, comprising hundreds of corporate or unincorporated communities. Fifty of these systems are operated by co-operative associations, some of them once small, now grown to considerable size. The remainder are operated by municipalities, several of which give county-wide service. *National* standards laid down by Congress in TVA's Act are maintained by means of provisions in the Authority's wholesale power contracts. In this way substantial uniformity of policy among its retail electricity distributors prevails in such important matters as rates, accounting, distribution of surplus revenues, and payments in lieu of taxes. But the ownership and control of the local electricity distribution systems are vested in the locality, usually through boards of trustees composed of local citizens. Within the area served by each of these one hundred and forty-six separate local agencies the citizens using electricity can place responsibility upon their own fellow citizens who represent them. If service within a city is inadequate, the local management is there close at hand and can readily be held accountable.

Each year a comparative financial and operating statement is issued, in which, in parallel columns, results are recorded for each of the one hundred and forty-six communities. If administrative costs per unit are higher in Community A than in Community B, the trustees in A can (and do) ask their superintendent for an explanation. If Community B piles up surpluses, reduces rates considerably below the standard TVA rate, as a number of communities have done, that example is there before Community A and all the rest to emulate if they can. Since the accounts are all set up on a uniform basis, comparisons are readily made.

In a real sense electricity users in each community, therefore, within wide limits, themselves determine their own standards of efficiency of service and level of rates. They have an opportunity to learn at first hand the principles of public management and accountability, the evil consequences of allowing politics to enter into municipal services, the importance of putting electricity distribution in the hands of non-political boards made up largely of men with business experience. In contrast, the service departments of municipalities—water, streets, and the like—were in many communities headed by men whose previous experience was chiefly political. The comparison between the services rendered by the power boards and the other departments of the cities, in most instances, has been illuminating to the citizens.

In one Tennessee city the sentiment arising from this contrast was so marked that transfer to the power board of *all* the city's operating functions was actually proposed. In less drastic fashion, approval of these new standards of administration has led to the application of the public accounting practices that are now applied to electricity operations, to the non-electric operations of these communities.

The financial and operating results of this method of administering electricity supply have been good; many of them have been remarkable successes, with very high earnings and low unit operating costs. There is no occasion to go into the details here, but records are readily available as public documents.

The contagion of example has been active here as in almost every part of the changes in the region; and here again (as in the farm program) we have relied upon the benefits that come from learning by doing, rather than by "preaching" or coercion. These methods have tapped resources of local pride, ingenuity, and friendly rivalry with other communities which may mean as much to the Tennessee Valley as the billions of kilowatt hours.

But the influence of this instance of decentralization goes beyond abundant and reliable electricity at low rates. For by this device a whole group of citizens and communities have taken themselves out of their strictly personal pursuits, to serve the interests of their neighbors and their whole community and region, with no other compensation, in most cases, than the prestige of leadership and the satisfaction of the task. As local power board members, they are in partnership with their national government, under a contract which for both locality and nation embodies a common purpose: the wide use of electricity for human welfare. They are not window-dressing to give a "local slant" to what is really a highly centralized undertaking, with the decisions actually made for them at remote headquarters. Disagreements occur from time to time between TVA and these local boards; and, though negotiations usually lead to agreement, it is quite a commonplace for a recommendation of TVA's staff, as originally proposed, to be rejected.

The responsibility for distribution supply, from the city gate to the electric refrigerator or the factory drill press, is solely theirs, subject only to broad policies that are part of a contract voluntarily entered into, which binds both the federal government and the local community. These boards are made up of men with every kind of background and interest. A recent count of the some 900 directors and trustees of the municipal and co-operative systems showed 266 farmers—the largest occupational group—57 bankers, 33 manufacturers, 136 merchants, 8 newspapermen, 8 contractors, 6 doctors, 5 cotton brokers, and 2 labor union officials, along with a large scattering of other occupations. They have an opportunity to take an active role in the entire development undertaking, of which this electricity operation in their town is a part. Not a few of the power boards have thus become a center of community initiative in industrial development, community planning, public recreation, postwar planning, and so on.

And thus still another group of the valley's citizens learn the lessons of the unity of resource development: the close interrelation between electricity and industry, between industry and farming, between farming and the building of the soil, between the soil and flood control. It will be seen that grass-roots democracy is throughout a story of the self-education of citizens. Men and women and children see their valley remade; they take part in that work. From this undertaking they have an opportunity to learn for themselves more of the basic lessons of nature and of human relations.

Chapter 14

DECENTRALIZATION: ANTIDOTE FOR
REMOTE CONTROL

But it is not wise to direct everything from Washington.
—PRESIDENT ROOSEVELT, Message to
the Congress respecting Regional
Authorities, June 3, 1937

WHAT I have been describing is the way by which the people of one region have been working out a decentralized administration of the functions of the central government.

The chief purpose of such methods of decentralization is to provide greater opportunity for a richer, more interesting, and more responsible life for the individual, and to increase his genuine freedom, his sense of his own importance. Centralization in administration tends to promote remote and absentee control, and thereby increasingly denies to the individual the opportunity to make decisions and to carry those responsibilities by which human personality is nourished and developed.

I find it impossible to comprehend how democracy can be a living reality if people are remote from their government and in their daily lives are not made a part of it, or if the control and direction of making a living—industry, farming, the distribution of goods—is too far removed from the stream of life and from the local community.

"Centralization" is no mere technical matter of "management," of "bigness versus smallness." We are dealing here with those deep urgencies of the human spirit which are embodied in the faith we call "democracy." It is precisely here that modern life puts America to one of its most severe tests; it is here that the experience in this valley laboratory in democratic methods takes on unusual meaning.

Congress established the TVA as a national agency, but one confined to a particular region. This provided an opportunity for decentralization. A limited region, its outlines drawn by its natural resources and the cohesion of its human interests, was the unit of federal activity rather than the whole nation.

To the degree that the experiment as administered helps to solve some of the problems raised by the flight of power to the center and the isolation of the citizen from his government, history may mark that down as TVA's most substantial contribution to national well-being and the strengthening of democracy.

TVA's methods are, of course, not the only ones that must be tried. There will be different types and other methods of administration suitable to other problems and different areas. Diversity will always be the mark of decentralized administration, just as surely as uniformity (often for its own sake) is the mark of central and remote control.

Decentralization in action is anything but an easy task. Its course will never be a smooth one, without setbacks and disappointments. Everywhere, nevertheless, the problem must be faced if we are to conserve and develop the energies and zeal of our citizens, to keep open the channels through which our democracy is constantly invigorated.

Overcentralization is, of course, no unique characteristic of our own national government. It is the tendency all over the world, in business as well as government. Centralization of power at our national capital is largely the result of efforts to protect citizens from the evils of overcentralization in the industrial and commercial life of the country, a tendency that has been going on for generations. Chain stores have supplanted the corner grocery and the village drug store. In banks and theaters, hotels, and systems of power supply—in every activity of business—local controls have almost disappeared. Business centralization has brought advantages in lower unit costs and improved services, and in new products of centralized research. Except by the village dressmaker, or the owner of the country store or hotel, the advantages of centralization, at the beginning, at least, were gratefully received. People seemed to like a kind of sense of security that came with uniformity.

The paying of the price came later when towns and villages began to take stock. The profits of local commerce had been siphoned off, local enterprise was stifled, and moribund communities awoke to some of the ultimate penalties of remote control. When a major depression struck in 1929, business overcentralization may well have made us more vulnerable than ever before to the disruption that ensued. Power had gone to the center; decisions had to be made far from the people whose lives would be affected. Cities and states seemed powerless. The federal government had to act. The tendency to centralization in government was quickened.

It was ironic that at this juncture, twenty years ago, centralized businesses should become, as they did, eloquent advocates of the merits of decentralization in government. From their central head-quarters they began to issue statements and brochures. And a wondrous state of confusion arose in the minds of men: they ate food bought at a store that had its replica in almost every town from coast to coast; they took their ease in standard chairs; they wore suits of identical weave and pattern and shoes identical with those worn all over the country. In the midst of this uniformity they all listened on the radio to the same program at the same time, a program that bewailed the evils of "regimentation," or they read an indignant editorial in their local evening papers (identical with an editorial that same day in a dozen other newspapers of the same chain) urging them to vote for a candidate who said he would bring an end to centralization in government.

I am not one who is attracted by that appealing combination of big business and little government. I believe that the federal government must have large grants of power progressively to deal with problems that are national in their consequences and remedy, problems too broad to be handled by local political units. I am convinced, as surely most realistic men must be, that from time to time in the future further responsibilities may have to be assumed by the central government to deal on a national basis with issues which our complex economic system calls into being.

The people have a right to demand that their federal government keep clear the channels by which they can enjoy the benefits of advances in science and research, the right to demand protection from economic abuses beyond the power of their local political units to control. But they have the further right to insist that the methods of administration used to carry out the very laws enacted for their individual welfare will not atrophy the human resources of their democracy.

It is folly to forget that the same dangers and the same temptations exist whether the centralization is in governemnt or in mammoth business enterprises. In both cases the problem is to capture the advantages that come with such centralized authority as we find we must have, and at the same time to avoid the hazards of over-centralized *administration* of those central powers.

It can be done. It can be done and is more latterly being done in many business operations, as well as in government activities. I have described the way in which the operations of the Tennessee Valley's power system have been brought close to the people of this valley. Certainly that makes clear that no blind fear of bigness underlies my conviction of the necessity for decentralized administration. Here we have centralized only the activities in connection with electric supply which are common to a large integrated area and can best be carried on by a single agency, that is, producing the power and then transmitting it from the dams and steam-electric plants to the gates of communities. But, as I have pointed out, in the Tennessee Valley system the ownership and management of the distribution systems are decentralized. Here, I believe, is one example, among many, of an effective combination of the advantages of the *decentralized administration of centralized authority*.

The distinction between authority and its administration is a vital one. For a long time all of us—administrators, citizens, and politicians—have been confused on this point. We have acted on the assumption that because there was an increasing need for centralized authority, the centralized execution of that authority was likewise inevitable. We have assumed that, as new powers were granted to the government with its seat at Washington, these powers therefore must also be administered from Washington. Out of lethargy and confusion we have taken it for granted that the price of federal action was a top-heavy, cumbersome administration. Clearly this is nonsense. *The problem is to divorce the two ideas of authority and administration of authority.*

Our task is to invent devices of management through which many of the powers of the central government will be administered not by remote control from Washington but in the field.

A national capital almost anywhere is bound to suffer from lack of knowledge of local conditions, of parochial customs. And in a country as vast as the United States, in which local and regional differences are so vital and so precious, many citizens and administrators are coming to see more and more that powers centrally administered from Washington cannot and do not take into account the physical and economic variations within our boundaries. The national strength and culture that flows from that very diversity cannot be nourished by too greatly centralized administration.

It has become common observation that in Washington it is too easy to forget, let us say, the centuries of tradition that lie behind the customs of the Spanish-American citizens in New Mexico and how different their problems are from those of the men and women whose lives have been spent in the mountains of the South. It is hard, from a distance, with only memoranda before him, for an administrator to be alive to the fact that the ways of suburban New Jersey are alien to the customs of the coast of eastern Maine. And yet the fact that the ancestors of these people brought dissimilar customs from their homelands, that they have earned their living in different manners, that the climates in which they live are not the same—this is all deeply important when a national program is brought to the men and women in cities and villages and farms for application, when their daily lives are visibly affected. When those differences in customs are not comprehended, statutes seem irrelevant or harsh. They destroy confidence, and disturb rather than promote people's welfare.

Centralization at the national capital or within a business undertaking always glorifies the importance of pieces of paper. This dims the sense of reality. As men and organizations acquire a preoccupation with papers they become less understanding, less perceptive of the reality of those matters with which they should be dealing: particular human problems, particular human beings, actual things in a real America—highways, wheat, barges, drought, floods, backyards, blast furnaces. The reason why there is and always has been so much bureaucratic spirit, such organizational intrigue, so much pathologic personal ambition, so many burning jealousies and vendettas in a capital city (any capital city, not only Washington), is no mystery. The facts with which a highly centralized institution deals tend to be the men and women of that institution itself, and their ideas and ambitions. To maintain perspective and human understanding in the atmosphere of centralization is a task that many able and conscientious people have found well-nigh impossible.

Making decisions from papers has a dehumanizing effect. Much of man's inhumanity to man is explained by it. Almost all great observers of mankind have noted it. In *War and Peace* Tolstoy makes it particularly clear. Pierre Bezukhov is standing a captive before one of Napoleon's generals, Marshal Davout.

At the first glance, when Davout had only raised his head from the *papers where human affairs and lives were indicated by numbers,* Pierre was merely a circumstance, and Davout could have shot him without burdening his conscience with an evil deed, but now he saw in him a human being . . .

To see each citizen thus as a "human being" is far easier at the grass roots. That is where more of the functions of our federal government should be exercised.

The permanence of democracy indeed demands this. For the cumulative effect of overcentralization of administration in a national capital is greatly to reduce the effectiveness of government. It is serious enough in itself when, because of remoteness and ignorance of local conditions or the slowness of their operation, laws and programs fail of their purposes. We are threatened, however, with an even more disastrous sequence, the loss of the people's confidence, the very foundation of democratic government. Confidence does not flourish in a "government continually at a distance and out of sight," to use the language of Alexander Hamilton, himself a constant advocate of strong central authority. On the other hand, said Hamilton,

the more the operations of the national authority are intermingled in the ordinary exercise of government, the more the citizens are accustomed to meet with it in the common occurrences of their political life, the more it is familiarized to their sight and to their feelings, the further it enters into those objects which touch the most sensible chords and put into motion the most active springs of the human heart, the greater will be the probability that it will conciliate the respect and attachment of the community.

When "the respect and attachment of the community" give place to uneasiness, fears develop that the granting of further powers may be abused. Ridicule of the capriciousness of some government officials takes the place of pride. Democracy cannot thrive long in an atmosphere of scorn or fear. One of two things ultimately happens: either distrustful citizens, their fears often capitalized upon by selfish men, refuse to yield to the national government the powers which it should have in the common interest; or an arrogant central government imposes its will by force. In either case the substance of democracy has perished.

We face a dilemma; there is no reason to conceal its proportions. I do not minimize the complexities and difficulties it presents. We need a strong central government. This is plain to everyone who sees the changed nature of our modern world. But I have deep apprehension for the future unless we learn how many of those central powers can be decentralized in their administration.

Every important administrative decision need not be made in Washington. We must rid ourselves of the notion that a new staff, with every member paid out of the federal treasury, has to administer every detail of each new federal law or regulation. We who believe devoutly in the democratic process should be the first to urge the use of methods that will keep the administration of national functions from becoming so concentrated at the national capital, so distant from the everyday life of ordinary people, as to wither and deaden the average citizen's sense of participation and partnership in government affairs. *For in this citizen participation lies the vitality of a democracy.*

Federal functions can be decentralized in their administration. But it requires a completely changed point of view on the part of citizens and their representatives. For this business of centralization is not wholly the fault of government administrators. Statutes are rarely designed to provide an opportunity for ingenuity in the development of new techniques in administration. Only infrequently do you find a new law which in its terms recognizes the hazards of overcentralization.

Most public men and editorial writers prefer the privilege of berating administrators as "bureaucrats" to suggesting and supporting ways through which the vices of bureaucracy would have less opportunity to develop. Congress has usually taken the easy course, when new laws are passed, of piling upon the shoulders of an already weary (but rarely unwilling) official the responsibility for supervising a whole new field of federal activity. He has been given a fresh corps of assistants perhaps, but upon his judgment decisions of great detail ultimately rest.

This country is too big for such a wholesale and indiscriminate pyramiding of responsibilities. In the general atmosphere of bigness, men continue to come about the same size. There is a limit to the energy and wisdom of the best; the ancient lust for power for its own sake burns in the worst.

In the case of TVA, Congress did enact a statute which permitted a decentralized administration. Had not Congress created that opportunity, the TVA could not have developed its administration at the grass roots. An area of manageable proportions—the watershed of a river as its base—was the unit of administration. Decisions could be made and responsibility taken at a point that was close to the problems themselves. That is the test of decentralization.

It is not decentralization to open regional offices or branches in each state, if decisions have to be made in Washington and the officers in the field prove to be merely errand boys. It is not decentralization nor genuine regionalism to set up an Inter-Agency Committee, as has been done in the Missouri River Basin, each of the members of the Committee being responsible to a different and separate Washington Department or bureau. The Hoover Commission's Task Force on Natural Resources, criticizing the ineffectiveness of this Inter-Agency device said that such a Committee could not see to it that "the basin is a unit for coordinated management despite the admission of informed public officials that it should be so regarded. The really important plans and decisions are made by separate Federal agencies responsible to a Washington desk or by the Congress or the President. Thus the present [Committee] organization *encourages centralization and the habits of dependence on centralized authority and largesse.*" (My italics.)

This proposition applies equally to the decentralization of huge business undertakings. Genuine decentralization means an entirely different point of view in the selecting and training of personnel. It means an emigration of talent to the grass roots. But if the important tasks, the real responsibilities, are kept at the center, men of stature will not go to the "field."

Neither is it decentralization when bureaus or departments are moved out of crowded Washington. It may be necessary and entirely wise—but it is not decentralization. You do not get decentralization as we know it in the TVA unless you meet two tests:

First, do the men in the field have the power of decision?

Second, are the people, their private and their local public institutions, actively participating in the enterprise?

There is generous lip service to decentralization on every hand. But little will be done about it unless there is real understanding of what it means, and an urgent and never ceasing demand from citizens.

When methods such as those the TVA has used are proposed, the chief objection usually made is that local communities, state agencies, or the field officers of federal agencies cannot be trusted to carry out national policies. Usually the reason is dressed up in more tactful language, but, however disguised, it is the doctrine of the elite nevertheless. The burden of proving that the men who at the time are federal officials in Washington are the only ones competent to administer the laws enacted by Congress certainly lies upon those who advance that reason. Actually such statements often prove the desperate hazards of centralization to the health of a democracy, for they exhibit, in the minds of those who put them forward, a low esteem or affectionate contempt for the abilities of anyone outside the capital city, or else a slavish concern for the existing rituals of bureaucracy.

There are of course many instances where the facts appear to support the claim that good administration of national concerns cannot be obtained through the co-operation of local agencies. Local politics, ineptitude, lack of interest and experience in public matters and in administration, brazen partisanship, even corruption —all these stand in the way. I am sure these hazards exist. I am sure, for most of them were encountered in this valley. But what are the alternatives? Fewer citizens participating in governmental administration. Less and less local community responsibility. More federal employees in the field armed with papers to be filled out and sent to Washington for "processing," because only there is "good administration" possible. The progressive atrophy of citizen interest. An ever wider gulf between local communities and national government, between citizens and their vital public concerns. Such are the alternatives.

The often flabby muscles of community and individual responsibility will never be invigorated unless the muscles are given work to do. They grow strong by use; there is no other way. Although it is true that decentralization at times is ineffective because of the quality of local officials or field officers, the virtues, by comparison, of what can be done in central headquarters are somewhat illusory. For, without the co-operation of citizens (an admittedly difficult goal) and of institutions familiar to them, no detailed and far-reaching economic or social policy and no democratic planning can be made effective.

The shortcomings of highly centralized administration of national policies are not due simply to the stupidity or wrong-headedness of particular individuals. Naming a villain whenever a mess is uncovered, a favorite American custom, is of little help; it usually misses the mark. We need perspective about such things, lest we foolishly take out our anger and frustration for ineptitudes upon this man and that, this party or that, instead of turning our attention where it often belongs, *viz.*, upon the limitations and dangers of centralization.

These evils are inherent in the overcentralized administration of huge enterprise, because it ignores the nature of man. There is light on this matter in the words of de Tocqueville, writing a century ago of the relatively simple society of the United States.

However enlightened and however skillful a central power may be [he wrote in his *Democracy in America*] it cannot of itself embrace all the details of the existence of a great nation. . . . And when it attempts to create and set in motion so many complicated springs, it must submit to a very imperfect result, or consume itself in bootless efforts. Centralization succeeds more easily, indeed, in subjecting the external actions of men to a certain uniformity . . . and perpetuates a drowsy precision in the conduct of affairs, which is hailed by the heads of the administration as a sign of perfect order . . . in short, it excels more in prevention than in action. Its force deserts it when society is to be disturbed or accelerated in its course; and if once the co-operation of private citizens is necessary to the furtherance of its measures, the secret of its impotence is disclosed. Even while it invokes their assistance, it is on the condition that they shall act exactly as much as the government chooses, and exactly in the manner it appoints. . . . These, however, are not conditions on which the alliance of the human will is to be obtained; its carriage must be free, and its actions responsible, or such is the constitution of man the citizen had rather remain a passive spectator than a dependent actor in schemes with which he is unacquainted.

Out of my own experience in the Tennessee Valley I became acutely aware of the difficulties of securing the active participation of citizens at the grass roots. I know "what a task" (again using the words of de Tocqueville) it is "to persuade men to busy themselves about their own affairs." But that experience has in it more of encouragement than of despair. For in this valley, in almost every village and town and city, in every rural community, there has proved to be a rich reservoir of citizen talent for public service. The notion that brains, resourcefulness, and capacity for management are a limited commodity in America—and this it is that is behind most of the skepticism about decentralization—is a myth that is disproved in almost every chapter and page of the story of the development of this valley.

The fact that TVA was not remote but close at hand has been the most effective way to dissipate the considerable initial suspicion of this enterprise and secure from citizens of every point of view the continued wide measure of warm co-operation. In the case of the power program of the TVA, for example, if TVA were not in the region and of it, if it could not make decisions until Washington, hundreds of miles away, had "processed" the papers and reached a conclusion, I wonder if more than a handful of these valley communities would have signed a contract with the TVA for power supply. Remote control from Washington might not have seemed greatly to be preferred to remote control from a holding company office in New York. And if TVA had not in turn decentralized its own operations the plan would work badly. TVA's division and area managers and other field officials were not merely office boys with imposing titles but no standing or authority. They were selected, trained, given broad responsibility and discretion.

The decentralized administration of federal functions is no infallible panacea. Of course mistakes are made at the grass roots too. But even the mistakes are useful, for they are close at hand where the reasons behind them can be seen and understood. The wise decisions, the successes (and there are many such), are a source of pride and satisfaction to the whole community. If, as I strongly believe, power of all kinds, economic and political, must be diffused, if it is vital that citizens participate in the programs of their government, if it is important that confidence in our federal government be maintained, then decentralization is essential.

I speak of decentralization as a problem for the United States of America. But the poison of overcentralization is not a threat to us here alone. Decentralized administration is one form of antidote that is effective the world over, for it rests upon human impulses that are universal. Centralization is a threat to the human spirit everywhere, and its control is a concern of all men who love freedom.

Chapter 15

REGIONAL PILLARS OF DECENTRALIZATION

I hope this will be an age of experiments in government.
—THOMAS JEFFERSON

YOU cannot, of course decentralize the functions of the federal government if the whole nation is the operating unit for the carrying out of national powers. Obviously some smaller area than the whole country must be used. In the case of the TVA, Congress and the President determined that in the development of resources that smaller unit should be based upon the natural region; this region is described in the language of the 1933 enactment as "the Tennessee River drainage basin and . . . such adjoining territory as may be related to or materially affected by the development consequent to this Act. . . ."

The use of the region as an autonomous unit of development was a deliberate "experiment." The results of this departure in national policy were to be reported to the nation and become the object of study as to its effectiveness. It was anticipated at the time that if the experiment commended itself by its results the method might be followed or adapted to other regions. The idea that the Tennessee Valley region was set up as a kind of testing ground for the nation has been often expressed, and appears in the President's original message: "If we are successful here," he said, "we can march on, step by step, in a like development of other great natural territorial units within our borders."

The application of TVA's results in decentralized regional development to other parts of the country has become a question of some practical consequence, since from time to time bills providing for regional developments have been introduced in Congress. These proposals, are sometimes described or are promoted as measures that provide a "TVA" for this or that area of the country.

References to TVA in connection with such proposals are hardly appropriate, however, and may even be misleading unless they do in fact adopt the TVA idea in its essentials,

—a federal autonomous agency, with authority to make its administrative decisions within the region

—responsibility to deal with resources, as a unified whole, clearly fixed in the regional agency, not divided among several centralized federal departments or agencies with their headquarters in Washington

—a policy, fixed by law, that the federal regional agency work co-operatively with and through local and state agencies.

The entire TVA experiment, as I interpret it, makes it clear that no proposal for regional resource development may be described as a kind of "TVA" unless it embodies these fundamentals, which are clearly written into the TVA Act and have been the very heart and spirit of years of transforming that law into action.

My concern here is not whether in future legislation Congress decides to follow or to abandon these principles embodied in the TVA; the purpose of this book goes deeper than merely to serve as a polemic urging more regional authorities along TVA principles. But there is a responsibility to point out that, in the discussions of resource policy, merely adopting the nomenclature "regional authority" or "regional administration" or calling a project a TVA for this or that river does not constitute an adoption of the essentials of the TVA idea.

What constitutes a region? How large should it be for most effective development? No one can work out a formula for what is in reality a judgment that does not lend itself to such precise measurement. On this issue of what constitutes a region and upon the general philosophy of regionalism there is a substantial literature to which those who wish to pursue the subject are referred.

There is, however, one generalization which experience in the TVA does support: unless there are countervailing physical or economic factors that simply cannot be gainsaid, the regions should not be so large that they are not, in a management sense, of "workable" size.

After twenty years experience the original TVA region has not been very substantially enlarged. This "region"—the watershed plus the area of electric service that extends outside the drainage basin substantially as that area is now constituted—is probably as large as it ever should be. The proposal to add to the TVA's responsibility the development of the Cumberland River is sound. That river lies within the region and adjoins the drainage line, emptying into the Ohio a few miles from the mouth of the Tennessee. The people of the Cumberland Valley are already participating in parts of the enterprise, and they understand it. But, with that exception, I feel that further substantial additions to the territorial scope of the TVA might impair rather than increase its effectiveness.

Those who come to have confidence in the TVA idea and seek to have it put into effect in their own regions are certainly aware that the task is one of adaptation and not of copying or imitation. Indeed, it is the strength of the regional idea that it tends to nourish regional differences in traditions, culture, and ways of living, without sacrifice of national unity on other fundamentals. National unity, but unity through diversity, is the essential meaning of the nation's motto, *E Pluribus Unum.*

I would be rendering a disservice if I gave the impression that the TVA's methods offer a ready-made pattern to be copied literally, in all manner of situations, or that genuine decentralization in the administration of every and any kind of national function is feasible. Many functions of the federal government present entirely different problems from the development and improvement of land, water, forests, minerals. Resources have a fixed *situs* and can only be dealt with adequately at that *situs.* TVA's methods can be readily adapted to such problems. But whether regional decentralization in the genuine sense is feasible for many other functions is not a subject for generalization. While different devices must be invented, TVA's methods and experience may be of considerable aid in that process.

All through the public service and in business able men are concerning themselves with such inventions, often with notable results. The practices of decentralized administration have made considerable headway; the tendency, however, continues the other way. Lip service is paid to decentralization by legislators and administrators; they then proceed to draw to Washington the very elements of discretion and the power to decide which impose centralization in its worst forms.

The following paragraphs are from a United Press Association dispatch from its Washington, D. C., bureau, February 13, 1953:

WASHINGTON, Feb. 13 (UP)—Douglas McKay, Secretary of the Interior, banned today the award of Interior Department contracts for more than $10,000 without direct approval from his office.

The order, which covers contracts for construction, supplies and services, will strike hardest at the Reclamation Bureau, which has charge of vast irrigation projects throughout seventeen Western states.

Previously, the bureau's chief engineer and regional directors had authority to award contracts up to $200,000 without consulting the Secretary or Reclamation Commissioner. . . .

He also called for weekly reports on contracts of $10,000 or less "with a showing as to the need of the work, supplies or services covered." He stressed that *contracts submitted* for approval must include "a complete and detailed justification."

Members of Congress will inveigh against the evils of "concentrating power in Washington," and then almost in the same breath speed up that very process by passing legislation that sets up additional managerial controls in a central Washington bureau. This is often due to the desire of Representatives and Senators to have the executive officials close at hand in Washington; exerting pressure for patronage or pork is otherwise made more difficult.

A Member of Congress, avowedly interested in the necessity of federal decentralization, once introduced a comprehensive resolution proposing a broad study of the means of achieving decentralization in the government; but only a few months later the same Member introduced another measure to combine all federally owned power operations in a central "power administration" in Washington!

The issue of regional decentralization is further clouded by simple naïveté. The mere moving of personnel out of Washington to some other city as a result of wartime congestion was regarded by many as "decentralization." This may simply be a rather expensive form of centralization. And then there is a tendency to obscure the issue and distract attention from the heart of the problem by arguments about quite irrelevant or relatively unimportant details. Thus there is sometimes a great to-do about whether a regional agency should be headed by a board of three members or by a single administrator. This of course has nothing whatever to do with the region as a unit of decentralization.

Another effort to obscure the issue is to set up a regional committee, called an "interagency committee." But since the membership of such a committee continues to be bound to Washington centralized departments for policies and authority, this is as spurious a method of decentralization as it is ineffective as a means of achieving a unified development of resources.

There is another and more subtle way of avoiding the real issue in regionalism: to paint a glowing detailed picture of the opportunities for regional development and the virtues of regionalism, and then to fail to discuss *how* these happy results are to be secured. This blandly ignores the fact that the particularized benefits so persuasively portrayed have, as a matter of historical fact, never been achieved by any of the traditional bits-and-pieces, Washington-centered methods of resource development. If this manner of presentation does not show lack of candor it displays a failure to understand the essential relation that means bear to results. The public is entitled to a realistic and candid discussion of precisely what is involved in regional decentralization. If a particular goal is described specifically, the method for reaching it should be disclosed with equal particularity; it cannot be ignored as an "administrative detail."

There are some opponents of decentralization and regionalism who face the issue squarely. I shall not, of course, attempt to state or to answer any but the principal of their objections, some of which are put in the highly technical jargon of expertise. Behind the multiplicity of words there is often concealed some bureau's or department's "vested right" in centralized government, or some private contractor's interest in retaining a piece of the "rivers and harbors" barrel of political pork.

The objection that regionalism will "Balkanize" the country is a familiar and candid one usually sincerely raised. The argument is that regionalism is a kind of provincialism that divides rather than unites the country, underlining sectional animosities and obstructing a really national outlook. But such a position shows a lack of understanding of our history and of the nature of regionalism. It assumes first of all that regions, rather than the individual states, have not always been the units of important national policy development, as scholars such as Turner have made clear and as public men understand so well. In the Congressional Record we read of "the Gentleman from Indiana" or New York or Texas. The newspapers, however, are more realistic. They report the plans, meetings, and votes of the "Senators from the Corn Belt," or the "cotton bloc," the "silver bloc," or the "New England delegation in Congress."

For the practical purposes of most federal legislation, this is a country of regions, not states.

The growth and development of our national economic policies is not the result of conflicts between states; it represents an attempted reconciliation between the interests of the various natural regions. Debates on such subjects as the tariff, inland waterway improvements, or measures relating to agriculture almost always foreshadowed votes cast for the most part on a sectional basis. It was not a war between separate states which settled one great economic and political conflict in this country. It was strife between sections. And, although only once in its history has this country resorted to arms to settle regional differences, our national policies have always been arrived at through compromises—often very costly ones to the nation's interest—between the points of view of different sections of the country. Each region has fought for its own interests, frequently with scant regard to the effect on the country as a whole. This is sectionalism. We avoid the word today, hoping perhaps that the evils of disunity and local selfishness will vanish if the syllables are forgotten. But it is not so easily exorcised.

Modern regionalism, by contrast, rests squarely upon the supremacy of the *national* interest. It admits that there are problems and resources common to areas larger than any single state—a river basin, for example. It recognizes that certain points of view develop in some portions of the country and are not shared by the nation as a whole. It affirms and insists, however, that the solution of regional problems and the development of regional resources are *matters of concern to the whole country.* It proposes to harmonize regional advancement with the national welfare. That concern for and supremacy of the national interest distinguishes "regionalism" from "sectionalism." Under the banner of sectionalism, states throughout our history have combined to support or to oppose federal action. Under the modern concept of regionalism, the federal government acts to meet regional needs to the end that the entire nation may profit.

The organization of the Tennessee Valley Authority is an example of this modern idea of regionalism. To create it seven states did not unite to demand special privileges to distinguish them from the country as a whole, regardless of the ensuing consequences to the national welfare. The federal legislature itself created an autonomous regional agency whose basic objective was to conserve the natural resources lying in the valley of the Tessessee and to develop those resources *in conformity with broad national objectives and policies.* This is the very opposite—indeed it is the antidote—of "Balkanization."

The idea of regionalism embodied in the TVA—a federal agency decentralized in fact—offers a rational way of harmonizing regional interests with the national interest. For the first time a federal implement is at hand for that task, to take the place of the usual method of political bargaining, so often wholly crude and without a basis in facts, policy, or principle.

An interesting illustration of how TVA functions in this balancing of regional and national concerns is afforded by the process by which the TVA Act was amended in 1940, to increase the payments in lieu of taxes on TVA's property which it is authorized to make to local and state agencies of the valley. The issue presented a sharp conflict between regional and national interests. Since, of course, federal property may not be taxed by the states, the Tennessee Valley region wanted Congress to consent to the largest possible tax payments from the federal government's TVA. The national government's interest, on the other hand, was in having returned to its treasury the maximum amount of TVA's surplus power revenues, and that meant consent to only a minimum tax payment to the valley. An analogous conflict has been before the national Congress on many occasions. In one case the bitter controversy reached a climax when Oklahoma's Governor called out state troops, the state by this show of force displaying its dissent to federal policy.

But in adjusting this kind of region-nation conflict in the Tennessee Valley, for the first time Congress could determine the issue on a record of facts and with a consideration of principle. For it was TVA's duty to prepare itself to make a balanced presentation. Hence consideration of the problem was not on the level of a mere show of voting strength, or log-rolling, or some haphazard and casual solution. To be successful in the discharge of this function it was necessary that TVA have the confidence of the region, and yet prove to Congress that it was putting national interests first.

TVA made an exhaustive analysis of the facts respecting local tax problems as a result of TVA property purchases, the prospects for the future, the benefits received by the region from federal funds. The details of the varying tax laws of several different states were analyzed closely. Then TVA representatives conferred with the governors and fiscal officers of all the states, of many counties with peculiarly difficult problems, with tax consultants, and with federal tax officials. As a result a measure was drafted which embodied principles that TVA as a national agency could recommend. And, although far short of the original claims of local tax bodies, its fairness led all the states to concur. After exhaustive Congressional committee hearings, the bill as recommended by the TVA and agreed to by the states was passed. Under this law TVA has paid, to the end of the fiscal year 1952, out of its power revenues, a total of $25,291,000 in tax payments to states and counties of the valley; in the single fiscal year ended June 30, 1952, the total of these payments was over three million dollars.

There are many other instances of the way a federal regional agency, though understanding and sympathizing with regional concerns, can *further the national interest in a cohesion of all regions;* this is in contrast with the evils of sectionalism, for it adds to national strength. Early in its history, for example, the TVA took a firm stand against any policy of tax favoritism or subsidies to existing industry located in other regions to induce them to move to the Tennessee Valley. Important as industrial development in this region seemed, it was clear that our national obligation would be violated by such a practice of pirating industry locally. It is significant that this policy, initially viewed with disapproval, now has wide, though not universal, support from the valley itself. The practices of inducing industry to change location by offering tax exemptions, free land and buildings, and the lure of "cheap and docile labor," practices that stir up interregional animosities and distrust, are today under a cloud of disapproval by most of the business interests of this valley.

The facts are clear that the remarkable growth of industry in the Tennessee Valley region has been principally the consequence not of relocation but of the establishment of new industrial plants, many of them to serve new markets in the Valley itself. To this proposition even the textile industry's shift from New England to the South is not a significant exception. This relocation, going on steadily over a period of a generation, has been chiefly outside the Tennessee Valley. In the area served by TVA power, employment in the textile industry increased by only 8.5 per cent from 1939 to 1947 (the latest date for which detailed figures are available); the increase in the Southeast as a whole was twice that great. The most rapid and substantial expansion of industry in the valley has not been in textiles but in the chemical and primary metals industries, in each of which employment more than doubled between 1939 and 1947.

In still another way the TVA, by relating the interests of this region to the national interest, has been able to promote national strength. An illustration is afforded by the development of processes suitable to convert the phosphate ores of the Far West into fertilizer materials. The starting point was, of course, the need of the Tennessee Valley region. The high-grade phosphate ores of Tennessee are too limited in extent to continue to support the land needs of so large a part of the United States as they are being called upon to serve. In Idaho and Montana, chiefly on the public domain, there existed almost limitless supplies. The TVA electric furnace was well adapted for the processing of these Far Western deposits for use either as industrial chemicals or as fertilizer on farms of the Middle West.

The first electric phosphorous furnace in the West, patterned on TVA furnaces, was put into operation at Pocatello, Idaho, in 1949, by Westvaco, a division of the Food Machinery and Chemical Corporation. TVA had run tests to determine the suitability of Idaho phosphate shale as feed for the plant; the Corporation sent its technical respresentatives to TVA for study of furnace operations; some of TVA's ablest technicians became employees of Westvaco, carrying with them their know-how in electric furnace techniques. Since 1949 Westvaco has added other furnace units, and other leading chemical companies, Monsanto Chemical Company, Victor Chemical Company, Manganese Products, Inc., Permanente Metals Corporation, have built a series of electric furnaces in the West utilizing TVA engineering and pilot plant experience. Thus has the regional interest in preventing the premature exhaustion of the Tennessee phosphate resources been harmonized, in part at least, with the national interest in developing the Western ore reserves and making available for the lands of the Midwest and Far West an industry capable of providing an ample source of phosphatic materials at reasonable cost.

It is worth while to contrast the performance of a regional national agency with the unhappy record of state embargoes on local resources and other trade barriers that have been resorted to in the past, in a local or sectional spirit, in analogous and sometimes parallel situations.

Regionalism can try out and demonstrate on a limited scale methods of development and of administration that are then open to use for the whole nation. The origin of the TVA itself illustrates the point. Franklin D. Roosevelt in New York State and George W. Norris in Nebraska saw the importance and value of regional planning of resources. They urged the setting up of a national experiment, in a southern region, which would be available for appraisal by every region. Experimentation and demonstration of the value of complete river planning, chief reliance upon storage reservoirs for flood control rather than downstream levees, multiple-purpose dams instead of limited-purpose structures—once these have been tried out on a drainage-basin scale in this valley region, they can and are being applied elsewhere. Similarly with new methods of administration: some of the specific steps toward regional decentralization, among other federal agencies, are directly attributable to public knowledge and approval of the successful experience in this one valley.

Regionalism is strengthening, not dividing, the nation. TVA was launched in such a setting of national interest; as President-elect

Roosevelt said in January, 1933, in an informal speech in the South, it was

more today than a mere opportunity for the Federal Government to do a kind turn for the people in one small section of a couple of States . . . [It was an] opportunity to accomplish a great purpose for the people of many States and, indeed, for the whole Union. Because there we have an opportunity of setting an example of planning, not just for ourselves but for the generations to come, tying in industry and agriculture and forestry and flood prevention, tying them all into a unified whole over a distance of a thousand miles so that we can afford better opportunities and better places for living for millions of yet unborn in the days to come.

In many matters of detail the TVA demonstrates the contrast between selfish sectionalism and national regionalism. TVA's personnel by a deliberate policy is selected from every part of the United States, whereas a narrow, sectional interest would follow the provincial practice in many cities and states of confining public employment to local citizens. The way in which the TVA has "loaned" its technical personnel to many other government agencies points in the same direction; the Bonneville Administration in the Northwest, the Santee-Cooper development in South Carolina, the Colorado River Authority in Texas are examples. In one degree or another these and other agencies have shared the lessons of the Tennessee Valley's experience and methods, even in such details of management as land purchasing, electric rate schedules, personnel management, accounting. Because the TVA has thus been called upon for aid in problems in other parts of this country and in foreign countries, the danger that this regional agency might fall into a narrow provincialism, the very antithesis of a national outlook, has been kept to a minimum.

"If there were a number of regional authorities like the TVA how could they possibly be co-ordinated?" This question is usually asked as if there could be but one answer, and that one a complete refutation of regionalism. It is sometimes coupled with the assertion, intended to show friendliness to the regional idea: "TVA has proved to be effective; but that is because there is only one TVA."

These critics offer the spectacle of a nation in which a considerable number of regional authorities would each be going its separate way, resulting in chaos or requiring elaborate administrative "co-ordination" in Washington. These fears call for some comment, based upon TVA's experience.

Surely it is not fear of conflicts on *policy* on which these concerns center. The policies that a regional authority must pursue are, of course, national policies. The broad structure of these policies must be determined by Congress. It is, of course, the highest function of Congress and the President to resolve just such conflicts in policy affecting the whole nation. The regional authority provides an instrument for assisting in reasoned settlement of such differing policies. Provided the legislation creating the regional pillars of decentralization is so drawn that Congress passes upon and defines fundamental policies, there would seem to be little basis for fears in this direction.

If not policy co-ordination, just what, then, is the nature of these apprehensions of conflicts between regional authorities, this fear of "lack of co-ordination"? The real issue is not lack of co-ordination in policies, but the fact that the decentralized administration of federal functions will not result in *operating uniformity*. The actual concern is that in one region problems will be administered in a different way from what they are in another.

It is important to examine this apprehension. And it clarifies the nature of the objection to observe that almost without exception the fears are held by those who do not believe in decentralization as a policy of administration.

Decentralization frankly seeks to promote diversity; centralization requires uniformity and standardization.

It follows quite simply that if your idea of "co-ordination" is *national uniformity* in *administration*, regionalism *will* create insuperable problems of "co-ordination." If you cannot conceive of a well-governed country that in every region is not standardized, identical, and uniform, then you do not want decentralization, and of course you would be opposed to regional authorities. If, on the other hand, diversity under broad national policies rather than uniformity in administration, adaptation to regional differences, and discretion and flexibility through the broad reaches of this greatly varied country are what appeal to you as sound, humane, and de-

sirable, then the problems of co-ordination that cause the centralizers such concern become relatively simple and manageable.

It is difficult to exaggerate the lengths to which some men with
administrative responsibility feel it is necessary to go in order to
secure what they call co-ordination. This extends to matters of
managerial detail. What such men would mean by the "co-ordination" of methods of federal land-buying—I use this only by way
of a wholly hypothetical illustration—would be to erase differences
as to the methods that might exist between federal land buyers dealing with small upland farms in east Tennessee and those applied
in the flat sectionalized reaches of northern Indiana. To them a regulation respecting personnel management is not a good regulation
if it does not apply uniformly throughout this whole country.

Now if your mind operates that way you would be opposed to
regionalism. For only a centralized government can pour the country into such a single mold. If differences in how a public program
is administered in the Tennessee Valley and in the Arkansas Valley, in Illinois and in New Mexico, disturb you, if those differences
appear to be a "conflict," then you are right in assuming that regional decentralization will promote conflict.

This is not to say that under regionalism there will not be conflicts between regions. The major ones of these conflicts must be
decided by Congress, as they have been since the very establishment of our central government. Other major conflicts involving
the Executive Department would have to be decided by the President, as they always have been under centralized government administration.

So long as we harbor the administrative obsession that uniformity
in administration is essential, the amount of co-ordination of this
kind with which Congress and the President must deal and must
continue to deal will be very great. Nor will regionalism eliminate
all or most of these conflicts. But I do venture the assertion that
it will considerably lessen them. This is true because the best place
to co-ordinate is *close to the point where the conflict arises,* and
not in the top levels and central offices. Industrial managers know
this and practice it daily. The same thing proves true in government.

And so, looking at the whole picture, it can be said with confidence that in the national interest the difficulties of co-ordination are certainly not increased, and I think upon consideration it will be seen that they are actually diminished, by regionalism. Let the reader reflect upon the way in which the TVA has brought into the task of resource development a great host of local communities and state agencies. The problems of co-ordinating these efforts have not proved to be insuperable because TVA is a decentralized federal agency operating in the Tennessee Valley region with power to make its decisions in the field. The serious conflicts in administration are the ones which, unresolved in the local communities, find their way into remote and often unreal atmosphere where men are dealing in "jurisdiction"—which is so often just a euphemism for the monumental personal vanity of some Cabinet officer or bureau chief.

Co-ordination between a regional agency and other federal regional agencies or centralized departments is not, of course, automatic. The TVA has, from the outset, developed a comprehensive scheme of active co-operation with every other federal agency, either in Washington or in field offices, that has a responsibility or a function which could be helpful in the building of this region. In an earlier chapter I have alluded to the extent to which the changes in the valley have been due to these other federal activities; I wish to repeat and emphasize that here. The TVA has entered into hundreds of contracts with more than a score of other federal departments and bureaus. These inter-federal agency contracts and the relations carried on under them have from time to time developed serious differences on matters of importance. The task of reaching agreement has not always been an easy one. Yet there has rarely been a difference that could not be worked out, usually between the staffs of the agencies. No conflict between the TVA and these many federal departments and bureaus made necessary a single conference with the President.

The subject of regionalism has the widest ramifications, since it touches fundamental issues; a complete discussion is beyond the scope of this book. But TVA's experience indicates clearly that the asserted danger of conflicts and the difficulties of co-ordination arising from regional decentralization are exaggerated and largely unreal.

Chapter 16

MODERN TOOLS FOR A MODERN JOB

A NEW and modern task requires new and modern tools; a spirit of enterprise and a creative modern outlook are quite as necessary in devising the mechanics of getting things done as in establishing policies and goals. What the TVA was directed to do was such a new and modern task. For such an undertaking Congress and the President invented an entirely new kind of government implement: the regional development corporation.

This corporate public agency, the Tennessee Valley Authority, was thus set up to be as different in its organization and the way it was to do its work as the scope and the nature of the task it was directed to do was different from previous American efforts in resource development. It is not, however, the fact that the TVA was cast in the mold of a corporation that is distinctive. The corporate device for public undertakings was, of course, neither new nor unique, and the term "authority" to describe such a public corporation was quite familiar and well established, e.g., the Port of New York Authority.

The TVA is a significant departure as an instrument of twentieth-century democracy in this: that, in creating the TVA, Congress adopted and carefully wrote into law the basic principles and practices of modern management. A public agency with broad responsibilities was given a full set of the tools that American business has found essential to good management.

There have been few pieces of legislation in which so much consideration has been given, through long Congressional committee hearings and debates on the floor, to principles of management and the kind of organization needed to carry out a new national policy. This in itself is an event of importance, rare in American government annals, and one that made easier TVA's task of translating the law into results.

In even the most carefully considered legislation, where the policy issues may be extensively debated, the method proposed for accomplishing the policies is seldom given attention. Frequently the administrative provisions of a proposed law, which may make effective or doom to failure the policies so hotly contested, are prepared by some drafting clerk, who simply copies the language of some earlier law or bill that seems to him to present a rough analogy. Or quite as frequently the method of administration finds its way into the bill not to promote the purposes of the proposed legislation, not because it is custom-built to promote the specific objectives of the bill, but upon the urging of some existing government agency eager to expand the field of its jurisdiction or to protect "vested" bureau rights.

The stupefying complexity of government procedure, the over-centralization and the multiplicity of "clearances" and approvals required before anything can be done, have bred intolerable delays, jurisdictional rows, and the practice of "passing the buck." These can be traced in considerable part to inattention to these potential evils when the devil's brew is being cooked, in the course of the legislative process. This Congressional failure or unwillingness to recognize the importance of principles of modern management in public affairs has visited upon this country the greatest consequences in the administration of these vital interests which have been entrusted to government.

The TVA, then, affords a demonstration of a truth that needs full understanding: that the *method* of getting a job done is of the greatest consequence, and not to be ignored or passed over casually. Further, the choice of method will determine whether resource development and industrialization, public or private, will be dictatorial—for the benefit of some especially privileged "elite," economic or political—or will be democratic—with the people actively participating and deriving the benefits.

A task cannot be done democratically if the method chosen for doing it is bureaucratic. And by this I mean performed exclusively by members of a bureau, governmental or private, whereby things are done "to" people, not with them. An undertaking cannot nourish a democratic spirit in men if, by law or custom, it must be carried out in a bureaucratic way.

The choice of tools is vital. The choice may be such that makes it impossible to decentralize and bring the experts and responsible administrators close to the people, where they must share the people's problems. The method chosen may thwart any hope of achieving unity in the development of resources because the agency of development is not permitted to adopt management practices that will effect that unity. Method is not a dull matter of "administration"; it is as inseparable from purpose and ends as our flesh is from our blood.

The reasons why the laws creating bureaus, commissions, and departments have, by almost invariable custom, failed to follow modern principles of management are not too difficult to understand. The policies of lawmaking in the immediate past have been largely regulatory and negative: "This shall *not* be done." The atmosphere of Congress has therefore been heavy with this regulatory spirit, expressed in carefully limited responsibility, lack of trust, and forever setting one man to watch and checkmate another, and still another to watch the watcher.

The tradition and climate of the skill of management, however, are remote from all such negation. Management is affirmative and initiatory: "This *is* to be done." It is in the process of defining, with skill and sense, what is to be done, and with it the *fixing of responsibility* for results, with wide freedom for judgment in the managers as to how it may best be done, that you have the essence of the best modern management.

In TVA's charter Congress stated clearly what was to be done in the Tennessee Valley: idle resources were to be set to work— rivers, land, minerals, forests. The job to be done was defined, clearly, simply, and yet in broad, inclusive terms. Navigation: a 9-foot minimum channel, from Knoxville to the Ohio. Flood control on the Tennessee and lower Mississippi. Power: the maximum consistent with other uses of the river's water. Agricultural and industrial development, operation of the Muscle Shoals plant, research, and so on. Congress told TVA's administrators what was expected of them, and by what measure they would be judged and held accountable.

Not only *what* was to be done but the fundamental policies to be followed were likewise set out. Thus, as to the disposition of electricity, Congress did not attempt to handle the business detail of fixing the particular rates to be charged, but directed the policy TVA should observe in fixing those rates. The Board of TVA was not instructed by law as to where dams should be built, nor was their daily operation prescribed. It was told, however, that certain broad policies should govern in their construction and operation; e.g., they must be multiple in purpose, and flood control and navigation should have priority over power production if there were conflict. TVA's detailed financial records were not prescribed, but policies of financing and cost keeping were defined. Who was to be employed and how selected were not written into our charter, but employment, it was stipulated, must be solely upon merit and without political considerations. A policy of democratic methods in administration was encouraged, by repeated authorization in the law for co-operation with existing state and local agencies, with farmers and farm groups, with public and non-profit organizations. But the precise manner in which these and other policies should be carried out was not fixed.

Such is the method of good business management. Most agencies of government, however, new as well as old, have not been thus dealt with by Congress. Although no sensible private board of directors would determine details of management—how much, for example, could be expended on some single item or class of operating cost, such as travel or maintenance of equipment—that is just the practice generally followed in the annual appropriations for federal establishments. The exact dollar amount, which may not be exceeded, for thousands of detailed managerial items of cost is fixed by law. Operating the details of a huge enterprise in this way is, of course, utter nonsense. It is no wonder that the civilian heads of our multibillion-dollar military program, for example, find it so difficult to improve the efficiency of the services, when they must operate under such antiquarian and stupid ideas as are regularly written into appropriation language by Congressional "enemies of waste and extravagance" who are without the foggiest idea or a shred of actual experience in management.

This practice, in the case of an enterprise such as the TVA, would distort and magnify out of all proportion these separate elements of the task represented by the fixed items of appropriation. The administrator who should be concentrating upon the best way to obtain the overall result is, by reason of particularized statutory limitations and managerial directions, necessarily distracted and preoccupied with items of detail rather than with the results of the whole undertaking. The unifying and generalizing function of management—its vital role—is deadened by the pressures and confusions of clinical details that have thus been given the dignity of legal mandate.

Such detailed direction has not been the Congressional practice followed in respect to the TVA, except in a few isolated instances. In 1942, for example, the maximum expenditure for travel was fixed by law, against TVA's recommendations. This departure from modern management principles, offered as an economy measure, actually resulted in higher costs and waste; any good manager will see why this was inevitable. Less than a year later Congress reconsidered and itself rescinded its action; steps were authorized to correct the error and these were made retroactive. It became apparent to the legislators that in the TVA the cost of keeping personnel in the field (in traditional government terminology called "travel cost") is but one item of many that go into the cost of building a dam or transmission line, or operating a chemical plant.

The job having been defined and the broad policies laid down, Congress in the TVA Act did what is new in our history: it fixed upon one agency the responsibility for results in resource development in a region. What seems the plainest sense to a manager, i.e., fixing responsibility in one place for an entire undertaking of many parts all interrelated and interwoven—land, water, minerals, forests —was virtually a revolution in government administration.

In the development of the river, not flood control alone, or navigation or power, but all the water's uses, together, were to be the responsibility of one public agency. Not water resources in one compartment of government, dealt with separately from soil or forests, nor farming separately from industry, nor industry separate from transport and electricity. The TVA's responsibilities for results were to be measured by the concept of the unity of resources. TVA's corporate charter makes this plain not only by the specific directions given but also by the indication of a broad purpose expressed in such statutory language as the following: "To aid further the proper use, conservation and development of the natural resources of the Tennessee River drainage basin . . ."; "the economic and social well-being of the people living in said river basin"; "physical, economic and social development of said areas"; "provide for the agricultural and industrial development of said Valley," and the like.

The best antidote for buck-passing and alibis for failure to get results is the fixing of responsibility. Regrettably, this well-established principle appears to be still a novelty in many areas of public administration. It was by thus fixing responsibility that Congress cut off any excuse by which TVA might escape accountability. If the building of the dams created a public health hazard from malaria, say, it was no excuse for TVA to reply that public health was the responsibility of some other agency. If in the use of the river to produce power, floods were not adequately controlled, there was no alibi available that flood control was someone else's responsibility. If power costs were too high to permit liquidation of the investment, there was no escaping accountability because someone else built the dams inefficiently. Similarly with the everyday matters of management—the selection of personnel, for example.

The Board of TVA and not the Civil Service Commission, by a specific provision of the Authority's charter, was made responsible for the employment, promotion and discharge of all its personnel, from general manager to messenger boy. The TVA was to establish what the law called a "merit" system, and it did; but if the men selected were incompetent or insensitive to the public's problems, or if it took a month to employ a stenographer or lineman when it needed to be done in a day, the blame could not be passed on to the Civil Service Commission's rules, nor could our supervisors escape their accountability to the TVA Board in that way. The notion that the TVA Board was to be entrusted, for example, with the building of the Kentucky Dam, costing $110,000,000, but not with employing the men who were to design and build it seems fantastic. And yet so rarely does our government follow the ordinary practices of fixing responsibility that TVA even today is one of the few permanent federal agencies that remain solely responsible for the selection and promotion of its personnel.

Senator Lister Hill, who in 1933 as a Representative was one of the conference managers for the original bill, said in a communication to the Senate Judiciary Committee that it was

the intent of the whole [TVA] statute—to create an agency which would be free of some of the Government red tape about which we complain, which would have authority commensurate with its responsibilities. We made certain that it could not "pass the buck" to another bureau or department in the event of failure, and that it would not be required to waste time and energy in jurisdictional disputes. It was intended that the Board alone be held responsible for the effective administration of the policies laid down by Congress.

Congress was consistent in extending this managerial principle of fixed and undivided responsibility to include the everyday operations of the undertaking. Land buying for TVA reservoirs (including examination of titles and condemnation where necessary), for example, is not separated from the rest of the task and put in other hands, which is the general federal practice. If the land is not acquired rapidly enough to meet the construction schedules of the dam builders, or if the land owners are not fairly, speedily, or courteously dealt with, the TVA Board cannot blame any other agency of government. And so with the purchase of machinery, supplies, etc., and the settlement of damage or contract claims against TVA. Such managerial functions in most government undertakings are detached from those who are in charge of individual tasks—buildings, plants, etc.—and centralized in several separate and independent agencies which do not have responsibility for the *total* result. To business managers accustomed to quite different methods, this splitting up of a single task is a source of constant frustration in their dealing with the government.

Following the principles of sound management, Congress, despite persistent proposals to the contrary by antagonists of the Authority, has declined to relieve TVA of responsibility for the legality and appropriateness of its expenditures, and this position meets with the approval of the incumbent Comptroller General of the United States, who audits the TVA's accounts on behalf of Congress. Thus TVA is given managerial discretion but is held strictly accountable not only for what it does but for *how well* it does it.

Such fixing of responsibility increases initiative and gives an opportunity for enterprise and experiment. The field of co-operative labor relations is one example. Every modern management knows that achieving good results in a difficult undertaking depends largely upon a working relation with employees that establishes confidence and fosters enthusiasm and zest for the task. A strike or any interruption of work on TVA's power system or upon a dam under construction would be an injurious and costly occurrence, for which TVA administrators would be held solely responsible. The development of productive labor relations, therefore, became one of TVA's major concerns at the very outset.

Active labor-management co-operation between organized workers and the TVA, now widely known and generally approved, could never have come about if Congress had provided for any division of responsibility for personnel management as between TVA's management and some other agency. Fixing of responsibility has thereby furthered "administrative democracy," in those vital relations between TVA management and employees. It should be obvious that, unless *within* TVA democratic methods are followed (not only as between labor and management but within TVA's management itself), it is impossible to expect that TVA can further strengthen the democratic spirit in the life of the valley.

Congress refused to divide responsibility in the TVA undertaking because it may have seen that such a course has in the past inevitably produced a senseless uniformity, and its offspring, rigidity and sterility. For when functions are thus severed from the main body of responsibility that nourishes them and gives them life and reality, any agency thus exercising disembodied authority must attempt to write "regulations" detailed enough to prevent mistakes and abuses of discretion. And, since such rules are commonly prescribed on a nation-wide basis to secure the fancied benefits of standardization, the lowest common denominator of conduct inevitably governs. The rituals of regulations, jurisdictional disputes, and the glorification of red tape thrive in such an atmosphere of divided responsibility.

I am not implying, of course, that there is anything peculiar about American public service. In Great Britain in the administration of government functions the British Civil Service, sometimes described as the best in the world, has shown the same tendencies, where management principles have not been applied. An observer makes this comment on conventional governmental methods in Britain, indicating how universal are these matters:

The civil service tradition [in Great Britain] implies a rigid hierarchical organization of authority. . . . The possibility of Parliamentary interpellation upon any detail of administration crystallises rigidity and overcentralization; an ex-Postmaster-General declares that as a result of this direct legislative control, "the minutiae of administration come right up to the highest officials, diverting their minds from broad matters of policy." However well suited to routine administration, the complete security of tenure characterising the civil service, with a tendency to promotion by seniority rather than merit, probably fails to offer an adequate spur to expression or originality, a first necessity in broadcasting, or to the salesmanship needed to create demand for a service.[1]

A distinguished Manchester businessman with extensive experience in public affairs, Sir Ernest Simon, on a visit to the TVA, commented upon the spirit of initiative in the TVA staff. He has since summarized his firsthand observations in this valley in a printed statement which reads in part:

The [TVA] Directors . . . have done all they can to delegate responsibility right down through the staff . . . [and] to cut out Civil Service red tape and the spirit of bureaucracy. The whole staff is encouraged to take responsibility, and not to worry if they make mistakes. The Directors have managed, I think, to get a spirit of constructive initiative throughout the staff as good as anything in the best private businesses.

Whatever the shortcomings in TVA's management, whatever delays, waste, and operating inefficiency there have been, is the direct responsibility of the Board of TVA itself. For Congress provided the conditions that make competent management possible. The at-

[1] Lincoln Gordon, *The Public Corporation in Great Britain* (London: Oxford University Press, 1938), p. 321.

titude of Congress and of the President toward TVA has been substantially that of a good business board of directors toward its management. "Here's your job. Here is the broad method we expect you to follow. On managerial detail it is up to you to pick the best way, within the framework of the policies we have set out and the terms of the company's charter. You are the manager. Get the job done. If you cannot and do not, you and you alone will be held responsible."

The corporation is a vehicle well adapted to such fixing of responsibility. The fact that TVA was set up as a corporation, however, is not alone any guarantee that it would not be subjected to the same rituals of divided responsibility, clearances, and detailed management by Congress as any bureau; in fact, some of our public corporations are thus encumbered. But, while no guarantee, there was a psychological advantage in using the corporate device, since by established practice and custom the corporation has come to embody in people's minds this idea of managerial responsibility.

Congress in 1933 took advantage of the opportunity that its selection of the independent corporate device created, and freed the TVA of the conventional procedures of government agencies and bureaus. The TVA continues in this autonomous status; it is not part of any of the existing bureaus and departments, and the head of the TVA reports directly to the President and to Congress.

Suppose these principles of management and decentralization, which Congress made it possible for TVA to put into effect in this valley, should be extended throughout the government. Would it mean the virtual abolition of the historic departments in Washington? How would it affect existing bureaus? Discussion of these and similar questions is beyond the scope of this book. But it should be evident that, even if these principles were extended to every federal activity to which they could appropriately be applied, many central departmental and bureau functions would be entirely unaffected. It is also evident that the size of some of the Washington departments would be reduced, and the nature and character of the work they perform would change.

It is to be hoped that these questions concerning management in government will continue to be the subject of study and objective discussion. The management of our federal government should be increasingly the subject of critical study by Congress and the people; experimentation and change (some of it drastic) are urgently needed.

The work of the Hoover Commission on the reorganization of the federal establishments, like the Brownlow report which preceded it, has had a tonic effect. This is not so much because of specific proposals (most of which were put into effect) as by the ensuing widespread discussion of management principles as applied to public affairs.

The people's everyday life has now become too intimately related to the way the government functions for the subject to be longer regarded as the exclusive field of professionals. Standpatters within government can sometimes manage to make official life uncomfortable and abbreviated for the administrators and managers who insist that there can be no such thing as a personal or political vested right in established government practice, however venerable; but this will not stem the tide of the public's demand that their government adopt the essentials of modern management.

Chapter 17

WHAT ABOUT "POLITICS"?

C AN politics be kept out of TVA?
This is a question that is often asked and has been extensively debated. By "politics" people mean nothing vague nor abstract. They mean such things as these: the appointment of engineers, land buyers, and workmen because they (or their friends or relatives) have helped to elect certain men to office; the preparation of specifications in a way that will favor the bid of some manufacturer who is politically "right"; the location of dams where they will win the most votes; in short, the use of TVA for partisan political purposes.

Opponents of the TVA during the long years of debate insisted that it was inevitable that partisan politics would infect TVA, and indeed any government undertaking of this character. This was in fact one of the chief arguments leveled by President Hoover and others against the proposals for a publicly owned enterprise as urged by Senator Norris. To prevent these forebodings from becoming a reality has been an important preoccupation of the administrators of the project. The success to date is due largely to the decision of Congress itself that politics must be kept out, a decision written into the explicit language of the law.

A river has no politics. Whether an engineer is a Democrat or a Republican, a conservative or a liberal, or indeed whether he has any interest in or knowledge of political matters at all, is entirely unrelated to his ability to design a dam. In this sense, experts as well as rivers have no politics. But the question of whether a river should be developed *is* a political question, and hence a proper subject of "politics." Whether a series of dams should provide only navigation, or instead should serve all the unified purposes to which the river can be put—this *is* a political question, and should be decided by Congress. The TVA Act is filled with such broad political decisions, made, as they should and must be made, by the elected representatives of the whole people. The decision to develop resources as a unified whole was a political one; the opportunity afforded for regional decentralization, the fixing of responsibility on a single agency in a region, even the decision that TVA must keep politics out of the selection of personnel—all these were political decisions.

Facts and experienced judgment, not political views, are the foundation of dependable technical decisions and action. Whether the rock at a particular site is a safe dam foundation or whether a certain kind of truck or transmission tower is best fitted for a job— these are not political questions and should not be decided politically or by political bodies. And, conversely, experts and administrators should not directly or by indirection decide political issues; moreover it is vital that they be held strictly answerable for their performance to prevailing public opinion, as expressed from time to time through democratic political methods.

Are these compatible principles? *Can science and politics live together* without one dominating the other? Can experts and managers be kept accountable to the public despite the great power over the lives of all of us that technical knowledge puts in their hands?

The TVA has, of course, inevitably faced these fundamental questions many times. The answers thus far have been in the affirmative. It is quite generally conceded that a high standard of technical and managerial competence has been maintained, and that the TVA has been guided by public policies laid down by Congress. It has certainly remained responsive to the wishes of the people it serves, who year in and year out have warmly supported TVA's resistance to political influence. The words used by the late Senator Bankhead of Alabama in a Senate debate fairly summarize the situation:

The TVA has no political activities; it has no policy-making programs except to carry out those declared in the Act, and they have been carried out to the very general satisfaction, as we have heard from all sides . . .

In the Tennessee Valley, regardless of politics, the program has the approval of the people, and the effort to bring under the confirmation power of the Senate [embodied in a bill to which the Senator was addressing himself] the engineers and architects and accountants and others connected with TVA is bitterly resisted by the people . . .

I have not heard a word from any citizen in the whole Tennessee Valley in favor of the proposed program [respecting Senate confirmation], but, on the contrary, countless letters, by the hundreds, possibly by the thousands, have come to me in opposition to any such program as that proposed, which would have a tendency to indicate that the TVA is to be made a political organization.

Too broad conclusions about politics in its relation to technology, however, should not be drawn from TVA's successful course in this respect in its first twenty years. It is always within the power of Congress to change the policy of keeping politics out of TVA. The issue, even as to TVA, may never be safely deemed as "settled."

Public understanding is the only possible safeguard against the mixing of politics and technology, and against the parallel evil of lack of accountability of administrators to the people. Considerations of theory will hardly determine whether the policy thus far successful in the TVA will be applied and followed in other comparable fields of public technical and managerial activities. Such public understanding must be constantly refreshed by concrete instances of the wisdom of the right course and the high cost of the wrong one.

This is no abstract question of "political science." Will the many technical questions with which modern government is constantly dealing be decided by political methods? On the other hand, will experts and industrial managers seek to disguise underlying policy questions by calling them "technical" or "economic," and thereby themselves decide political issues? Will these problems be dealt with in a kind of free-for-all fight between politics and managerial and technical judgment? The light of TVA's analogous experience is here of not a little practical importance.

As I have previously indicated, the appointment of all TVA officers and employees was vested exclusively in the hands of the Board of Directors. By an unusual provision Congress expressly excluded political considerations in all such appointments. The language was forthright: "No political test or qualification shall be permitted or given consideration, but all such appointments and promotions shall be given and made on the basis of merit and efficiency." Violation of this provision subjects a member of the Board of Directors to removal from office by the President and any employee to removal by the TVA Board. Under this authorization a complete system of personnel selection was set up, based upon methods that have been generously commended in managerial circles in both public and private business.

At the outset there was a disposition on the part of some Members of Congress to assume that TVA's Board and staff would look the other way, and disregard or give lip service to this explicit provision against any political appointments. When it became evident, however, that the intention was to hew consistently to the line, and that there would be no exceptions, the initial impatience diminished. After a trying year or two the policy came to be well recognized and generally accepted. Many Members of Congress have expressed approval of the policy.

What Senator (later Vice-President) Barkley (the then majority leader) said on the floor of the Senate is representative of the experience and the position of many legislators:

Mr. President, I have had my moments of disagreement and impatience growing out of perfectly natural and human reactions on account of the Tennessee Valley Authority. When the Gilbertsville Dam [now known as the Kentucky Dam] was authorized and construction of it was begun, unemployment was rife and widespread in the Tennessee Valley region and in my State. I live within 23 miles of the Gilbertsville Dam. Thousands of persons came to me thinking that I could obtain employment for them in the Tennessee Valley Authority. To all of them I pointed out the fact that when we enacted the law in the beginning we were so anxious to keep the TVA out of politics that we put in the law a provision that no political consideration should be given by the Tennessee Valley Authority to the employment of any person who might apply for employment under it.

The TVA has been so anxious to obey that injunction of the Congress and to be meticulous in the observance of that law that a recommendation by a Member of the Senate or the House was a disadvantage rather than an advantage to those who sought employment. The Tennessee Valley Authority did not want the people to get the idea that anybody could come there and obtain a job because he had a letter from a Senator or Representative. . . . I mention that because the TVA has been kept absolutely out of politics. It has given no consideration to politics in employing anybody, whether he was a Democrat, Republican, or otherwise.

The Senator then proceeded to express his strong opposition to legislation that he believed would inject politics into TVA.

To retain technicians and managers of high caliber would have been impossible if it had not been for this policy. But far more is at stake than the appointment and promotion of employees on their merits. An employee who owes his appointment to his political standing is a man whose allegiance may not be solely to the merits and the public purposes of the undertaking. The whole enterprise would be infected by half-technical, half-political judgments. There would be no foundation upon which TVA could stand. Public confidence in its integrity would soon fade. Once politics enters, the entire edifice of an enterprise built upon expert skills becomes unsafe.

Now there are of course all kinds of "politics." Administrators and technicians, however high-minded their purposes may seem to them, cannot piously abjure party politics, and then indulge in their own variety. "Taking care of the boys" at public expense is an evil in any guise, whether it is on the basis of personal friendship, business or social ties, or some amateur political notion about an "elite of brains" (self-selected), a kind of Phi Beta Kappa version of Tammany Hall.

The usual forthrightness of Congressmen is wholesome compared with the "holier-than-thou" attitude toward politicians of those who occasionally practice their own personal brand of politics. I was reminded of this hypocrisy a few years ago, when I read a signed magazine editorial which denounced the political patronage system, in the most righteous terms. The writer of this piece is a man who in 1933 had been a powerful figure in the government. When TVA was first created this Galahad sent word to the TVA Board that it must put one of his relatives on our pay roll. A jaunty young satellite brought us the message. We made the same reply that we had been giving to similar requests from Members of Congress: Let the relative file his application and be judged along with other applicants. The messenger tried to wave all this aside. He had been told (he said) to let us know that such rules about examinations were not intended to apply to men of such high social purposes! Both of these men have long since discredited themselves and are out of public service, but before this happened they had done not a little damage to the reputation for disinterestedness of all public administrators.

The employment of relatives is a form of personal politics; one of TVA's first actions was to establish a strong policy against the practice of nepotism. And then there are those businessmen who come into the government to perform a technical job of defense production who find nothing incongruous in injecting into a conference a partisan attack on the President or Members of Congress, or who even use a government post to further a particular political candidacy—these too are men who surely fail to comprehend the harm they are doing to public confidence in technicians in public affairs.

Congress itself determined to keep its kind of politics out of TVA's technical administration. It was, in turn, our responsibility as administrators to keep TVA out of political matters. Accordingly TVA in 1936 adopted a policy forbidding political activity by anyone connected with the TVA, even in municipal affairs. No TVA employee could be a candidate for any office, or be active in elections of any kind, except of course, to vote. This was a number of years before the Hatch Act placed similar but less extensive limits upon political activity of all federal employees. It is arguable that the TVA's policy is too extreme in that it forbids thousands of citizens living in the Tennessee Valley from useful participation in strictly community governmental affairs, but on balance this restriction seems justified by the dangers it averts.

TVA, if it had been politically managed, might have been anything but a blessing to this valley. Just what would it mean if politics had been injected into TVA's selection of personnel, or into detailed administration of funds by which the job is carried out? It would mean that the thousands of miles of transmission lines built by TVA's forces might have been located not for economic and engineering reasons, but upon a political basis. A city that votes "right," a county that delivers the "right" number of votes for a particular organization or candidate, an industry that "comes through," could be rewarded by advantages in the location of transmission lines, though such a location was not justified by the business facts. A city and its industries that do not vote "right" might find that its electric substations were not adequately maintained, that service was poor, that its industrial growth had stopped. These things would probably never actually happen, but the disintegrating suspicion that politics was under the surface would always be there.

If the TVA were under political management its transactions for purchase of materials and equipment—tens of thousands of contracts totaling many hundreds of millions of dollars, every one awarded on business principles of cost and relative quality of products—would have been potential political rewards. Even the location of dams might be the subject of political decisions rather than based on streamflow, character of the foundation, cost compared with other sites, and similar factual engineering considerations. Indeed in one instance—the building of the Douglas Dam in 1942—TVA earned the costly and lingering opposition of the then senior Senator from Tennessee, Kenneth D. McKellar, who was Chairman of the Senate Committee on Appropriations, because it persisted in recommending the location of the dam solely upon engineering considerations, contrary to the wishes of the Senator's political friends.

In the spring of 1942 Senator McKellar introduced into Congress a bill to change TVA's method of financing in such a way as to inject political considerations into the technical and business operations of TVA. Public understanding of this issue of politics in TVA took on unprecedented forms. Full-page advertisements protesting against the measure appeared in the daily papers, sponsored by and paid for by the valley's Chambers of Commerce and local service clubs. The valley press almost unanimously expressed strong opposition in repeated editorials. The bill was also opposed by a national magazine which speaks for the private electric industry and opposed the creation of TVA: "TVA has a trained personnel and a competent engineering staff operating under a capable management . . . TVA should be free from political control."[1] The theme of the newspaper advertising, the letters, the editorials, the resolutions of Sunday-school classes and women's clubs was: "Keep politics out of

[1] *Electrical World*, May 16, 1943, pp. 56-7.

TVA." The Senator's proposal, like his earlier ones to similar effect, was not enacted.

It is accurate to say that TVA has demonstrated to the satisfaction of those most directly affected that the task of getting resources developed should be kept non-political. It is now "good politics" for political leaders themselves, in the Tennessee Valley, to urge that politics be kept out of TVA. Probably the most thoughtful and informed leadership on the basic issues of the valley's development is coming from a group of its younger political leaders and elected officials. They know that their support of TVA will not be rewarded by jobs or favors, and have long since ceased to think in those terms. If TVA does a good job, one that the valley and the country judges to be competent, that constitutes their political reward. And to the surprise of many "realistic" people, it turns out that helping to keep politics out of TVA is a political asset to candidates for public office in the valley, men such as Senators Hill and Sparkman of Alabama, and Senators Kefauver and Gore of Tennessee. It is another case where "no politics is good politics." As long as the people these elected officials represent have confidence in the TVA idea and the technical and managerial craftsmanship behind it, the danger of politics in administration is not great; whenever that is lost, the injection of political decisions and methods is not far off.

But it would not be safe or wise to give to the administrators of the TVA such broad independence of action in carrying out political decisions made by Congress unless they were held strictly accountable for results. (And what is true of TVA seems to me applicable to managers and experts generally.) Moreover, TVA's freedom from interference in carrying out policies determined by Congress makes it imperative that the policies themselves be under constant control and review by Congress as the instrument of politics. When managers and technicians, in business or in government, are permitted to use the leverage of their authority and expert knowledge to lodge irresponsible power in themselves, the foundation of democracy is threatened at once.

Accountability begins with a full report of results. The TVA each year makes several such reports, public documents with a wide circulation. The Authority's regular report of its activities, made annually to Congress, is in great detail. Reports on special subjects are made from time to time. Financial reporting is comprehensive; it embodies the most progressive business methods: detailed unit cost accounting; a monthly and annual financial statement, including balance sheet and income account; and an audit by the Comptroller General of the United States. Until 1945, on TVA's initiative, the books were audited by a leading firm of commercial accountants. Since that time the commercial audit has been made by the Corporation Audits Division of the General Accounting Office in accordance with the Government Corporations Control Act. An elaborate accounting of results is also made each year before the Appropriations Committees of both Houses of Congress, as well as to the President through the Bureau of the Budget. Such reports as these have been the occasion of extensive debate over TVA in Congress, in the press, and in other public forums.

There are few enterprises, public or private, which have been subjected to more vigorous and persistent public review or about which more detailed reports have been made. Thus in 1938 a Joint Congressional Committee to investigate the TVA, equipped with a considerable technical staff, spent a year investigating the TVA. Its report, proceedings, and engineering analysis totaled 7,500 printed pages.

From time to time the entire TVA program has been reviewed in Congress in the course of consideration of statutory amendments or appropriations. In the ensuing hearings and debate the effectiveness of its management has been inquired into, new public policies have been written into TVA's basic charter, existing ones confirmed. In 1938, for example, a contract entered into by the TVA to purchase properties of the Tennessee Electric Power Company was reviewed by Congress. Every question in a lengthy contract, on which the late Wendell Willkie (on behalf of the company) and my associates and I had spent years of negotiation, was thus publicly examined, debated, and confirmed. Another instance of Congressional review of policy occurred in 1940 when the law respecting tax payments by TVA was changed. The committee hearings in Congress and the debates constituted a reappraisal of fundamental policy and an accounting of stewardship by TVA's managers covering virtually every phase of the enterprise.

It has been demonstrated by these and other instances that it is

entirely feasible to hold this public enterprise to strict accountability and responsibility without resort to political controls of the
details of operation from the floor of Congress. But it is in far less
formal ways that the most effective responsibility to the people is
established. *Working at the grass roots is the surest guarantee of
that day-to-day adjustment to the needs and aspirations of the
people which is the liveliest form of public accountability.* When
the managers and the experts are close to the people and their
problems, it does not ordinarily take the formality of a Congressional hearing to determine whether the program undertaken is
succeeding or needs adjustment, whether staff members are alive to
their opportunities or are arrogant and self-seeking.

Decentralization is a kind of mirror in which one can see, each
day and each hour, how well or how badly the work responds to its
broad purpose. Because it is a regional agency, doing its work and
making its decisions in the valley, TVA cannot escape the sight of its
mistakes or irresponsibly turn its back upon the stream of daily life.
Success can come only through a technical leadership in which the
people, not in the mysterious aura of distance but under the reveal-
ing and commonplace light of proximity and familiarity, have confidence. At the grass roots a new kind of accountability is born,
more significant than reports, reviews, criticism by Congress. It is
the day-to-day accountability of working partner to working partner.

Will the managers and experts of business and government enterprises, whose skills give them such great power, become a new
ruling class, exploiting the rest of society for their own benefit? In
his book, *The Managerial Revolution*, Professor James Burnham
asserts that such a "drive for social dominance, for power and privilege, for the position of ruling class by the social group or class of
managers" has already taken place in Germany and Russia, and, so
Professor Burnham states, is far along on its inevitable way in the
United States. The functions of our "new masters," Burnham says,
are now being performed in the earlier stages of this "managerial
revolution" by the executives of enterprises of which he singles out
General Motors and the Tennessee Valley Authority as examples.

In the past, similar predictions have been made, predictions
likewise adorned with analogies drawn from nations that are with-

out the experience or talent for democracy that exists in this country. But what gives Burnham's restatement of this thesis any importance is that it is sometimes taken in dead seriousness by men in important managerial and technical posts. The idea of managerial domination certainly cannot be lightly written off. The amount of influence which so cynical a thesis can have upon the vain, the naïve, and the power-hungry is not to be discounted. I trust it is clear that the methods of TVA are calculated to promote that accountability of the manager, public or private, and that diffusion of power which are the precise opposite and may well be an effective antidote to "managerial revolution."

More hazardous to democracy than such a dream of a ruling elite of managers and technicians, but not unrelated to it, is a growing contempt of "politics" and of Congress. This is nothing new or surprising from defeatists about democracy, and from reactionary forces generally. But to find this deprecation of politics spreading is a danger sign. The strongest expressions of disgust and impatience with politics and with Congress I have ever heard have come recently from men of great executive or technical ability in government service and in business who tried to get an urgent defense job done quickly, only to be delayed and even frustrated by what they describe as "political pressure," by sometimes pointless, demagogic, or just plain stupid Congressional committee hearings, and endless conferences with legislators. This is trying, of course. And it is true that when the line I have tried to draw in this chapter is crossed—the line between political policymaking and administrative execution of that policy—there is ample cause for this discouragement. But genuine democrats are under a peculiarly heavy responsibility to recognize, with scrupulous care, the role of politics in the fixing of basic policies. They must be the first to see that, if the institution of politics becomes discredited, the enemies of democracy have won an important victory.

Chapter 18

PLANNING AND PLANNERS

TVA is supposed to be a planning agency for this region. Yet nowhere on your organization chart do I find a Department of Planning; and when I ask for a copy of the TVA Plan no one can produce it: Some such comment has been made many times by friendly and earnest visitors to TVA.

The reason *the* TVA Plan is not available is that there is no such document. Nor is there one separate department set off by itself, where planners exercise their brains. To one who has read thus far in this account, it is evident this does not constitute the TVA idea of planning.

The TVA *is* a planning agency. The great change going on in this valley is an authentic example of modern democratic planning; this was the expressed intent of Congress, by whose authority the TVA acts. But through the years the TVA has deliberately been sparing in the use of the terminology of "plans" and "planning" within TVA and outside, and those terms have appeared infrequently thus far in this book. For the term "planning" has come to be used in so many different senses that the nomenclature has almost lost usefulness, has even come to be a source of some confusion.

It is necessary, however, to attempt to translate the ideas of this book into the terminology of planning and the language that planners employ.

To some the content of the word "planning" has been pared down until it means merely ordinary foresight, and thereby the term has lost any broad significance. Others have gone to the other extreme; they approve or violently condemn "planning" because to them it means a complete reconstitution of our social system, comprehensive state socialism, or over-all centralized economic planning with powers of enforcement.

The term "planning," however various are the meanings ascribed to it, is here to stay; but, since it has apparently come to mean all things to all men, I have, in preceding chapters, set out just what I have in mind in using the word, and what planning means in this valley. "Unified development" as I have described the idea in action is, in substance, the valley's synonym for "planning."

We have always made plans in America. The question for us is not: Should we plan? but: *What kind of plans* should we make? What kind of planners? What method of "enforcement of plans"? On these matters what has transpired in the Tennessee Valley, as I have tried to describe it, casts the light of actual experience.

Economic and social planning in America is by no means new and strange, but is indeed as old as the Republic. Generally speaking, planning in this country in the past has been practiced by two great groups: first, by elected public officials, variously called "politicians" or "statesmen"; and, second, by businessmen, called by some "empire builders," by others "exploiters of our resources."

Let us look for a moment at some of the instances of planning carried on by public men, selected to represent the economic interests and the social point of view of their constituents. Land planning, for example. By Royal Proclamation in 1763 the colonists were barred from free access to the western lands. Then, by the Ordinance of 1787, the politicians established a different conception of land planning: the opening of the western lands to settlers. The economic and social views of the people of that time called for land planning which would encourage and stimulate the settlement of the West.

Or take another illustration of public planning by elected officials, industrial planning. In the early days of American manufacturing, a plan was devised to stimulate industry. Certain of the public men of that day, like Hamilton and Webster and their sectional constituents, wanted a particular result: manufacturing in the Northeastern States. With the home market "protected," they planned an industrial future for the Northeast, and the method they used to effectuate the plan was the protective tariff.

The Homestead Act of 1862, the Income Tax Amendment, the

Sherman Anti-Trust Act, the Granger Laws—one can recite instance after instance of public planning through our political institutions, through acts of Congress, acts of state legislatures, local ordinances. One thing particularly characteristic of such planning by elected representatives is that they did not as a regular practice call into their councils the assistance of technically trained men—scientists, economists, engineers, administrators—to assist them in formulating these plans.

How well did these early planners do their job? Were the plans well conceived and in the public interest? This much is certain: their plans were not sterile, they were not merely reports and recommendations, written to be filed away and to gather dust. They were put into action, and out of that action in less than 150 years grew the greatest industrial and agricultural nation of all time.

Great as were some of the accomplishments of public planners in the past, we know that we suffer today from the consequences of some of those plans. The state of our natural resources has become a national emergency, grave and critical. Hindsight tells us that some of the public land policies embodied in such planning as the Homestead laws were extravagant and wasteful. Such piecemeal planning for the immediate year-to-year demands of particular groups of constituents we now know was not wise planning. Catastrophic floods, denuded forests, soil exhaustion—these are part of the price we are paying. For more than a generation a change in those plans has been urged. Overtones prophetic of President Roosevelt's message to Congress concerning TVA were heard, faintly it is true, as early as 1909 when President Theodore Roosevelt's Conservation Commission made this recommendation:

Broad plans should be adopted providing for a system of waterway improvement extending to all uses of the waters and benefits to be derived from their control, including the clarification of the water and abatement of floods for the benefit of navigation; the extension of irrigation; the development and application of power; the prevention of soil wash; the purification of streams for water supply; and the drainage and utilization of the waters of swamp and overflow lands.

As in the case of planning by public men, we should remember that when businessmen become planners they are not venturing into new and strange fields. Long-range planning is a familiar and established practice of progressive business. Perhaps the best-known example is that of the American Telephone and Telegraph Company. This vast communication service has expended large sums of money in continuous and intensive study of the future, and on the basis of such study develops plans five years, ten years, and even longer in advance—plans for new construction, for the revision of its exchanges, for the building of additional capacity. In other businesses there has long been comparable economic planning with substantial organizations devoted to the task. Surveys are made of the market, financial trends, technological changes, all the complex factors which will affect the future activities of a great business enterprise.

Planning by businessmen, often under some other name, is recognized as necessary to the conduct of private enterprise. It has the virtue of a single and direct objective, one that can be currently measured that is producing and marketing goods or services at a profit. A plan that is impressive in the form of a report but which does not work, as judged by the financial reports of the company, is an unsuccessful plan. It has been just as simple as that. The business planner has rarely felt it necessary to complicate his problem by trying to determine whether the making of profit under his plan benefits the whole of society, or injures it. And, as I have said, it is not often that a single business or even an entire industry is in a position to pass intelligently upon such a question.

This is admittedly a grave defect of planning by the businessman. For his legitimate and essential object, namely a profitable business, is not necessarily consistent with the object of society, that is, a prosperous and happy people. The plans of the A. T. & T. and of the small manufacturer may both be quite effective within those enterprises. But factors affecting the plans of the A. T. & T. and the small manufacturer go far beyond their businesses. Over this multitude of external factors the businessman has little or no effective control. As this and a thousand valleys demonstrate so tragically, private planning, even when temporarily sound from the viewpoint of a particular enterprise, has often resulted in great injury to many other enterprises, and therefore to the public welfare.

The idea of unified resource development is based upon the

premise that by democratic planning the individual's interest, the interest of private undertakings, can increasingly be made one with the interest of all of us, i.e., the community interest. By and large, things are working out that way in the Tennessee Valley. The income of the private business of farming has increased, largely as a result of a program of aiding the region's soil. Sales by private fertilizer companies have increased more rapidly than at any other time in their history, a result attributed largely to TVA's development and demonstration of new fertilizer products designed to further the over-all public interest in the land. Promotion of education in forest-fire protection and scientific cutting methods has furthered conservation and at the same time aided the private business of lumbering, and chemical industries dependent upon a permanent supply of forest products. Community planning has made towns more attractive and pleasant for everyone, and at the same time increased land values for individual owners. These results and many others I have described have been in the general public interest; all have furthered the interest of particular business enterprises.

Effective planners must understand and believe in people. The average man is constantly in the mind of the effective planning expert. Planners, whether they are technicians or administrators, must recognize that they are not dealing with philosophical abstractions, or mere statistics or engineering data or legal principles, and that planning is not an end in itself.

In the last analysis, in democratic planning it is human beings we are concerned with. Unless plans show an understanding and recognition of the aspirations of men and women, they will fail. Those who lack human understanding and cannot share the emotions of men can hardly forward the objectives of realistic planning. Thurman Arnold, in *The Symbols of Government*, has well described this type of earnest but unrealistic person:

They usually bungle their brief opportunities in power because they are too much in love with an ideal society to treat the one actually before them with skill and understanding. Their constant and futile cry is reiterated through the ages: "Let us educate the people so that they can understand and appreciate us."

A great Plan, a moral and indeed a religious purpose, deep and fundamental, is democracy's answer both to our own homegrown would-be dictators and foreign anti-democracy alike. In the unified development of resources there is such a Great Plan: the Unity of Nature and Mankind. Under such a Plan this valley moves forward. True, it is but a step at a time. But under democratic planning responsibility by each citizen is assumed not simply for the little advance made each day, but for that vast and all-pervasive end and purpose of all our labors, the material well-being of all men and the opportunity for them to build for themselves spiritual strength.

Here is the life principle of democratic planning—an awakening in the whole people of a sense of this common moral purpose. Not one goal, but a direction. Not one plan, once and for all, but *the conscious selection by the people of successive plans.* It was Whitman the democrat who warned that "the goal that was named cannot be countermanded."

If this conception of planning is sound, as I believe, then it is plain that in a democracy we always must rest our plans upon "here and now," upon "things as they are." How many are the bloody casualties of efforts to improve the lot of man, how bitter the lost ground and disillusionment because of failure to understand so simple and yet so vital an issue of human strategy. So frequently have men sought an escape from the long task of education, the often prosaic day-by-day steps to "do something about it," by pressing for a plan—usually in the form of a law—without considering whether the people understand the reason for the law's plan, or how they are to benefit by it.

An unwillingness to start from where you are ranks as a fallacy of historic proportions; present-day planning, anywhere in the world for that matter, will fall into the same pit if it makes the same gigantic error. It is because the lesson of the past seems to me so clear on this score, because the nature of man so definitely confirms it, that there has been this perhaps tiresome repetition throughout this record: the people must be in on the planning; their existing institutions must be made part of it; self-education of the citizenry is more important than specific projects or physical changes.

And it is because of this same conviction that the TVA has never attempted by arbitrary action to "eliminate" or to force reform upon those factors or institutions in the valley's life which are vigorously antagonistic to a plan for unified development.

We move step by step—from where we are. Everyone has heard the story of the man who was asked by a stranger how he could get to Jonesville; after long thought and unsuccessful attempts to explain the several turns that must be made, he said, so the anecdote runs: "My friend, I tell you; if I were you, I wouldn't start from here." Some planning is just like that; it does not start from here; it assumes a "clean slate" that never has and never can exist.

The TVA idea of planning sees action and planning not as things separate and apart, but as one single and continuous process. In the President's message to the Congress in 1933, this fact was stressed. The words bear repetition here: The TVA, he said, "should be charged with the broadest duty of planning for the proper use, conservation, and development of the natural resources of the Tennessee River drainage basin and its adjoining territory for the general social and economic welfare of the Nation." Then follows this sentence: "This Authority should also be clothed with the necessary power to carry these plans into effect." And the law enacted this principle.

This is fundamental. And yet it is here that much of the disagreement with TVA has arisen from outside, and in its first years internal disagreement as well. The idea that planning and responsibility for action may and should be divorced—the maker of plans having little or nothing to do with their execution—follows the analogy of the planning of a house, an office building, any fixed structure. But the analogy is a mistaken one. For the development of a region is a course of action; it has no arbitrary point of beginning and goes on and on with no point of completion. The individual acts that make up regional development are the day-to-day activities of plowing a particular field, harvesting timber from a particular tract, the building of a factory, a church, a house, a highway. TVA's purpose was not the making of plans but that a valley be developed.

Plans had to be made, of course, many of them. But plans and action are part of one responsibility. TVA is responsible not alone for plans but for results. Those results depend chiefly upon the people's participation. Getting that participation was to be almost wholly on a voluntary basis. To get a job done in this way was a unique assignment, one that required the invention of new devices and new methods. If TVA had been a "planning agency" in the sense that its responsibility had been limited to the making of plans —the usual meaning of the term—those plans would probably have met the fate of so many other plans: brochures decorating bookshelves, adornments of what is so often mere sterile learning.

In *The Coming Victory of Democracy*, Thomas Mann put his finger on this deep-lying error of intellectualism that treats planning apart from action. His words are moving, for they tell much of the causes beneath the catastrophe of European culture:

Democracy is thought; but it is thought related to life and action. . . . No intellectual of the pre-democratic era ever thought of action, nor of what kind of action would result if his thinking were put into practice. It is characteristic of undemocratic or of democratically uneducated nations that their thinking goes on without reference to reality, in pure abstraction, in complete isolation of the mind from life itself, and without the slightest consideration for the realistic consequences of thought.

In the TVA the merging of planning and responsibility for the carrying out of those plans forces our technicians to make them a part of the main stream of living in the region or community; this it is that breathes into plans the breath of life. For in the Tennessee Valley the expert cannot escape from the consequences of his planning, as he can and usually does where it is divorced from execution. This has a profound effect on the experts themselves. Where planning is conceived of in this way, the necessity that experts should be close to the problems with which they are dealing is evident.

In my opinion the idea of planning is still struggling for popular support in America in part for this reason: that many of the most spectacular plans have been drawn by men who did not have the responsibility for carrying them out. They did not have the salutary discipline which the experts of this valley had who have had to ask themselves: "Is this a plan that I can take responsibility for seeing carried out? Will the people understand it, will the people help to make it effective? Will they make the plan their own?"

In the work of the TVA we have taken to heart and sought to put into practice what seems to me one of the most profound utterances upon the problem of freedom through democracy. They are the words of the late John Dewey.

The conflict as it concerns the democracy to which our history commits us [he wrote] is *within* our own institutions and attitudes. It can be won only by extending the application of democratic methods, methods of consultation, persuasion, negotiation, communication, co-operative intelligence, in the task of making our own politics, industry, education, our cultures generally, a servant and an evolving manifestation of democratic ideas. . . .

. . . democratic ends demand democratic methods for their realization. . . . Our first defense is to realize that democracy can be served only by the slow day-by-day adoption and contagious diffusion in every phase of our common life of methods that are identical with the ends to be reached. . . . An American democracy can serve the world only as it demonstrates in the conduct of its own life the efficacy of plural, partial, and experimental methods in securing and maintaining an ever-increasing release of the powers of human nature, in service of a freedom which is co-operative and a co-operation which is voluntary.[1]

What of the enforcement of economic and social plans in this valley? In the building of dams and other structures, TVA of course has the power which even private utilities and railroads have, to take property of landowners who are unwilling to sell, at a price fixed by court proceedings. It can refuse to sell power except under the policies set out in the TVA Act. But, beyond such things, in no significant particular is TVA planning for the development of this region enforceable by law. And this, in my opinion, has not been a handicap.

This is not to say dogmatically that there is never any justification whatever for regulatory measures, or that voluntary methods have not resulted in a good many mistakes and waste that good planning would have avoided, if the people who made those decisions had been persuaded to make different ones. It is pointed out to us constantly that the course of education and voluntary action is too slow, that only the force of law will meet the crisis of soil depletion.

[1] *Freedom and Culture* (New York: G. P. Putnam's Sons, 1939), pp. 175-6.

Critics, admitting that not a little progress has been made by the TVA methods, point to the many farmers who still persist in plowing higher and higher on their hills, planting more corn and cotton, destroying more and more land; to the timber interests which continue to spurn the advice of forest technicians that would sustain the yield of lumber; to the manufacturers who still pollute the streams with waste and show scant interest in technical means of ending this contamination. More than once industries have been located at points where it seemed clear that sound planning should discourage industrial location.

This lack of power to enforce plans has disturbed a good many observers and students of the enterprise, especially in the early years, and still mystifies and irritates some of them. But the TVA has continued to rely upon and to emphasize the methods described in this book, the ways of contract, persuasion, incentives, encouragement, methods based on the people's confidence in TVA's comprehension, its good faith, and the quality of its technical leadership. I feel strongly that the admitted limitations of voluntary methods, distressing and tragic as their consequences sometimes are, do not invalidate the wisdom of a *minimum of coercion* in carrying out plans for resource development. For coercion is insatiable. In whatever guise, once coercion becomes the accepted reliance for making planning effective, more and more coercion is needed. I am deeply persuaded that high as the price of voluntary methods may be, in delays and errors, in the end the price of arbitrary enforcement of planning is nothing less than our freedom.

Chapter 19

TVA AND WORLD RECONSTRUCTION

THIS chapter was written while World War II was being fought. Read in 1953, therefore, many references to the war, in the present tense, and to a future coming postwar period of reconstruction, are obviously dated.

I have concluded, however, to let the chapter stand as it was originally written, except for reference to such new facts or events as could be indicated by footnotes. For the chapter may be useful, unchanged, as reflecting one American's thinking and outlook, at that time and under those circumstances, on issues that since the war have become of the greatest possible importance. Those issues are referred to in this chapter as "world co-operation," or as American economic and technical aid to other countries in their resource development. Today, of course, these matters would be identified by speaking of particular institutions and programs born since the war, such as the United Nations and its various agencies, or the Marshall Plan and its several successors, Point IV, and so on.

Though there is a note of apprehension about the future implicit in the very theme of the chapter, nowhere is there expressed any premonition of the coming catastrophe of a cold war and the bloodshed of Korea. This is a reflection of the generally sanguine mood that prevailed at the time the chapter was written.

A new chapter (Chapter 20) follows this one. It is a look at the current manifestations of the TVA idea elsewhere in the world, foreshadowed by what I had to say on that subject in the original chapter. An extensive Appendix, C, compiles information on the impact of the TVA idea in other lands.

Among the more than eleven million people[1] who have visited the TVA in recent years have been representatives of almost every country in the world. Since the war there has been a marked increase in foreign visitors.[2] They come in a steady procession: a Chinese general returning to Chungking, complete with military cape and battle dagger, an agricultural commissioner from New Delhi, the British Ambassador, a group of Swedish journalists especially observant of the modern architecture of the new power-houses, a Brazilian scientist, a prominent Australian politician, a Czech electrical expert—hundreds of men from the most distant lands.[3]

The TVA has also served as a training ground for foreign technicians; twoscore engineers and agriculturists from a dozen republics of South America; a similar contingent from China, singularly enthusiastic and intense. There has been a group of Russian engineers working with TVA technicians on Lend-Lease hydroelectric plants that in 1944 will be producing power on streams "somewhere beyond the Urals."

This steady stream of "visiting" reminds you of the way in which a farmer crosses the ridge to take a look at a neighbor's demonstration farm, to see "how he does it," so he can try it out in his own way on his own place—except these neighbors may be from Auckland on the other side of the globe, or from Göteborg, Buenos Aires, or Tegucigalpa. Among the visitors from abroad are not only policy-makers but experts in the many specialized fields embraced in this undertaking: from public health to mapping, from resettlement to community planning. Here they observe how their particular

[1] Thirty-nine million, as of 1953.

[2] In 1947 the number was 728, which rose, steadily, to 2,114 in fiscal 1952.

[3] Among recent foreign visitors have been President Miguel Aleman of Mexico; Queen Juliana and Prince Bernhard, Netherlands; Prime Minister David Ben-Gurion of Israel; Prime Minister Joseph Pholien of Belgium; President Gabriel Gonzales Videla of Chile; Dr. Franz Bluecher, Vice-Chancellor of Western Germany; Prime Minister Pandit Jawaharlal Nehru of India; President Enrico Gaspar Dutra and Governor Arnon De Mello, State of Alagoas, of Brazil. Right Honorable Hector McNeil, British Minister of State; the Khan of Kalat, Ruler of Kalat, Pakistan; Prince Charles, Regent of Belgium; Abdel Meguid Pasha Saleh, Egyptian Minister of Public Works; Prince Seif Al-Islam Abdullah Hamiduddiq of Yemen; George Pezopoulous, director of power of Greece.

specialized interest can be made an integral part of the whole task of resource development.

This same world-wide interest is reflected in thousands of letters from many nations. The questions propounded, the material requested, the inquiries about how TVA proceeded, reflect a remarkable degree of interest in regional resource development. In recent months this correspondence has been largely from officials of post-war commissions of reconstruction, representatives of governments in exile, and legislators of Western Hemisphere nations. Writers in foreign magazines and newspapers describe TVA and set out what they believe are the lessons for their homeland in what is going on in this far-away and hitherto little known region. A leading English publication, *The Architectural Review*, for example, devoted its entire June, 1943, issue to a lengthy description and interpretation of TVA by Julian Huxley, the distinguished scientist and publicist. In a concluding paragraph he says:

Last, but not least, the TVA idea, of the planned development of natural regions such as river valleys, has already found its way into the world's general thinking. TVA ideas and methods are helping to guide the growth of new planning agencies such as the Middle East Supply Council; studies are being made of how a set-up of general TVA type could be adapted to serve as an international instead of a national agency (thus among other things undercutting and transcending nationalist sovereignties, as the TVA undercuts and transcends States' rights and boundaries), and adjusted to promote the planned development of regions of greater backwardness, like parts of Africa.

Our foreign visitors see with particular clarity that TVA speaks in a tongue that is universal, a language of *things close to the lives of people*: soil fertility, forests, electricity, phosphate, factories, minerals, rivers. No English interpreter is needed when a Chinese or a Peruvian sees this series of working dams, or electricity flowing into a single farmhouse, or acres that phosphate has brought back to life. For it is not really Norris Dam on a Tennessee stream or a farm in Georgia that he sees, but a river, a valley, a farm in China or Peru. The changes that are taking place here are much the same as those which men all over the world are seeking. The technical problems, too, at bottom are essentially similar, whether one is dealing with soil erosion along the Yangtze or the Hiwassee, the malaria

mosquito in Burma or Mississippi's Tishomingo County, power production in Norrland in Sweden or Swain County, North Carolina.

TVA's development of democratic methods of consent and participation by the people also touches a desire that is widely shared.
Again and again our visitors have made substantially this comment:
"We are even more interested in TVA's way of working with people than we are in its dams and furthering of industrial development." That resource development should not only be *for* the
people of the valley but *by* them appeals to most of our foreign
visitors. For like human beings almost everywhere they want to
see the changes they hope to work out for their own countries done
in their own way. This is important for Americans to remember,
especially those who want to do the world over exactly on our own
pattern, either on a cost-plus basis, or as a kind of paternalistic imperialism.

The TVA experience in resource development is being earnestly
examined for the lessons it may hold for a battered world facing
the giant contours of a historic period of reconstruction. For it is
coming to be recognized ever more widely that our hope of future
peace or the certainty of new wars rests to an important degree
upon the wisdom the world can summon to the task of resource development. This is not the whole story of course; the effect of racial
antagonisms and conflicting cultures on political systems goes deep.
But at the root of much of the world's turbulence lies the way we
deal with the physical base of every man's and hence every nation's
livelihood.

The subject has the broadest ramifications; to pursue them is
outside the scope of this book. It is obvious, however, that the pressure of people upon resources that do not adequately support them
has long nourished a spirit of armed aggression against other nations. It is a commonplace that the development of one people's
land and forests and minerals for the sole benefit of another people
has started many a fire of hatred that later exploded into war. It
has not, however, been quite so apparent that methods of unified
development to create sustained productivity rather than quick exhaustion, that technical advance which makes low-grade ores, for
example, as useful as the scarce higher grades, or that expert skills
which can restore now wasted land and greatly increase its pro-

ductivity, relieve war-creating tensions of impoverishment and may be the foundation stones upon which peace in a modern world can be slowly built. It is the light which this valley's experience throws on such matters—the brass tacks of world reconstruction—that has made it a center of interest to foreign visitors.

The TVA has come to be thought of (here and abroad) as a symbol of man's capacity to create and to build not only for war and death but for peace and life. This is of great importance in the postwar period. For despair and cynicism in our own ranks will be a deadly enemy after Germany and Japan surrender. The immediate task of fighting keeps us tense. Once that tension is relaxed we must be prepared for a let-down, a bitter loss of faith and hope. When that time comes it will be desperately important as a matter of mental antisepsis that there be, in this country and abroad, many living proofs, of which the TVA is one, of the creative powers of mankind and of democracy's demonstrated and practical concern for the everyday aspirations of people.

The value of TVA as a symbol of what man can do to change his physical environment is increased by the knowledge that in this valley we have had to face so many of those same problems which plague other regions of the world: low income, resignation to the *status quo* as "inevitable," complacency on the part of other more favored areas. A demonstration that such gains can be made without forcible changes in social status or property rights, without liquidating all those who do not agree completely with one's plans, will be evidence to support the conviction of those who have no faith in catastrophe as an instrument of human social improvement.

What I have said in the preceding chapter on "planning," on the importance of starting from where you are and of taking a step at a time, *one change promoting the next,* applies with peculiar force to our economic and political thinking about the post-war world. What is dumfounding to me, however, is that men who show they understand this as applied to our own affairs, when they consider the future of world society will abruptly slip these hawsers of experience and reality. They would be quick to condemn TVA if it had sought to make this valley over according to a pattern of TVA's own design. Yet they seem quite eager that America try the even more quixotic task of building a world order on the same kind of undemocratic foundation.[4]

There is yet another way the TVA may throw the light of experience on the conditions for a lasting peace. For TVA is a demonstration, and one that can be readily understood, of this truth: *in any perspective of time, unified resource development anywhere helps everyone everywhere.* A stronger, more productive Tennessee Valley region has benefited the whole American nation and all its regions. So it will be when any region of the world strengthens the basis of its livelihood. Regional economic developments, whether within the nation or the family of nations, are not something to fear but to encourage.

When people of the more developed regions of the earth cease their fear that resource development and greater productiveness elsewhere injure them, and realize instead that they are benefited by them, then international political co-operation will be on the way to full realization. For it is that fear which nourishes extreme nationalism, with its harvest of hatred between peoples, tariff barriers, restrictive trade, autarchy, and finally—war. The physical shrinking of the world only multiplies the opportunities for inflaming these deep anxieties.

It is upon a wide popular comprehension and practice of the economics of the Golden Rule—and particularly among our fellow Americans—that it seems to me the prospects for world peace largely rest. The essential structure of political co-operation between nations will be weakened, may indeed begin to crack the day it is set up, unless those political arrangements rest upon increasingly effective economic co-operation.

[4] Cf. Mr. Justice Douglas before First National Conference on International Economic and Social Development, Washington, D. C., April 7, 1952, from which the following is quoted:

". . . If the conditions existed in America that exist in the Middle East and Asia, we would be forming an American revolutionary committee—a committee to promote a revolution—to lead a revolution—to destroy the octopus that was overpowering us. . . . You can't stop [the Red tide of communism] by talking about democracy and peace. You have to talk about it in terms that are understandable at the village level. We can't do that unless we are prepared to go into the villages of Asia and the Middle East with a program of political action. If you can't go in that way, stay out. When you go in, go in whole-heartedly in the American way. With a few dollars and few great ideas, you can save the world from this horrible spectre of Soviet imperialism."

The experience of the Tennessee Valley helps to make these matters clearer to American public opinion, and thus serves a useful educational purpose in world reconstruction. It was a favorite argument against the TVA in its earliest years that the development of this valley would endanger the prosperity of the people elsewhere—in Ohio and Connecticut and New York. If an additional factory is built in Alabama—so the oft-repeated story ran—that will mean less factory employment in Ohio; if Tennessee produces more dairy products, that means a loss to the dairying industry in Wisconsin. Such ideas, seriously put forward in editorials and speeches about the TVA, rested upon the assumption that there is a market for just so much goods, and that America had now reached its highest level of production and of consumption.

Until the falseness of such ideas *within our own country* is understood at the grass roots, it is politically naïve to expect American public opinion to support the idea of encouraging world-wide economic co-operation in the interest of lasting peace. That many of us would prefer that such a policy be adopted primarily upon ethical grounds, and would favor it even if it hurt us economically, is quite irrelevant.

These things can be best understood by demonstrations that are close to us. Therein lies the value of TVA. For many people in Ohio, for example, or Connecticut, or New York, have come to see that increased productivity in the Tennessee Valley has not endangered their own standard of living as they were repeatedly told it would. The millions of people in this region who have been producing more, who thereby have been able to buy and enjoy more automobiles, radios, refrigerators, and clothes, make for a more prosperous nation and a stronger Ohio, Connecticut, New York. The figures I have cited of increase in the level of income among the valley's people can be readily translated into the language of more production in *every* region.

Ten years age the Tennessee Valley was regarded in the electrical appliance industry as the "zero" market of the country; a few years later it was the leading market of the entire country, with the spectacular increases in purchases that I have previously recited. The men in the General Electric shops at Schenectady, New York, or at the Westinghouse Company in Mansfield, Ohio, who produced many of those additional tens of thousands of electric ranges, water pumps, and refrigerators, now can see that it was in their interest that this valley had become productive enough to buy and pay for the products of their shops. This meant that men in Schenectady would buy overalls and aluminum goods made in this valley; could perhaps afford a fishing vacation on one of the new TVA lakes.

There was at the outset bitter opposition to the TVA from the coal industry, an opposition which further illustrates how mistaken it is to cling to the ideal of restricted development. The argument was made that by developing electricity from the water of the river TVA would rob the coal industry of its existing market for coal for steam-generated electricity. Actually, of course, sound development of one asset, water power, and a rate policy that increased its use enormously, inevitably stimulated the use of other resources, coal included. The valley market for coal for industrial and other purposes rose to heights never before experienced. Even the use of the region's coal for power generation has exceeded all records, as TVA's electric rate example multiplied power use over wide areas where coal is the principal source of electricity. Never has as much coal been used for the generation of electricity, as since the river has been developed. TVA itself has built and acquired steam-electric plants to supplement the river's power; in 1940 TVA purchased 574,000 tons of coal; in 1941, 693,000 tons; in 1942, 1,319,000 tons, chiefly for power production.[5]

This is the way—by one object lesson after another—we learn that the dangers to us of economic development elsewhere in the world are imaginary. When Americans see that it has helped, not hurt, the people of Ohio, say, to have this southern valley more productive, we shall see that much the same thing will be true if, in their own way, Mexicans and Brazilians and Russians and Chinese develop their resources and trade with us and with each other. That comprehension can best be learned at first hand.

It is folly to expect Americans clearly to see the tragedy, *for the world,* of an intense nationalism until restrictive sectionalism *within the nation* is also seen as a self-defeating policy. A demand for an end of a colonial system far from home is not nearly so important as an understanding of the colonial system within the

[5] For more recent figures, which have sharply increased, see TVA Annual Report for 1952.

United States, and the reasons why it is so injurious to this nation's interest. And colonialism, or exploiting the hinterland, is substantially the basis upon which the South and the West have been so long predominantly a raw-materials source for the dominant manufacturing regions of the North and Northeast.

American public opinion on world co-operation will not be strengthened by the kind of double talk that displays fervid concern for self-development for India along with lack of interest, even hostility, toward industrial development for undeveloped American regions. Such a cynical attitude will justify the suspicion that far-off China's cause is espoused and that of near-by Georgia and Arkansas ignored because there are fewer American vested interests —political and economic—to be antagonized. Equality of opportunity for all the nations of the world will yield few benefits to the average man if that great principle is dissociated from specific issues of equality of opportunity for regions within our own country.

World co-operation cannot be built on mere expansiveness of spirit, or upon escapes from the reality of hard work close at hand. It is in our own backyard that we can best prove the sincerity of our aims for the wide world, and best learn the great truth of universal interdependence. In the teaching of this truth, by action and not words alone, TVA has a limited but useful role.

We have still a long way to go in public understanding of these matters. As recently as the spring of 1943 the Governor of one of our great eastern industrial states, a man of national leadership, warned against the growth of industry in the South and West upon the ground that it would injure his state, apparently on the assumption that greater industrial activity here inevitably meant net losses to his state. His remarks were occasioned in part by a series of TVA reports to Congress. In these reports we urged, in the national interest, the end of a system of regional freight rates that are much higher in the South and West than in the industrial North and East. We recommended a national rate without discrimination against any region.[6]

---

[6] See two TVA special reports: *Interterritorial Freight Rate Problem of the U. S.*, 75th Congress, House Document 264 (1937); *Regionalized Freight Rates: Barrier to National Productiveness*, 78th Congress, House Document 137 (1943).

With freight rates on goods manufactured in the South almost 40 per cent higher, mile for mile, than on goods manufactured north of the Ohio (though railroad unit costs are almost identical), a manufacturer to establish himself in the South and in other similarly disadvantaged regions must carry a heavy handicap. No wonder progress in southern industry has been so slow and difficult, and the pressure to pay low wages so great. Moreover, since it is manufacture that gives opportunity for those skills which yield the highest returns, income in the American colonial regions is far below that of the industrial regions of the North. It was inevitable that with this disadvantage against manufacture, the South and West have had to drain their natural resources of soil fertility, timber, minerals, and oil, unwisely and often disastrously. By contrast, favorable freight rates on raw materials encouraged this exploitation.

The elimination of this man-made handicap of regional rates,[7] TVA believes, would enable the South and West to increase the amount of manufacturing of their raw materials, since then the internal tariff walls of freight rates would no longer bar their manufactured goods from free movement to their economic markets. The people's income would accordingly rise, for low income and reliance upon raw materials are the marks the world over of the colonial system.

TVA has insisted that this change would not rob Peter in the North to swell the lean pockets of Paul in the interior, but would *benefit both regions*. And here precisely is the importance of the freight rate issue in the development of an American public opinion favorable to world economic co-operation. It must become clear to Americans generally that the increased productiveness of the undeveloped regions of this country is to the advantage of the whole country and all of its regions. Otherwise it is a forlorn hope to believe that the equivalent principle in world affairs will receive effective and continuous American popular support.

To what extent and under what terms should private investors or the government of this country finance the development of re-

[7] On May 30, 1952, the Interstate Commerce Commission, after lengthy consideration of the problem raised by the TVA reports referred to above, made final an order establishing a uniform freight classification and uniform class rates for the entire country east of the Rockies.

sources in other parts of the world as a means of buttressing the pillars of peace? A complete discussion of this is obviously beyond the scope of this book. The point I seek to make is simply this: the issue ought not be thought of in terms of fear of "creating competition against our own businessmen and farmers." This fear has as little general validity in the international field as it has between regions here at home. The policy of reciprocal trade, for example, takes on meaning only when there is trade, i.e., productiveness, to reciprocate. The flourishing regions and nations can only *remain* vigorous and strong by encouraging the regions and nations that are less productive.

Whether we encourage or discourage it, or are foolish enough to regard it with indiscriminate fear, world-wide development of natural resources and industrialization will go forward rapidly after the war. The United States can in some ways speed the process and influence its course. But it is nonsense to believe that we hold a broad veto over what other great nations decide to do in developing their rivers or their other resources. To accept such shallow talk as this is to close our eyes to the central fact that sets our time off from all that went before—the drive, the world over, toward resource development through the machine and science.

There are, however, questions that are still open: what *course* the development will take, both here and abroad; the *methods* that will be used; for whose *benefit* the development will be carried out. Unless the people demand a course that will benefit them, one that will not exhaust their resources wastefully, the old exploitative methods of the elite few are likely to be followed.

It is for this reason that the TVA experience ought to be known. For a knowledge of the methods followed in this valley's development will enable the people to be critical, to demand answers to their questions—questions such as these: Will economic development be unified, seen as a whole? Will resources be regarded as a means of benefiting the human beings who depend upon them, or will the development of each resource be deemed as an end in itself, its benefits drained off by a few with no recognition of broad ethical purpose? Will resource development be treated as merely a physical task for technicians and businessmen; or will it be seen to be a democratic opportunity as well, the essence of which is the participation of the people, the acceptance of their evolving ideas of what is good, of what it is they want?

Will these new projects be administered by the methods of remote control and extreme centralization, invitations to tyranny; or will decentralized administration of central policies be the general principle? Will these developments be energized and directed by modern tools for getting things done; or by archaic methods of administration, crusted with tradition and fortified by bureaucratic "rights"? Unless the decisions are to go by default to those who always watch out for their own selfish interests, these are some of the questions that should be faced by the people, in our country and in others, as the time draws ever closer when action can take the place of plans for post-war development.

The use abroad of the public corporation as a tool to accomplish resource development after the war, in both mature and undeveloped regions, has been the object of extensive discussion. In other countries there has been much the same reaction as in the United States against the traditional bureau as an instrument to accomplish modern needs. There is a growing recognition that the autonomous corporation can get certain kinds of things done that other more customary government agencies somehow do not. In other countries, too, it has apparently been almost impossible in any other way to secure the adoption of modern management methods in government. Whether in Britain, China, or Australia, there appears to a remarkable degree the same need to cut away from the ritualism of traditional agencies' methods. The public corporation appears to be one of the ways of achieving this purpose. The TVA's adoption of business methods and management devices has accordingly been the subject of considerable firsthand study by foreign observers.

The public development corporation, following the broad lines of the TVA, is also a possible medium for administering *international* resource projects, i.e., the development of resources lying in more than one country, in which control and responsibility must be divided between several nations or their citizens. This has been given a good deal of consideration, particularly in Great Britain, in discussions of the development of Central Europe—the Danube River

Valley, for example. Various forms of international development corporations have been proposed. "Such an international public corporation," writes Mr. Lewis L. Lorwin, "may prove as useful a device for opening up international economic activity in the twentieth century as did the private corporation in the nineteenth century." He concludes that the public corporation, based upon "its proved value on the national level, as demonstrated by the Tennessee Valley Authority in the United States and by the British Broadcasting Corporation in England . . . offers, in the international field . . . an opportunity to achieve social purposes, under public control, by business operations with a maximum of flexibility and a minimum of restraint by standardized bureaucratic procedures."

But the use of the public corporation, in itself (while it might be very useful), would have only an incidental relation to the TVA idea unless it were the instrument of the basic idea of unified development within a natural region.

Whether a river is wholly within a single nation or flows through several countries does not affect the technical problems of its development or the necessity of dealing with it as a unity. A river has no nationality. The Danube River, for example, is oblivious of the national animosities or the many boundary lines along its course from the Black Forest through Bavaria, Austria, Hungary, Yugoslavia, Bulgaria, and Rumania, until its three mouths pour its water into the Black Sea. The sound of its name changes as it flows along —Donau, Dunau, Dunav, Dunarea—but the river itself is as little affected by political differences as by the different names by which it is known. Such a river valley has a unity that is of nature; its development in accordance with this oneness would require an international agency; the TVA public-private prototype might be the best available.

These are interesting speculations, but they must not be taken to prove too much. The differences between the people in such a natural region, their ancient disunity, racial antagonisms, barriers of custom and language, are as real in human affairs as they are unreal to a river or a forest. The common development by all these peoples of a single river may serve to ease these old tensions. But it would be tragic, by any oversimple analogies between nature and men's institutions, to underestimate the difficulties.

A final word about the place of the TVA idea in the development of world economic co-operation. Resource development in the United States in accordance with the principle of unity can mean a period of expanding industry and agriculture. It can mean more income, more jobs, adventures in new enterprise for trained brains and hands. Contrariwise, if we neglect or ignore the signs of resource exhaustion, and if we persist in wasteful use of what nature has provided for us, we increase the hazard of contraction, retrenchment, "hanging on to what we have," and the fears and uneasiness which that kind of stability creates. Such a climate of caution and scarcity will increase greatly the political difficulties of American participation in world affairs. It may even make them impossible. Workmen without jobs or afraid they may soon be, businessmen harassed by the problems of retrenchment and failing markets, farmers worried about raising crops without any assurance that city people will have the money to buy them—these are not people who are in a mood to co-operate with other nations.

What American public opinion will support in world affairs may well depend upon whether at the hour of decision the dominant feeling at home is optimism and good will, or the fearful grasping of worried men intent on "saving their own necks" by letting the world go hang. Such an escape is only an illusion, but frightened men will embrace it. In all but the best-disciplined spirits panic kills the natural, warmhearted impulse to work with one's neighbors. An expanding prosperous nation is not necessarily one that is willing to take its share of world responsibilities; but we can be sure that never will a frightened nation play a great role in world affairs.

In the Tennesseee Valley this development has created an expansive spirit, a note of confidence and hope in the future. To the extent that resource development in America after the war can aid in this way to stimulate confidence among businessmen, farmers, and workers, it may have important spiritual consequences that go beyond the bare bones of economics. It may thereby improve the chances of creating and maintaining an American public opinion upon which may rest the world's hopes for peace.

Chapter 20

THE TVA IDEA ABROAD

The United States has no better ambassador-at-large in Asia than the one which bears the initials T.V.A.
— M. R. Masini, *former Mayor of Bombay, in* Foreign Affairs, *April 1952.*

IN THE original opening chapter of this book I wrote (speaking of 1943) that the newly awakened expectations of people the world over for better living would become the central issue with which politicians and statesmen would have to contend. Events since that time have, it seems to me, borne out that estimate.[1] TVA offered one way to meet those expectations, by its example of a concrete course of action, based upon principles that have application "in almost any of a thousand other valleys where rivers run from the hills to the sea."

Many American travelers have brought back with them confirmation of this role of TVA as a symbol of the hopes, the desires, and the expectations of peoples in other countries.

One of the most interesting of such reports is that related by Supreme Court Associate Justice Douglas. Justice Douglas has spent several summers traveling on horseback in the remote areas and the villages of Asia through what he describes as "the vast underbelly of Russia that extends from Lebanon and Syria on the west through India on the east," a distance of hundreds of miles, a region in which live tens of millions of people of many varying cultural and

[1] Appendix C, consists principally of portions of a digest of information, prepared by the TVA Technical Library, about developments in many parts of the world where the TVA idea appears to have influenced the planning or execution of such programs, to a greater or less degree.

economic patterns of life. "Everywhere I went," Justice Douglas reports, "people asked, 'Why can't we have a TVA?'"

He continued: "A Druze chieftain, south of Damascus, inquired about it. I was asked about it many times as I traveled the length of the Tigris and Euphrates, the site of the ancient Mesopotamia, reputed cradle of civilization on this globe. Below Baghdad I saw 50,000 people homeless by reason of a flood. They too had heard of the TVA and wanted one for themselves.

"In Persia I traveled the length of the Zagros range—from the Russian border in the north to the Persian Gulf on the south. In practically every valley I heard the same plea, 'We need a TVA.'

"The Tennessee Valley Authority," says Justice Douglas, "has caught the imagination of all the people across this broad belt of Asia. They think of it as a device for insuring crops in a land where crop failures mean death from starvation. TVA also means to them increased productivity of the land, new forests, the end of erosion, modern methods of farming . . . it means the harnessing of floods, the storing of rain water, and the installation of modern irrigation systems."

But it was the symbolic significance that this great observer and traveler emphasized. According to Justice Douglas, TVA means more to the people he visited than crops and new forests; it is thought of, he reports, as "a symbol of a new order, a new way of life—security and independence for themselves and their children." Based upon this observation, he goes on to say:

"If we are bold enough to make this device an instrument of our Asiatic foreign policy, we can take the political initiative away from Soviet Russia, turn the tide and win country after country for the democratic cause. . . . TVA represents an idea that can be utilized as one of the major influences to turn back the tide of Communism which today threatens to engulf Asia."[2]

During my years with TVA I had many opportunities, of course, to talk with visitors to the Tennessee Valley from all over the world, and in this way to learn from them something of the opportunities and problems of their homeland that had caused them to travel so far to see this American experiment. Since that time, in extensive

[2] "Tennessee Across the World," address by Mr. Justice William O. Douglas before the General Assembly of the State of Tennessee, February 22, 1951.

travel as a private individual, I have had a chance to "return the visit" of a good many of these observers or students of TVA from distant parts of the world.

On my first morning in Karachi, capital of Pakistan, I was greeted by a half dozen smiling and friendly young men, whose faces seemed vaguely familiar; it turned out that I had met them in the Tennessee Valley, where they had spent months as observers and "trainees" of TVA.

One of them said, "When you bade us good-by in Knoxville and we tried to thank you for the hospitality shown us, you said, 'No, don't thank us; one of these days I'll turn up in Pakistan to see what you are doing with the Indus River, and then we'll be even.' Well, here you are, and now we're going to show you."

And they—and other young men very like them in neighboring India—certainly did "show" me, through hundreds of miles of the back country of that huge subcontinent, on foot, in pony carts, by automobile, and on airplane flights up the winding course of the Indus, or into the Himalayas, at more than 20,000 feet, to within nine miles of the summit of Mt. Everest, on the return circling over dam sites these young men intend to transform, in years to come, into the largest source of hydroelectric energy in the world.

In the Highlands of Scotland I visited the Sloy project, a new development scheme above Loch Lomond, since completed and in operation. I was there as guest of the man responsible for this so-called "TVA for the Highlands"; he had been my guest at TVA some years before. As the guest of the Republic of France I traveled the length of the Valley of the River Rhône, now undergoing a development that will provide "a stairway of calmed water, descending, step by step to the sea."[3]

This undertaking, often described as the "TVA of France," includes not only the magnificence of the Genissiat Dam but also the grandeur of concept and execution of the Donzere-Mondragon project. There I met executives and engineers whom I had first come to know on their several visits to TVA. In Japan leading industrialists, engineers, and economists talked with me of their plans and hopes for a fifteen-year multipurpose river development,

[3] Quoted from *Indian Journal of Power and River Development*, Calcutta, September, 1952, p. 17.

following TVA lines, to help achieve self-sufficiency and the economic renaissance of Japan. Students told me of TVA research study groups in the colleges.

On a trip to Mexico in early 1946 I spent several days visiting some of Mexico's river control projects. In the remote back country I encountered not only former TVA engineers and young Mexicans who had trained with TVA, but construction equipment purchased from us, with the letters "TVA" still on the trucks and gondolas. I talked over with the then candidate for President, Miguel Aleman, and his engineering adviser, Adolfo Orive Albe, their dreams for the development, along TVA lines, of the basin of the Papaloapan River, a great valley that extends from the high mountains of the states of Pueblo and Oaxaca into the swamplands of Vera Cruz. Not long after he became President, Aleman created the Papaloapan Commission. Our invitation to them to visit TVA was acted upon, first by a technical staff of experts, then by the President and Engineer Orive Albe, who had become his Secretary of Hydraulic Resources. Before Aleman's term of office had expired, in 1952, Mexico had made not a little construction progress on this ambitious plan, commonly referred to as the Mexican TVA.

Whether in my talks with the Prime Ministers of India, Japan, Pakistan, or Great Britain, or with engineers of India's Damodar Valley Corporation, in the valley of the Rhône or the Scotch Highlands, or in West Punjab villages near Lahore in the Indus River basin, or with ranchmen in Central Mexico, I found far from home a quite remarkable knowledge of TVA methods and philosophy and objectives.

And, incidentally, the following circumstance struck me as not without significance: I had just completed more than three years as head of the American atomic energy program. Yet in none of the countries I visited was there evidenced the slightest interest in the atom; nor did anyone seem to think of their visitor in those terms. Their preoccupation was invariably with resource development and my experience with TVA.

It was strange, at first, for so typically provincial an American as I am to find, as I did at first hand, that so many people in distant countries not only know more about TVA than many of my fellow countrymen, but in some respects have an even better understanding of its fundamental objectives and distinctive methods. On reflection this is not too surprising, for in the United States the essential collateral public-versus-private power controversy naturally dominates the headlines, and the perennial Congressional hearings, inquiries and oratory. It thereby obscured the more fundamental meaning of this experiment. Abroad it is not this controversy over public electric power but the more significant and deeper issues, to which most of this book is devoted, upon which interest is concentrated.

Now it is true that the term "TVA" has often been loosely and inappropriately applied in the case of developments in foreign lands. There are even instances abroad in which any big dam has been called a "TVA," for no better reason than that there are also dams in the Tennessee Valley. But by and large the term has come to take on a valid symbolic meaning; has come to represent the aspirations and hopes, and a central guiding principle for unified development of natural resources and the raising of living standards. That this interpretation of TVA is largely symbolic, representative of its methods, purpose, and driving motivation rather than its specific technology, is clear. This is illustrated by the fact that some developments abroad, described as "patterned on the TVA," have as major functions the storage of water for irrigation and the furthering of agriculture in a semiarid country. As the leaders of these "TVA-like" developments well know, the Tennessee Valley is a region of abundant rainfall, not requiring the use of stored water for irrigation.

An excellent statement of the strength *and the limitations* of the TVA idea in other and quite different countries is contained in a statement of Dr. Sudhir Sen, Secretary of India's Damodar Valley Corporation, who in 1948 visited the Tennessee Valley for several months. For India, he wrote:

. . . TVA has shown us a new way: You take a whole river basin as the unit area, apply unified development first to the river system . . . and then to the entire watershed, salvage every possible benefit at every point, at the same time make sure that the resources are not used up too fast, but are developed and managed on a sustained-yield basis, and in this way you build up, on a relatively narrow resource-base, the highest possible level of wealth, employment and income. . . .

In India this approach was intended to be applied, for the first time, in the Damodar Valley. How far this experiment will succeed it is too early to say. One thing is clear: *We cannot imitate the TVA in every detail.* It is true that the behavior of rivers is essentially the same all over the world; and so, in harnessing the Damodar river system, we may closely follow the TVA. But as soon as we leave the river and come to the land, we notice big differences. The Tennessee Valley has some 3.5 million people in an area of 40,000 square miles; our Valley is only one-fifth in size, but it contains 5 million souls. I heard the land-use planners of the TVA plaintively speak of the pressure of population on land in their Valley and the small size of their farms, which on an average consisted of 75 acres; and I had no heart to tell them that the average "farmer" in the Damodar area has a miserable holding of 2.5 acres and that too sliced into odd pieces and scattered around in the village fields. These and other basic differences must make a correspond-ing difference, both in planning and the final economic results.

Just because of these facts, however, the essentials of the TVA ap-proach, though first tried out in the world's richest country, has an ever greater, and not less, relevance to an old, heavily populated, resource-poor country like ours. (My italics.)

There is a further aspect of the idea embodied in the TVA which may have application to certain of the problems of developing a growing measure of cooperation and understanding between the peoples of different nations, and thereby diminishing the prospects of war. This can be illustrated by reference to a proposal made by the author, based upon his TVA experience, for a partial recon-ciliation between Pakistan and India, the two nations created by the Partition of the subcontinent of India in 1948.

The antagonism and tensions bordering on actual war between these two brothers are customarily associated with their bitter po-litico-religious dispute over whether the territory of Kashmir be-longs within India or Pakistan. There is, however, another dispute between them which lends itself to an engineering or functional solution, and which is also physically related to the Kashmir issue. This is the controversy over the use of the life-giving waters of the Indus River and its tributaries, which flow through Kashmir, Pakis-tan and India.

All of the headwaters of the Indus system are in India or Kash-mir; closing off of the waters at their sources by Indian dams or diversions could devastate downstream Pakistan. Yet the Indus Basin, if developed according to a unified plan of water storage and release, joined in by both Pakistan and India, could be made to provide ample water for the needs of all.

After a visit to the Indus Basin in February, 1950, I proposed such a unified bi-nation approach to this increasingly angry controversy. This proposal was based upon engineering data and concepts largely developed by Pakistan and Indian engineers, at the time, prior to Partition, when they had been fellow-workers and neighbors. Back of the proposal was the hope that by working together on a joint engineering project such as this, in a professional rather than a political atmosphere, not only might this one cause of international enmity be eliminated or ameliorated, but a habit of once more working together on other matters might be re-instituted.

It was part of my proposal that the World Bank extend its good offices, on a technical and financial basis. This it did promptly. The Prime Ministers of Pakistan and of India agreed with President Eugene R. Black of the Bank to explore the plan, generally on the basis of the principles outlined in the proposal. Engineering joint conferences, chaired by the World Bank, opened in Washington; at this writing these are continuing in the subcontinent of India.

One must entertain considerable doubt whether a final agreement can be reached, in view of the steadily worsening relations between these countries on political and religious issues. The instance, however, does illustrate a possible area of political usefulness for the concept of the physical unity of a river system, and the potentialities of making use of this natural unity to promote an increased measure of cooperation between people of differing views and nationalities.[4]

Another instance of a proposal for the setting up of an international technical and industrial project as part of the search for peace and security is the suggestion for a United Nations Atomic Development Authority. This was proposed by Hon. Bernard M. Baruch, on behalf of the United States, in an historic address to the Security

[4] The proposal is described in "Another Korea in the Making," *Collier's Magazine*, August 4, 1951, p. 23 et seq. See also "Storm Along the Indus," by John C. Perham, *Barron's Weekly*, December 22, 1952, p. 7.

Council in June of 1946,[5] and was a part of the Branch Plan for international control of atomic energy (later adopted by all the U.N. member nations except the Soviet and its bloc).

An undertaking based upon analogous considerations, formulated with great insight by M. Jean Monnet of France, is the Schuman Coal-Steel Plan, which has since been adopted by the several European countries, and is now an operating organization.

As it enters upon its third decade most of TVA's huge output of electricity goes into the making of America's stockpile of atom bombs, the greatest concentration of the power of destruction in all history, and perhaps the greatest single deterrent to Russian world conquest by force. History may well record, however, that it is TVA *as an idea* that represents its greatest significance; that it is in its high symbolic value "in a thousand valleys" beyond the seas that TVA has rendered its greatest service in safeguarding and nurturing freedom in the world.[6]

[5] See also Report of the Board of Consultants on the International Control of Atomic Energy, made to a Special Committee headed by the then Under Secretary of State Dean G. Acheson, dated March 16, 1946, Department of State Publication 2448, and particularly p. 3.

[6] It is an interesting sidelight on these comments on the symbolic value of TVA abroad that the first edition of this book has been published abroad in many languages, including Danish, Chinese, Japanese, French, German (two separate editions), Spanish for Latin America, Spanish for Mexico, Hebrew (for Israel), and Italian; and that an American and an English paper-backed edition has appeared, in several editions, running into hundreds of thousands, distributed in most of the English speaking areas of the world.

Chapter 21

IT CAN BE DONE: DREAMERS WITH SHOVELS

IN THIS one of the thousand valleys of the earth the physical setting of men's living has improved. Each day the change becomes more pronounced. The river is productive, the land more secure and fruitful, the forests are returning, factories and workshops and new houses and electric lines have put a different face upon the Tennessee Valley.

Is this really genuine improvement? Has it enhanced the quality of human existence? Are men's lives richer, fuller, more "human" as a result of such changes in our physical surroundings? To most people, I am sure, the answer is in the clear affirmative. But, in appraising the meaning of this valley's experience, the doubts on this score can by no means be ignored, nor dealt with out of hand; some people not only raise such questions but answer them differently from the way most of us would answer them.

There are those who believe that material progress does not and cannot produce good, and may indeed stand as a barrier to it. To those, and there are many who hold such belief, mechanical progress, technology, the machine, far from improving the lot of men are actually seen as a source of debasement and condemned as "materialism."

The whole theme and thesis of this book challenges these ideas and the philosophy upon which they rest. I do not, of course, believe that when men change their physical environment they are inevitably happier or better. The machine that frees a man's back of drudgery does not thereby make his spirit free. Technology has made us more productive, but it does not necessarily enrich our lives. Engineers can build us great dams, but only great people make a valley great. There is no technology of goodness. Men must make themselves spiritually free.

But because these changes in physical environment in the valley do not in and of themselves make men happier, more generous, kinder, it does not follow that they have no relation to our spiritual life.

We have a choice. There is the important fact. Men are not powerless; they have it in their hands to use the machine to augment the dignity of human existence. True, they may have so long denied themselves the use of that power to decide, which is theirs, may so long have meekly accepted the dictation of bosses of one stripe or another or the ministrations of benevolent nursemaids, that the muscles of democratic choice have atrophied. But that strength is always latent; history has shown how quickly it revives. How we shall *use* physical betterment—that decision is ours to make. We are not carried irresistibly by forces beyond our control, whether they are given some mystic term or described as the "laws of economics." We are not inert objects on a wave of the future.

Except for saints and great ascetics, I suppose most people would agree that poverty and physical wretchedness are evils, in and of themselves. But because extreme poverty is an evil it does not follow that a comfortable or a high material standard of living is good. A Tennessee Valley farm wife who now has an electric pump that brings water into her kitchen may or may not be more generous of spirit, less selfish, than when she was forced to carry her water from the spring day after day. A once destitute sharecropper who now has an interesting factory job at good wages and lives in a comfortable house in town may or may not be more tolerant, more rational, more thoughtful of others, more active in community concerns. We all know that some of the least admirable men are found among those who have come up from poverty to a "high standard of living."

Whether happiness or unhappiness, freedom or slavery, in short whether good or evil results from an improved environment depends largely upon how the change has been brought about, upon the methods by which the physical results have been reached, and in what spirit and for what purpose the fruits of that change are used. Because a higher standard of living, a greater productiveness and a command over nature are not good in and of themselves does not mean that we cannot make good of them, that they cannot be a source of inner strength.

The basic objection to all efforts to use the machine for human betterment lies in an attitude of absolute pessimism: that life is an evil in itself; that therefore anything which seeks to mitigate its inescapable pain and utter dullness is misdirected and futile. To men who in sincerity and passion hold to this faith, there is no answer that will satisfy them. Although there are few people in America who would admit that they hold such sweepingly negative views, they are nevertheless important; for such a faith (or lack of faith) colors and affects far less drastic but far more widely held objections to material changes. Many people, for example, although not denying the worth of life itself, are committed to the closely related belief that mankind is essentially wicked and naturally and irretrievably inclined to evil. This "prodigious malignity of the human heart," they assert, marks down as folly and misguided any efforts to improve men's physical surroundings.

That there are evil tendencies in mankind few who have lived through the last quarter century would care to deny. But of this I am sure and confident: the *balance*, the overwhelming balance, is on the side of good. This is a matter of faith, for where is the statistician or logician who can prove or disprove on which side the balance stands? But by the very act of faith in the essential goodness of men we further that goodness, just as the Nazi faith in the wickedness of men nourished human animality and depravity by the very act of believing in it.

Democracy is a literal impossibility without faith that on balance the good in men far outweighs the evil. Every effort to cherish the overtones of human imagination in music, painting, or poetry rests upon that same faith, makes that same assumption. And so it is with what men have been seeking to do in the valley of the Tennessee. To call it "materialistic" answers nothing. The rock upon which all these efforts rest is a faith in human beings.

I recognize that I am dealing with a broad issue of religious and philosophical thought upon which a great debate has raged for centuries and still continues. But it cannot be ignored, even if it cannot here be adequately discussed. I must let the matter rest, for present purposes, by quoting the statements of two modern thinkers upon this matter, whose words state the essentials of my own conviction.

The first is that of the great contemporary philosopher of China, Dr. Hu Shih, former Ambassador to the United States. He refers to the argument embraced as truth by countless millions in the Orient, and by not a few among our own people, that improvements in physical surroundings are no aid to the spirit, and that those civilizations which regard such advances as important are "materialistic." Then he says:

For to me that civilization is materialistic which is limited by matter and incapable of transcending it; which feels itself powerless against its material environment and fails to make the full use of human intelligence for the conquest of nature and for the improvement of the conditions of man. Its sages and saints may do all they can to glorify contentment and hypnotize the people into a willingness to praise their gods and abide by their fate. But that very self-hypnotizing philosophy is more materialistic than the dirty houses they live in, the scanty food they eat, and the clay and wood with which they make the images of their gods.

On the other hand, that civilization which makes the fullest possible use of human ingenuity and intelligence in search of truth in order to control nature and transform matter for the service of mankind, to liberate the human spirit from ignorance, superstition, and slavery to the forces of nature, and to reform social and political institutions for the benefit of the greatest number—such a civilization is highly idealistic and spiritual.[1]

The words of Pope Pius XI, in the famous encyclical *Quadragesimo Anno*, are equally simple, and the conclusion convincing:

Then only will the economic and social organism be soundly established and attain its end, when it secures for all and each those goods which the wealth and resources of nature, technical achievement and the social organization of economic affairs can give. These goods should be sufficient to supply all needs and an honest livelihood, and to uplift men to that higher level of prosperity and culture which, provided it be used with prudence, is not only no hindrance but is of singular help to virtue.

[1] *Whither Mankind*, ed. Beard (New York: Longman's, Green and Co., 1937) pp. 40-1.

But in addition to the philosophical protests there is a further and more widely held objection to such an enterprise as the world sees in this valley. The hideous belief has been spread over the earth that the price of material progress and freedom from want must be the complete surrender of individual freedom. The acceptance of this doctrine by the people of Russia, Germany, and Japan, the leading technical nations of Europe and Asia, is surely the most disastrous event of the twentieth century.

Here in the United States, too, there are people of great influence who have essentially that conviction. They seek to persuade America, chiefly by subtle indirection, that modern technology demands that ordinary people (they do not, of course, think of themselves as such) abandon the ideal of individual freedom and the right to a voice in their own destiny, that only by yielding up such mistaken ideas is it possible for modern industry to raise their "standard of living." There is irony and yet an awful fitness in the fact that arch-conservatives and ultra-radicals are joined in agreement at this point. This spirit of defeatism about the individual in modern life and therefore about democracy is far too widespread to be ignored, and the support it receives in our own country too great to be dismissed lightly.

The technical results in the Tennessee Valley, the achievements of many kinds of experts, are of course matters of no little importance. But unless these technical products strengthen the conviction that machines and science can be used by men for their greater individual and spiritual growth, then so far as I am concerned the physical accomplishments and the material benefits would be of dubious value indeed.

There are few who fail to see that modern applied science and the machine are threats to the development of the individual personality, the very purpose of democratic institutions. It is for this reason that the experience of the last two decades in the valley of the Tennessee is heartening. In this one valley (in some ways the world in microcosm) it has been demonstrated that methods can be developed—methods I have described as grass-roots democracy—which do create an opportunity for greater happiness and deeper experience, for freedom, in the very course of technical progress. Indeed this valley even in the brief span of twenty years, supports a conviction that when the use of technology has a moral purpose and when its methods are thoroughly democratic, far from forcing the surrender of individual freedom and the things of the spirit to the machine, the machine can be made to promote those very ends.[2]

It is enormously important that we have that conviction, that we have evidence which clearly supports that conviction. For here is the reality: This job must be done, this task of changing our physical environment through science and the machine. It ought to be done by democrats, by those who believe that people come first, by those who have faith in the capacities of many men and not of only a few. It cannot be done by defeatists. And it ought not be done by those who believe that human beings are inherently wicked. But it is a job that must be done. And it will be done—*by someone*. The only questions open are: How will it be done? Who will benefit? The answers will largely be provided by that intangible known as faith.

Faith is the greatest power in the world of men, the most "practical" force of all. How is faith sustained and built ever stronger? By the redemption of faith through works. Take the simple case of a farmer on one of the valley demonstration farms. When you talk with him you can sense at once that his faith has been stirred. He has actually seen something happen on his own homestead that he never believed could come true for him. He has seen what science can do for his land, what it can do under his own rooftree, what it can do in his community among his neighbors. What he and his wife have seen with their eyes gives them added faith that other equally impossible things can happen, too, on their farm, in their community, in the nation. They come to feel—"It *can* be done."

Faith that individual personality can flourish side by side with the machine and with science is vital in this: that men have only to have a faith that is deep enough, a belief sufficiently firm, in their daily work and living, that these things can be done—and then they will be done. For no insoluble physical problems stand in the way. There is no insuperable material barrier. The only serious obstacles are in the minds of men. These are not inconsiderable, it is true, but thinking put them there; a new kind of thinking can remove them. The great thing that has transpired in the Tennessee Valley is this

[2] For a further exposition of the author's views on this issue, see Chapter 23, "Making Bigness Serve Modern Individualism," in *Big Business: A New Era*.

growing faith not only that the scientific progress of our time can be used as a tool to create higher income and more comfortable living, but that technology can give men a choice, a genuine choice of alternatives, and that it can be used to make men free as they have never been before.

But there must be more than a conviction, a sure confidence, that it can be done. There must be a *sense of urgency*, a sense that this is the day on which to turn the first shovel. There are some who dream great dreams but never feel this urgency "to do something about it." This is in character for the intellectual gone to seed, the perfectionist, the "cooler head," the defeatist, the nostalgic liberal, the cynic about human possibilities. They are preoccupied in conjuring up all the possible difficulties and multiplying them. But the dreamers with shovels in their hands know that to start is important. The dreamers with shovels want only a job that is magnificent enough, room enough to stand in, and a chance to make a start.

They see a start as only that. For this is a continuing process, this improving the physical environment of men. It is never finished. There is no end, no blueprint of a finished product.

I share with many of my former neighbors and associates in the Tennessee Valley a deep conviction that it can be done, the modern job of building our resources and making the machine work for all men. And because of this experience together we believe that it can be done by such methods and with such purposes as will enrich the things of the spirit. This experience has convinced me that science and invention can be consciously and deliberately directed to achieving the kind of world that people want. If it is decentralized industry men want, "family farming," or pleasant cities not too large, an end to smoke and congestion and filth—there are modern tools which can be turned to just such ends. The people, working through their private enterprises and public institutions which are democratic in spirit, can get substantially the kind of community and country they want.

The physical job will be done. If not democratically, it will be done in an anti-democratic way. Conceivably it will be done by a handful of corporations, controlling the country's resources; or by a tight clique of politicians; or by some other group or alliance of groups that is ready to take this responsibility which the people themselves decline to take. The smooth-talking centralizers, the managerial elite, cynical politicians, everyone without faith in the capacities of the people themselves to find a way will be hard at work seeking to draw off the benefits and control the development of the resources by which in turn they will control the lives of men.

No one can minimize the hazards to peace and to individual freedom of the gathering storm, or fail to see that troubled days lie ahead for democracy in our country. But catastrophe need not befall us. If as a people, in our daily living, we will only use the strength our democratic inheritance gives us, democracy can emerge revitalized by the test and conflict.

In the valley where this statement of faith was written, the people know the job of our time can be done, for they have read the signs and reaped the first token harvest. They know it can be done, not only *for* the people but *by* the people.

APPENDIX A

BIBLIOGRAPHY

Compiled by
BERNARD L. FOY
TVA Technical Librarian

This is not a comprehensive bibliography on the Tennessee Valley Authority. The majority of the titles listed here appear in standard books on TVA, government documents and periodicals, and may be found in many public and educational libraries.

The Agricultural Index, Industrial Arts Index, Engineering Index, Readers' Guide to Periodical Literature, Public Affairs Information Service Bulletin, and the *Education Index* will aid the reader in exploring any of the special phases of the TVA program. For important newspaper articles consult the New York Times Index.

HISTORICAL BACKGROUND OF THE TVA

Finer, Herman. *The T.V.A.: Lessons for International Application.* Montreal: International Labour Office, 1944, ch. 1, p. 1-17.

Govan, G. E., and Livingood, J. W. "TVA." (In their *Chattanooga Country, 1540-1951, From Tomahawks to TVA.* New York: E. P. Dutton & Co., 1951. p. 441-467.)

King, Judson. *A Brief Chronology of Muscle Shoals Legislation, 1916-1933.* Knoxville, Tennessee: TVA, 1933. 10p. mimeo.

King, Judson. *Legislative History of Muscle Shoals.* Knoxville, Tennessee: TVA, 1936. 5v.

Owen, Marguerite. *Muscle Shoals and the Public Welfare.* Washington: National League of Women Voters, 1929. 45p.

Pritchett, C. H. "Development of the Tennessee Valley Authority Act." *Tennessee Law Review,* 15:128-141, February 1938.

Pritchett, C. H. *The Tennessee Valley Authority; a Study in Public Administration.* Chapel Hill, North Carolina: University of North Carolina Press, 1943. ch. 1, p. 3-30.

Ransmeier, J. S. *The Tennessee Valley Authority; a Case Study in the Economics of Multiple Purpose Stream Planning.* Nashville, Tennessee: Vanderbilt University Press, 1942. chs. 1-3, p. 3-101.

U.S. President. (Franklin D. Roosevelt) "Muscle Shoals Development. Message from the President of the United States Transmitting a Request for Legislation To Create a Tennessee Valley Authority—a Corporation Clothed with the Power of Government but Possessed of the Flexibility and Initiative of a Private Enterprise." Washington: Government Printing Office, 1933. 2p. (73d Congress, 1st session. House. Doc. 15.)

GENERAL

Barr, Stringfellow. *Citizens of the World.* New York: Doubleday and Company, 1952. p. 135-154.

Bauer, Malcolm. "TVA—Model for CVA?" *Congressional Record,* 95:A3302-A3319, May 27, 1949.
Reprint of a series of articles appearing in *Portland Oregonian,* March 17-April 4, 1949.

Billings, Henry. *All Down the Valley.* New York: The Viking Press, 1952. 208p.

Brittain, Robert. "All the Rivers Run into the Sea." (In his *Let There Be Bread.* New York: Simon and Schuster, 1952. p. 117-141.)

Browning, Gordon. "Tennessee and the Tennessee Valley Authority." (In American Public Power Association. *Proceedings,* 1951. Washington: 1951. p. 105-110.)

Callahan, North. "Coming of TVA." (In his *Smoky Mountain Country.* New York: Duell, Sloan & Pearce, 1952. p. 172-184.)

Chase, Stuart *Rich Land, Poor Land; a Study of Waste in the Natural Resources of America.* New York: McGraw-Hill Book Company, 1936. 361p.

Chenery, W. L. "Taming of the Tennessee." *Collier's,* 116:22-23, August 11, 1945.

Clapp, G. R. "Administrative Resources of a Region: the Example of the Tennessee Valley." (In *New Horizons in Public Administration; a Symposium.* University, Alabama: University of Alabama Press, 1945. p. 79-95.)

Clapp, G. R. "Experience of the Tennessee Valley Authority in the Comprehensive Development of a River Basin." (In United Nations Scientific Conference on the Conservation and Utilization of Resources. *Proceedings*, Lake Success, New York, August 17-September 6, 1949. 1950. V. 1, p. 369-375.)

Clapp, G. R. "The Tennessee Valley Authority." (In Jensen, Merrill, ed. *Regionalism in America*. Madison, Wisconsin: University of Wisconsin Press, 1951. p. 317-329.)

Clapp, G. R. "TVA: a Democratic Method for the Development of a Region's Resources." *Vanderbilt Law Review*, 1:183-193, February, 1948.

Clapp, G. R. "TVA—a National Asset." (In American Public Power Association. *Proceedings*, 1951. Washington: 1951. p. 83-92.)

Clapp, G. R. "TVA After Two Decades." *New Republic*, 127:22-24, September 22, 1952.

Cole, W. E. "Impact of TVA upon the Southeast." *Social Forces*, 28:435-440, May 1950.

Cooke, M. L. "Multiple-Purpose River Valley Development." *Mechanical Engineering*, 71:129-132, February 1949.

Curtis, H. A. "TVA and the Tennessee Valley—What of the Future." *Land Economics*, 28:333-340, November, 1952.

Curtis, H. A. "TVA: the Tennessee Valley Authority." *World Crops*, 2:51-55, February 1950.

Daniels, W. M., comp. *Should We Have More TVA's?* New York: H. W. Wilson Company, 1950. 225p. (*The Reference Shelf*, V. 22, No. 2.) This is a collection of excerpts from articles, books and speeches. The book is divided into five parts: "The TVA," "The Proposed CVA," "The Proposed MVA," "The Proposed St. Lawrence Seaway," and the "Authority Idea in Perspective."

Douglas, W. O. "Tennessee Across the World." *Tennessee Law Review*, 21:797-802, June 1951. (Also in *Congressional Record* [Daily Edition], 97:A2529, May 1, 1951; and *Progressive*, 15:5-7, August 1951.)

Duffus, R. L. *The Valley and Its People*. New York: Alfred A. Knopf, 1946. 167p.

Finer, Herman. *T. V. A.; Lessons for International Application*. Montreal: International Labour Office, 1944. 289p.

Fitts, W. C., Jr. "TVA's Firm Foundation and TVA's Accomplishments." *Public Utilities Fortnightly*, 32:795-805, December 23, 1943; 33:85-98, January 20, 1944.

Fly, J. L. "Role of the Federal Government in the Conservation and Utilization of Water Resources." *Pennsylvania Law Review*, 86:274-294, January 1938.

"Government and Water Resources: a Symposium." *American Political Science Review,* 44:575-649, September 1950. Contents: Introduction, by James W. Fesler; Congress and Water Resources, by Arthur A. Maass; National Executive Organization for Water Resources, by Gilbert F. White; The Valley Authority and Its Alternatives, by Charles McKinley; Water Resources and American Federalism, by Albert Lepawsky.

Gunther, John. *The Story of TVA.* New York: Harper & Brothers, 1951. 32p.
Originally published in 1947, this new reprint from Gunther's *Inside U.S.A.* incorporates the author's revisions in the 1951 edition of his book.

Hart, H. C. "Legislative Abdication in Regional Development." *Journal of Politics,* 13:393-417, August 1951.

Herry, Hermann. "TVA's of the Future." *American Scholar,* 14:488-493, Autumn 1945.

Huxley, J. S. *TVA, Adventure in Planning.* Cheam, Surrey: The Architectural Press, 1943. 142p.

Lilienthal, D. E., and Marquis, R. H. "Conduct of Business Enterprises by the Federal Government." *Harvard Law Review,* 54:545-601, February 1941.

Lilienthal, D. E., and Clapp, G. R. "Progress in Regional Planning in the U. S. A." (In Eighth International Congress for Scientific Management. *Papers and Proceedings,* 2:235-243, 1947.)

McCarthy, C. J. "Land Acquisition Policies and Proceedings in TVA—a Study of the Role of Land Acquisition in a Regional Agency." *Ohio State Law Journal,* 10:46-63, Winter 1949.

McCarthy, C. J. "TVA and the Tennessee Valley." *Town Planning Review,* 21:116-130, July 1950.

McKinley, Charles. "The Tennessee Valley Authority as a Model: Its Job and Its Methods." (In his *Uncle Sam in the Pacific Northwest.* Berkeley, California: University of California Press, 1952. p. 480-542.)

Menhinick, H. K. "Tennessee Valley and Its Development." American Institute of Architects, *Journal,* 6:147-155, October 1946.

Pope, J. P. "Water Control and Resource Development." (In Inter-American Conference on Conservation of Renewable Natural Resources. *Proceedings,* Denver, Colorado, September 7-20, 1948. Washington: Department of State, 1949. p. 519-526.)

Pritchett, C. H. *Tennessee Valley Authority; a Study in Public Administration.* Chapel Hill, North Carolina: University of North Carolina Press, 1943. 333p.

Ransmeier, J. S. *Tennessee Valley Authority; a Case Study in the Economics of Multiple Purpose Stream Planning.* Nashville, Tennessee: Vanderbilt University Press, 1942. 486p.

Satterfield, M. H. *Soil and Sky; the Development and Use of Tennessee Valley Resources.* Knoxville, Tennessee: Bureau of Public Administration, University of Tennessee, May 1950. 120p. (*University of Tennessee Record, Extension Series,* V. 26, No. 3.)

Swidler, J. C., and Marquis, R. H. "TVA in Court: a Study of TVA's Constitutional Litigation." *Iowa Law Review,* 32:296-326, January, 1947.

"Symposium on Regional Planning." *Iowa Law Review,* 32:193-416, January 1947. Contents: Interstate Cooperation as a Child, by A. S. Abel; Interstate Cooperation in River Basin Development, by L. K. Caldwell; The Settlement of Disputes Between States Concerning Rights to the Waters of Interstate Streams, by Julius Friedrich; The Role of the Federal Power Commission in Regional Development, by Willard Gatchell; TVA in Court: a Study of TVA's Constitutional Litigation, by J. C. Swidler and R. H. Marquis; The Transplantability of TVA, by C. H. Pritchett; What Kind of "Valley Authority," by R. W. Greenleaf; Plain Talk About a Missouri Valley Authority, by M. L. Cooke; A Critical Review of the Proposed Missouri Valley Authority, by J. M. Drabelle.

Tennessee. Department of Conservation. *Answers to Questions Most Frequently Asked About TVA.* Nashville, Tennessee: September 1950. 8p.

Tennessee Valley Authority. *Annual Report,* 1933-Date. Washington: Government Printing Office.

Tennessee Valley Authority. *Report to the Congress on the Unified Development of the Tennessee River System.* Knoxville, Tennessee: TVA, 1936. 105p.

Tennessee Valley Authority. *TVA—Two Decades of Progress.* Washington: Government Printing Office, 1953. 76p.
An abridged edition of the 1952 annual report.

Tennessee Valley Authority Act, May 18, 1933, with Amendments. Washington: Government Printing Office, 1942. 41p. (Available from TVA.)

"Tennessee Valley Governors Report on TVA." *Congressional Record,* 93:3035-3037, April 2, 1947. (Reprinted from the *St. Louis Post-Dispatch,* December 31, 1944.)

"TVA Program—the Regional Approach to General Welfare." *Journal of Educational Sociology,* 15:129-192, November 1941.

U.S. Congress. House. Committee on Public Works. Subcommittee to

Study Civil Works. Study of Civil Works. Part 3: Federal Power Commission, Department of Interior, Tennessee Valley Authority . . . *Hearings* . . . 82d Congress, 2d Session. Washington: Government Printing Office, 1952. 693p.

Statement by the Chairman of the TVA Board of Directors relating to progress in the Tennessee Valley 1933-1952, p. 613.

U.S. Library of Congress. Legislative Reference Service. "Valley Authorities." Washington: March 1951. unp. (*Public Affairs Abstracts*, V. II, No. 3.) mimeo.

Abstracts of articles, addresses and books on the subject of valley authorities. TVA, the Missouri, Columbia and Delaware Basins are particularly stressed.

U.S. President's Water Resources Policy Commission. "The Tennessee River Basin." (In the Commission's *Report*. Washington: Government Printing Office, 1950. V. 2, p. 705-797.)

White, L. C., and Murray, J. L. "TVA Condemnation Practice Under the Federal Rules." *Tennessee Law Review*, 22:325-345, April, 1952.

Whitman, Willson. *God's Valley; People and Power Along the Tennessee River*. New York: The Viking Press, 1939. 320p.

AGRICULTURE

Alabama Polytechnic Institute. Agricultural Extension Service. Grassland Farming in Alabama, by D. R. Harbor. Auburn, Alabama: November 1951. unp. (Circular 427.)

Alabama Polytechnic Institute. Agricultural Extension Service. New Wealth from Soils. Auburn, Alabama: June 1949. unp. (Extension Circular 380.)

Ball, C. R. *A Study of the Work of the Land-Grant Colleges in the Tennessee Valley Area in Cooperation with the Tennessee Valley Authority*. Knoxville, Tennessee: TVA, 1939. 76p.

Clapp, G. R. "The Purpose of TVA Fertilizer." *National Fertilizer Review*, 27:6-7, July-August-September 1952.

Curtis, H. A. "Rainfall, Watershed and Stream Flow." *World Crops*, 4:47-49, 91-94, February and March 1952.

Georgia. University. Agricultural Extension Service. *Growth; Unit-Test Demonstration Farms in Georgia*, by Russell Lord. Athens, Georgia: June 1944. 36p. (Bulletin 506.)

Georgia. University. Agricultural Extension Service. *Strength for Living*, by J. R. Johnson. Athens, Georgia: June 1947. unp. (Bulletin 541.)

Hill, Lister. "Increased Food Production—Phosphate Essential of a Fighting Soil." *Congressional Record*, 89:3783-3800, April 29, 1943.

Jones, R. J., and Rogers, H. T. "New Fertilizers and Fertilizer Practices." (In *Advances in Agronomy*. New York: Academic Press, Inc., 1949. V. 1, p. 39-76.)

Kentucky. University. Agricultural Experiment Station. *Sources of Incomes on Upland Marshall County Farms*, by Glenn L. Johnson. Lexington, Kentucky: 1952. 21p. (Progress Report 1.)

North Carolina State College. Agricultural Extension Service. *Mountain Agriculture Moves Forward; a Report of Agricultural Development and Watershed Protection in the Tennessee Valley Area of North Carolina, 1935-1948*. Raleigh, North Carolina: undated. 84p.

Rogers, H. T. "Crop Response to Nitraphosphate Fertilizers." *Agronomy Journal*, 43:468-476, October 1951.

Tennessee. University. *Progress in Agricultural Development and Watershed Protection in the Tennessee Valley Area of Tennessee*. Knoxville, Tennessee: July 1949. 41p.

Tennessee. University. Agricultural Experiment Station. *Fused Tricalcium Phosphate*, by O. H. Long and Eric Winters. Knoxville, Tennessee: April 1951. 4p. (Circular No. 107.)

Tennessee. University. Agricultural Extension Service. *Building a Better Tennessee Through Rural Community Improvement*, by Almon J. Sims. Knoxville, Tennessee: January 1950. unp. (Publication 321.)

Tennessee Valley Authority. *Agriculture, Fertilizer and Forestry Activities of the Tennessee Valley Authority*. Knoxville, Tennessee: TVA, January 1950. 53p. processed.

Tennessee Valley Authority. *Soil . . . People, and Fertilizer Technology*. Washington: Government Printing Office, 1949. 57p.

Tennessee Valley Authority. Department of Agricultural Relations. "Approach to Agricultural Development in the Tennessee Valley." (In Soil Science Society of America. *Proceedings*, 1946. 1947. p. 369-373.)

Tennessee Valley Authority. Department of Agricultural Relations. *Food at the Grass Roots; the Nation's Stake in Soil Minerals*. Knoxville, Tennessee: TVA, 1947. 100p.

Tennessee Valley Authority. Division of Agricultural Relations. *Results of Conservation Activities in the Tennessee Valley*. Knoxville, Tennessee: TVA, revised March 1950. 18p.

U.S. Department of Agriculture. *Soil, the Nation's Basic Heritage. A Story of the Restoration of Natural Water Control Through Soil Conservation and Improvement*. Washington: 1936. 58p.

Wengert, N. I. *Valley of Tomorrow; the TVA and Agriculture*. Knoxville, Tennessee: Bureau of Public Administration, University of Tennessee, July 1952. 151p. (*University of Tennessee Record*, Extension Series, V. 28, No. 1.)

Wengert, N. I. "The Land, TVA, and the Fertilizer Industry." *Land Economics*, 25:11-21, February 1949.

ARCHEOLOGY

Webb, W. S., and DeJarnette, D. L. *An Archeological Survey of Pickwick Basin in the Adjacent Portions of the States of Alabama, Mississippi, and Tennessee.* Washington: Government Printing Office, 1942. 536p. (Smithsonian Institution. Bureau of American Ethnology. Bulletin 129.)
Detailed report on the prehistory of the TVA Pickwick Basin. Similar surveys have been made of the Guntersville, Hiwassee, Norris, and Wheeler areas.

ARCHITECTURE

Gutheim, F. A. "Tennessee Valley Authority; a New Phase in Architecture." *Magazine of Art*, 33:516-531, September 1940.
Hackett, Brian. "TVA: Creator of Landscape." Town Planning Institute, *Journal*, 37:7-14, November 1950.
Hamlin, T. F., ed. *Forms and Functions of Twentieth-Century Architecture.* New York: Columbia University Press, 1952. 4v.
References to TVA appear in volumes II and IV.
Hamlin, T. R. "Architecture of the TVA." *Pencil Points*, 20:721-744, November 1939.
Reid, Kenneth. "Design in TVA Structures." *Pencil Points*, 20:691-720, November 1939.
Tennessee Valley Authority. *Architectural Forum*, 71:73-114, August 1939.
Tour, H. B. "TVA—Ten Years of Concrete." *Architectural Concrete*, 9:22-29, July 1943.
Wank, R. A. "Architecture in Rural Areas—A Report on TVA Experience." *New Pencil Points*, 23:47-53, December 1942.
Wank, R. A. "Some Recent Work of the Tennessee Valley Authority." *Pencil Points*, 22:475-482, July 1941.

CHEMICAL ENGINEERING RESEARCH

Clapp, G. R. "The Purpose of TVA Fertilizer." *National Fertilizer Review*, 27:6-7, July-August-September 1952.
Tennessee Valley Authority. *Agriculture, Fertilizer and Forestry Activities of the Tennessee Valley Authority.* Knoxville, Tennessee: TVA, January 1950. 53p. processed.

Tennessee Valley Authority. *Mineral Fertilizers and the Nation's Security.* Wilson Dam, Alabama: TVA, December 1, 1944. 9p. mimeo.

Tennessee Valley Authority. *Soil . . . People, and Fertilizer Technology.* Washington: Government Printing Office, 1949. 57p.

Tennessee Valley Authority. Division of Chemical Engineering. *Agglomeration of Phosphate Fines for Furnace Use,* compiled by E. L. Stout. Washington: Government Printing Office, 1950. 124p. (Chemical Engineering Report No. 4.)

Tennessee Valley Authority. Division of Chemical Engineering. *Corrosion Tests of Metals and Ceramics,* complied by L. D. Yates. Washington: Government Printing Office, 1951. 56p. (Chemical Engineering Report No. 9.)

Tennessee Valley Authority. Division of Chemical Engineering. *Development of Processes and Equipment for Production of Phosphoric Acid,* compiled by M. M. Striplin, Jr. Washington: Government Printing Office, 1949. 143p. (Chemical Engineering Report No. 2.)

Tennessee Valley Authority. Division of Chemical Engineering. *Development of Processes for Production of Concentrated Superphosphate,* compiled by G. L. Bridger. Washington: Government Printing Office, 1949. 172p. (Chemical Engineering Report No. 5.)

Tennessee Valley Authority. Division of Chemical Engineering. *General Outline of Chemical Engineering Activities,* by H. A. Curtis. Revised. Washington: Government Printing Office, 1949. 60p. (Chemical Engineering Report No. 1.)

Tennessee Valley Authority. Division of Chemical Engineering. *Phosphorus; Properties of the Element and Some of Its Compounds,* compiled by Thad D. Farr. Washington: Government Printing Office, 1950. 93p. (Chemical Engineering Report No. 8.)

Tennessee Valley Authority. Division of Chemical Engineering. *Preparation of Research and Engineering Reports,* by M. A. Tschantre. Wilson Dam, Alabama: TVA, 1950. 33p.

Tennessee Valley Authority. Division of Chemical Engineering. *Production of Elemental Phosphorus by the Electric-Furnace Method,* compiled by R. B. Burt and J. C. Barber. Wilson Dam, Alabama: TVA, 1952. 312p. (Chemical Engineering Report No. 3.)

COMMUNITY RELATIONSHIPS

Dolson, Hildegarde. "Meet a TVA Family." *Ladies' Home Journal,* 65: 183-187, June 1948.

Gray, A. J. "City Planning in the Southeast." *Georgia Local Government Journal,* 2:14-17, March 1952.

Gray, A. J. Local Planning in the Tennessee Valley." *Horizons*, 20:6-12, Winter 1948.

Hayes, W. J. "Planning Process in Tennessee Valley Communities." (In his *Small Community Looks Ahead*. New York: Harcourt, Brace and Company, 1947. p. 114-150.)

Hitch, Earle. "Expanding Rural Earning Opportunities." (In his *Rebuilding Rural America; New Designs for Community Life*. New York: Harper & Brothers, 1950. p. 201-216.)

Leonard, R. F., and Dobbins W. O. "Community Planning in North Alabama." *Public Administration Review*, 4:220-225, Summer 1944.

Shelton, Barrett. *Decatur Story*. Knoxville, Tennessee: TVA, 1949. 11p. An address by the editor and publisher of the *Decatur* (Alabama) *Daily* before the United Nations Scientific Conference on the Conservation and Utilization of Resources, at Lake Success, New York, September 5, 1949. It is also available in the *Proceedings* of the UN Conference, V. 1, p. 376-379.

Strong, Miriam. "Citizen's Organizations for Planning in Small Cities." *Planning and Civic Comment*, 12:1-10, July 1946.

EDUCATIONAL RELATIONSHIPS

Board of Control for Southern Regional Education. *Off-Campus Opportunities for Graduate and Professional Education in the Tennessee Valley Authority*. Atlanta, Georgia: September 1951. 39p. (Bulletin No. 2.)

"Education for Better Living Through the Use of Human and Natural Resources." *School Executive*, 67:27-58, January 1948.

"Education Helps Build a Region." *High School Journal*, 29:101-171, May 1946.

Gant, G. F. "Education for the Use of Resources." (In Reeves, F. W., ed. *Education for Rural America*. Chicago, Illinois: University of Chicago Press, 1945. p. 54-72.)

Ivey, J. E., Jr. *Channeling Research into Education*. Washington: American Council on Education, 1944. 187p. (Series I—Reports of Committees and Conferences—No. 19, V. 8, August 1944.)

National Education Association. *Large Was Our Bounty: Natural Resources and the Schools*. Washington: 1948. 216p. (Association for Supervision and Curriculum Development of the National Education Association. 1948 Yearbook.)

Rothrock, M. U. "Libraries and Regional Development." *Library Quarterly*, 12:666-674, July 1942.

Southeastern States Cooperative Library Survey. *Libraries of the Southeast, a Report* . . . 1946-1947, edited by L. R. Wilson and M. A. Milczewski. Chapel Hill, North Carolina: University of North Carolina Press, 1949. 301p.

Tennessee Valley Authority. "Resources; a Basis for Understanding." (In American Council on Education. *Report of Gatlinburg Conference II, 1944*. Washington: 1945. p. 45-57.)

Tennessee Valley Authority. Advisory Panel on Regional Materials of Instruction for the Tennessee Valley. *Applications of the Common Mooring*, prepared by Howard P. Emerson. Rev. ed. Knoxville, Tennessee: TVA, July 1943. 127p. mimeo.

ENGINEERING

Bennett, T. L. "Grave Relocation in TVA Reservoir Areas." *Surveying and Mapping*, 10:127-130, April-June 1950.

Blee, C. E. "Multiple Purpose Reservoir Operation of Tennessee River System." *Civil Engineering*, 15:219-222, 263-266, May, June 1945.

Blee, C. E., and Riegel, R. M. "Rock Fill Dams." (Preprint from Fourth International Congress on Large Dams, New Delhi, 1951. *Transactions*. Question No. 13, Report No. 22.)

Bowden, N. W. "Multiple-Purpose Reservoirs; General Problems of Design and Operation." American Society of Civil Engineers, *Proceedings*, 75:301-315, March 1949.

Bowman, J. S. "Trend Toward Multipurpose Developments." *Civil Engineering*, 22:152-155, September 1952.

Davis, H. E. "Reservoir Clearing in the Tennessee Valley; Completely Cleared Drawdowns Feature TVA Reservoirs." *Civil Engineering*, 16:27-30, January 1946.

"Design Developments—Structures of the Tennessee Valley Authority; Symposium." American Society of Civil Engineers, *Proceedings*, 71: 1193-1232, October 1945.

Elliot, R. A. "Value of Topographic Maps to the Tennessee Valley Authority Program." *Surveying and Mapping*, 10:3-9, January-March 1950.

Hays, J. B., and Schmidt, L. A. Jr. "Unusual Cutoff Problems; Dams of the Tennessee Valley Authority; Symposium." American Society of Civil Engineers, *Proceedings*, 69:1399-1446, November 1943.

Hopkins, R. A. "Hydroelectric Power Stations." (In Pender, Harold and Del Mar, W. A., eds. *Electrical Engineers' Handbook*. 4th ed. New York: John Wiley & Sons, Inc., 1949. V. 1, Section 13, p. 14-35.)

Hopkins, R. A., and Petersen, H. J. "Tennessee Valley Authority Hydroelectric Stations—Electrical and Mechanical Design." *American Institute of Electrical Engineers, Transactions,* 65:920-931, 1946.

Leonard, G. K. "Record Blast Provides 1.8 Million Cubic Yards of Rock for South Holston Dam." *Civil Engineering,* 20:187-191, March 1950.

"More Steam Plants for TVA Goals Set by Chief Engineer." *Engineering News-Record,* 149:57-62, July 24, 1952.

Petersen, H. J. "Johnsonville Steam Plant of the TVA." *Combustion,* 22:44-50, December 1950.

Petersen, H. J. "Shawnee—TVA to AEC." *Power Engineering,* 56:74-76, September 1952.

Reed, Oren, and McDougle, E. A. "TVA's Experience with Concrete Aggregate." *Roads and Streets,* 93:86, January 1950.

Rich, G. R., and others. "Design of Recent TVA Projects." *Civil Engineering,* 13:144-147, 165-167, 205-208, 257-260, 305-308, 373-376, 413-416, 465-468, March-October 1943.

Tennessee Valley Authority. *Engineering Data; Tennessee Valley Authority Projects.* Knoxville, Tennessee: TVA, March 1948. v.p. (Technical Monograph No. 55.)

Tennessee Valley Authority. *Engineering Geology and Mineral Resources of the Tennessee Valley Authority Region,* by E. C. Eckel. Knoxville, Tennessee: TVA, June 1934. 25p. (Geologic Bulletin No. 1.)

Tennessee Valley Authority. *Facts About Major TVA Dams.* Knoxville, Tennessee: TVA, 1951. Two-page table.

Tennessee Valley Authority. *A Report on the Development of the Cumberland River Below Nashville, Tennessee.* Knoxville, Tennessee: TVA, September 1950. 34p.

Tennessee Valley Authority. Technical Reports. Washington: Government Printing Office.
1. *The Norris Project.* 1939. 840p.
2. *The Wheeler Project.* 1940. 362p.
3. *The Pickwick Landing Project.* 1941. 431p.
4. *The Guntersville Project.* 1941. 423p.
5. Vol. 1. *The Hiwassee Project.* 1946. 367p.
   Vol. 2. *The Apalachia, Ocoee No. 3, Nottely, and Chatuge Projects.* 1947. 749p.
6. *The Chickamauga Project.* 1942. 451p.
7. *The Cherokee Project.* 1946. 411p.
8. *The Watts Bar Steam Plant.* 1948. 380p.
9. *The Watts Bar Project.* 1948. 545p.
10. *The Douglas Project.* 1948. 438p.

11. *The Fort Loudoun Project.* 1949. 521p.

12. *The Fontana Project.* 1949. 695p.

13. *The Kentucky Project.* 1950. 877p.

21. *Concrete Production and Control, Tennessee Valley Authority Projects.* 1948. 352p.

22. *Geology and Foundation Treatment, Tennessee Valley Authority Projects.* 1949. 548p.

23. *Surveying, Mapping and Related Engineering, Tennessee Valley Authority.* 1951. 416p.

24. *Design of TVA Projects.* Volume 1: *Civil and Structural Design.* 1952. 439p.

These Technical Reports may be procured, when available, from the Treasurer's Office, TVA, Knoxville, Tennessee.

Tennessee Valley Authority. Divisions of Engineering and Construction. *Measurements of the Structural Behavior of Norris and Hiwassee Dams.* Knoxville, Tennessee: TVA, August 1950. 462p. (Technical Monograph No. 67.)

Tennessee Valley Authority. Hydraulic Data Branch. *Operation of TVA Reservoirs, Annual 1951.* Knoxville, Tennessee: TVA, March 1952. 37p. 74 plates.

Tennessee Valley Authority. Hydraulic Data Branch. *TVA and the River,* by LeRoy Engstrom. Knoxville, Tennessee: TVA, 1951. 12p.

Titus, E. M. "Structural Steel Design of Hydro Projects of the Tennessee Valley Authority." *Saskatchewan Engineer,* 5:71-76, 1950.

Weber, A. H. "Correction of Reservoir Leakage at Great Falls Dam. "American Society of Civil Engineers, *Proceedings,* 76:101-118, January 1950.

Weber, A. H. "Hales Bar Dam: Rebuilt and Ready for More Power." *Engineering News-Record,* 145:37-39, October 19, 1950.

Wiersema, H. A. "Tennessee Valley Authority Hydroelectric Program." (In Midwest Power Conference. *Proceedings,* Chicago, Illinois: 1951. p. 121-130.)

Woodruff, W. W., and others. "Power Transmission." (In the *Standard Handbook for Electrical Engineers.* 8th ed. New York: McGraw-Hill Book Company, 1949. p. 1169-1324.)

Woodward, S. M., and Hare, V. C. "Great Public Utility: the Tennessee Valley Authority." *Queen's Quarterly,* 55:1-19, Spring 1948.

Woodward, S. M. "Operation of the Multi-Purpose Projects of the Tennessee Valley Authority." (In Midwest Power Conference. *Proceedings,* 1941. Chicago, Illinois: Illinois Institute of Technology, 1941. p. 76-82.)

FINANCIAL OPERATIONS

Kohler, E. L. "TVA and Its Power-Accounting Problems." *Accounting Review*, 23:44-62, January 1948.

Kull, D. C. *Budget Administration in the Tennessee Valley Authority*. Knoxville, Tennessee: Published by the Division of University Extension for the Bureau of Research, College of Business Administration, and the Bureau of Public Administration, University of Tennessee, 1948. 64p. (College of Business Administration. Bureau of Research. Study No. 15.)

Neuner, E. J. *Financial and Operating Characteristics of the Municipal and Cooperative Distributors of T.V.A. Power*. Knoxville, Tennessee: Division of University Extension, University of Tennessee, May 1949. 115p. (College of Business Administration. Bureau of Research. Study No. 20.)

Parker, T. B. "Allocation of the Tennessee Valley Authority Projects." American Society of Civil Engineers, *Proceedings*, 67:1813-1826, December 1941.

Society for the Advancement of Management. *Financial Control System of the Tennessee Valley Authority*. Revised ed. Washington: American University Press, 1945. 43p. (Federal Fiscal Series. Study No. 1.)

Tennessee Valley Authority. *Investment of the Tennessee Valley Authority in Wilson, Norris and Wheeler Projects*. Washington: Government Printing Office, 1938. 40p. (75th Congress. House Document No. 709.) Additional allocation reports have been issued from time to time pursuant to section 14 of the TVA Act and have been included in the Annual Reports of the Authority.

Tennessee Valley Authority. Comptroller. *Financial Statements for the Fiscal Years Ending June 30, 1938-Date*. Knoxville, Tennessee: TVA.

Tennessee Valley Authority. Comptroller. *Municipalities (Electric Departments Only) & Cooperatives, Purchasing Power from Tennessee Valley Authority*. Financial Statements for the Fiscal Years Ended June 30, 1938-Date. Knoxville, Tennessee: TVA.

U.S. Federal Power Commission. *Report of Review of Allocations of Costs of the Multiple-Purpose Water Control System in the Tennessee River Basin, as Determined by the Tennessee Valley Authority and Approved by the President Under the Provisions of the TVA Act of 1933 as Amended*. Washington: FPC, March 23, 1949. 46p.

U.S. General Accounting Office. *Report on the Audit of Tennessee Valley Authority, 1945-Date*. Washington: Government Printing Office.

FLOOD CONTROL

Barrows, H. K. "Tennessee Valley Authority." (In *Floods, Their Hydrology and Control.* New York: McGraw-Hill Book Company, 1948. p. 91-95, 177-182, 280-296.)

Rutter, E. J. "Flood-Control Operation of Tennessee Valley Authority Reservoirs." American Society of Civil Engineers, *Proceedings,* 76: 1-33, May 1950. (Separate No. 19.)

Tennessee Valley Authority. *Chattanooga Flood Control Problem.* Washington: Government Printing Office, January 9, 1939. (76th Congress. House Document No. 91.)

Tennessee Valley Authority. *Value of Flood Height Reduction from Tennessee Valley Authority Reservoirs to the Alluvial Valley of the Lower Mississippi River.* Washington: Government Printing Office, 1939. 64p. (76th Congress. House Document No. 455.)

FORESTRY AND WILDLIFE

Artman, J. O. "Forest Development in the Tennessee Valley." *Unasylva,* 5:147-153, October-December 1951.

Baker, W. M. *TVA Approach to Forest Development.* Durham, North Carolina: Duke University, School of Forestry, June 1946. 15p. (Duke University, School of Forestry Lectures, No. 6.)

Chase, S. B. "New Tree Crops in the Tennessee Valley." *Southern Lumberman,* 175:228-232, December 15, 1947.

Clapp, G. R. "Our Forests and the Future of the Tennessee Valley." *Journal of Forestry,* 45:329-334, May 1947.

Clapp, G. R. "Valley of Faith and Works." *American Forests,* 54:488-490, November 1948.

Darwin, W. N. "Tennessee Valley Authority's Interest in Forest Products Research." Forest Products Research Society, *Journal,* 2:76-85, April 1952.

Eschmeyer, R. W. *Fish and Fishing in TVA Impoundments.* Nashville, Tennessee: Tennessee Department of Conservation, 1950. 28p.

Eschmeyer, R. W. "Fishery Management Methods . . . Reservoirs." (In the *Fisherman's Encyclopedia,* edited by Ira N. Gabrielson. New York: Stackpole & Heck, 1950. p. 369-381.)

Eschmeyer, R. W., Manges, D. E., and Haslbauer, O. F. "Trends in Fishing on TVA Storage Waters." Tennessee Academy of Science, *Journal,* 22:45-56, January 1947.

Seigworth, K. J. "Reforestation in the Tennessee Valley." *Public Administration Review*, 8:280-285, Autumn 1948.

Tarzwell, C. M., and Bryan, Paul. "Changes in the Commercial Fishery on the Tennessee River." Tennessee Academy of Science, *Journal*, 20:49-54, January 1945.

Tennessee Valley Authority. *Agriculture, Fertilizer and Forestry Activities of the Tennessee Valley Authority.* Knoxville, Tennessee: TVA, January 1950. 53p. processed.

Tennessee Valley Authority. Division of Forestry Relations. Annual Report. Norris, Tennessee: TVA, 1946-Date.

Tennessee Valley Authority. Division of Forestry Relations. *Fish and Wildlife in the Tennessee Valley.* Norris, Tennessee: TVA, 1950. 17p.

Tennessee Valley Authority. Division of Forestry Relations. *Sawmill Facts; First Step Toward Good Management.* Norris, Tennessee: TVA, August 1951. 17p.

Tennessee Valley Authority. Division of Forestry Relations. *Tennessee Valley Forests*, by J. O. Artman. Norris, Tennessee: TVA, 1950. 17p.

Wiebe, A. H., Cady, E. R., and Bryan, Paul. *Waterfowl on the Tennessee River Impoundments.* Norris, Tennessee: TVA, February 14, 1950. 11p.

GOVERNMENTAL RELATIONSHIPS

Clapp, G. R. "Public Administration in an Advancing South." *Public Administration Review*, 8:169-175, Summer 1948.

Durisch, L. L. "Local Government and the T.V.A. Program." *Public Administration Review*, 1:326-334, Summer 1941.

Durisch, L. L. "Regional Research: the Experience of the Tennessee Valley Authority." *Public Affairs*, 8:234-238, Summer 1945.

Durisch, L. L. "States and Decentralized Administration of Federal Functions." *Journal of Politics*, 12:3-12, February 1950.

Durisch, L. L., and Macon, H. L. *Upon Its Own Resources; Conservation and State Administration.* University, Alabama: University of Alabama Press, 1951. 136p.

Edelmann, A. T. "Public Ownership and Tax Replacements by the TVA." *American Political Science Review*, 35:727-737, August 1941.

Johnson, H. B. "Federal-State-Local Cooperation: the Tennessee Valley." *State Government*, 21:214-218, October 1948.

Lepawsky, Albert. "Government Planning in the South." *Journal of Politics*, 10:536-567, August 1948.

Macon, H. L. "Payments in Lieu of Taxes by the Tennessee Valley

Authority." (In National Tax Association, *Proceedings*, 1943. p. 100-103.)

Ray, J. M. Influence of the Tennessee Valley Authority on Government in the South. *American Political Science Review*, 43:922-932, October 1949.

Satterfield, M. H. "Intergovernmental Cooperation in the Tennessee Valley." *Journal of Politics*, 9:31-58, February 1947.

Satterfield, M. H. "TVA-State-Local Relationships." *American Political Science Review*, 40:935-949, October 1946.

HEALTH AND SAFETY

Bishop, E. L. "Health and Safety Services of the Tennessee Valley Authority." *Public Personnel Review*, 4:9-16, January 1943.

Clark, R. N., and Kittrell, F. W. "Bacteriological Studies of the Fort Loudoun Reservoir." *American Journal of Public Health*, 38:342-350, March 1948.

Clark, R. N. "Stream Sanitation in the Tennessee Valley." American Society of Civil Engineers, *Proceedings*, 75:1278-1281, November 1949.

Derryberry, O. M. "Employee Health and Safety Program Developed in TVA." *Industrial Hygiene Newsletter*, 8:14-16, June 1948.

Derryberry, O. M., and Gartrell, F. E. "Trends in Malaria Control Program of the Tennessee Valley Authority." *American Journal of Tropical Medicine and Hygiene*, 1:500-507, May 1952.

Gartrell, F. E., and Johnson, A. H. "A Study to Evaluate Malaria Control Projects of Kentucky Reservoir in Terms of Collateral Uses and Socio-Economic Benefits." National Malaria Society, *Journal*, 9:259-267, September 1950.

Hinman, E. H., and Hess, A. D. "Biological Activities of the Public Health Program of the Tennessee Valley Authority." Tennessee Academy of Science, *Journal*, 24:195-205, July 1949.

Kiker, C. C. "Management of Water to Control Anopheline Mosquito Breeding." (In Fourth International Congress of Tropical Medicine and Malaria. *Proceedings*, May 10-18, 1948. Washington: Government Printing Office, 1948. p. 865-871.)

Kittrell, F. W., and Thomas, F. W. "Effect of River System Development on Water Quality in the Tennessee Valley." American Water Works Association, *Journal*, 41:777-791, September 1949.

U.S. Public Health Service. *Malaria Control on Impounded Water*, by the United States Public Health Service and Tennessee Valley Authority, Health and Safety Department. Washington: Government Printing Office, 1947. 422p.

INDUSTRIAL ECONOMICS

Clapp, G. R. "National Dividends from the Tennessee Valley." *South Atlantic Quarterly*, 49:1-7, January 1950.

Conference on the Measurement of County Income. *County Income Estimates for the Seven Southeastern States; a Report of the Conference* . . . by John Littlepage Lancaster. Charlottesville, Virginia: Bureau of Population and Economics, University of Virginia, 1952. 246p.
This study was sponsored by the state universities of the seven Valley States and the Tennessee Valley Authority.

Conference on the Measurement of County Income. *Methods for Estimating Income Payments in Counties; a Technical Supplement to County Income Estimates for Seven Southeastern States*, by Lewis C. Copeland. Charlottesville, Virginia: Bureau of Population and Economic Research, University of Virginia, 1952. 108p.

Copeland, L. C., and McPherson, W. K. "Industrial Trends in the Tennessee Valley." *Social Forces*, 24:273-283, March 1946.

Ferris, J. P. "The TVA Approach." (In *Institute on Regional Development of the Southeast*, July 28-29, 1949. Knoxville, Tennessee: University of Tennessee, May 1950. University of Tennessee Record, Extension Series, V. 26, No. 2, p. 72-83.)

McPherson, W. K. "Some Aspects of Economic Development in the Tennessee Valley." *Economic Leaflets* (University of Florida), 11: 1-4, May 1952.

Robock, S. H. "Regional Markets and Industrial Development." *Georgia Business* (University of Georgia, Bureau of Business Research), 9:6-8, June 1950.

Robock, S. H. "Rural Industries and Agricultural Development." *Journal of Farm Economics*, 34:346-360, August 1952.

Robock, S. H. "Tennessee Valley Study Shows Trend Toward Industrialization." University of Tennessee, *News Letter* (Tennessee Business), 30:1-4, April 1951.

Tennessee Valley Authority. Industrial Economics Branch. *Defense Expansion in the Tennessee Valley Region.* Knoxville, Tennessee: TVA, July 2, 1952. 12p.

Tennessee Valley Authority. Division of Regional Studies. *Local Govern-*

ment Services and Industrial Development in the Southeast. 27p. No imprint.

A joint statement by the state universities of the Valley States and TVA.

LABOR RELATIONS

Case, H. L. "Wage Negotiations in the Tennessee Valley Authority." *Public Personnel Review*, 8:132-137, July 1947.

Clapp, G. R. "Problems of Union Relations in Public Agencies." *American Economic Review*, 33:supp. 184-196, March 1943.

Clapp, G. R. *Union-Management Cooperative Program in TVA.* Transcript of Proceedings, Federal Personnel Council, Washington, D. C., April 24, 1952. Knoxville, Tennessee: TVA, 1952. 8p.

Dodd, Thelma Iles. "Teamwork Approach to Productivity." *Personnel Administration*, 15:1, January 1952.

Kampelman, M. M. "TVA Labor Relations: a Laboratory in Democratic Human Relations." *Minnesota Law Review*, 30:332-371, April 1946.

King, Judson. *TVA Labor Relations Policy at Work; Successful Cooperation Between Public Power and Organized Labor in the Public Interest. Revised ed.* Washington: National Popular Government League, April 19, 1940. 64p. (Bulletin 192-A.)

Tennessee Valley Authority. Central Joint Cooperative Committee. *Highlights of the Cooperative Program of TVA and the Tennessee Valley Trades and Labor Council.* Knoxville, Tennessee: TVA, August 1950. 30p.

Tennessee Valley Authority and Salary Policy Employee Panel. *Articles of Agreement . . . ,* December 5, 1950, Knoxville, Tennessee: TVA, 1950. 15p.

Tennessee Valley Authority and Tennessee Valley Trades and Labor Council. *General Agreement . . . and Supplementary Schedules.* Negotiated August 6, 1940, Revised July 1, 1951. Knoxville, Tennessee: TVA, 1951. 68p.

U.S. Congress. Senate. Joint Committee on Labor-Management Relations. *Labor-Management Relations in TVA.* Washington: Government Printing Office, 1949. 63p. (81st Congress. Senate Report No. 372.)

NAVIGATION AND TRANSPORTATION

Barker, C. T. "Navigation on the Tennessee River." *Engineering News-Record*, 136:285-288, February 21, 1946; 136:351-354, March 7, 1946.

Joubert, W. H. "Tennessee River—a New Frontier in Navigation."
Transport and Communications Review, 4:47-60, July-September
1951.

Menhinick, H. K. "Local Riverfront Development." *American City*, 65:
83-85, November 1950.

Taylor, C. T. "Transportation on the Tennessee." Federal Reserve Bank
of Atlanta, *Monthly Review*, 34:13-19, February 28, 1949.

Tennessee Valley Authority. *History of Navigation on the Tennessee
River System; an Interpretation of the Economic Influence of This
River System on the Tennessee Valley*. Washington: Government
Printing Office, 1937. 192p. bibliog. (75th Congress. House Document
No. 254.)

Tennessee Valley Authority. *Interterritorial Freight Rate Problem of the
United States*. Washington: Government Printing Office, 1937. 66p.
(75th Congress. House Document No. 264.)
The problem of discriminatory freight rates, particularly as they affect
the South, is discussed as to structure and economic results, and possible solutions are suggested. Two additional TVA studies have been
made of this problem:
*Supplemental Phases of the Interterritorial Freight Rate Problem of
the United States*. Washington: Government Printing Office, 1939.
61p. (76th Congress. House Document No. 271.)
Regionalized Freight Rates: Barrier to National Productiveness. Washington: Government Printing Office, 1943. 79p. (78th Congress.
House Document No. 137.)

Tennessee Valley Authority. Commerce Department. *Cheaper Transportation Via the Tennessee River*. Knoxville, Tennessee: TVA, February
1946. 45p.

Tennessee Valley Authority. Division of Regional Studies. *The Barge
Grain Case—Its Significance to the Tennessee Valley and the Southeast*. Knoxville, Tennessee: TVA, November 1951. 38p.

Tennessee Valley Authority. Division of Regional Studies. *Navigation in
the Development of the Tennessee Valley*. Knoxville, Tennessee: TVA,
May 1949. 14p.

Tennessee Valley Authority. Division of Regional Studies. *Transportation
and Container Problems, and Related Developments in the Fertilizer
Industry*. Knoxville, Tennessee: TVA, July 9, 1951. 7p.
Prepared at the request of the President's Materials Policy Commission.

PERSONNEL ADMINISTRATION

Case, H. L. "Cornerstones of Personnel Administration in TVA." *Personnel Administration*, 11:10-12, January 1949.

Chase, Stuart. "Down in the Valley." (In his *Roads to Agreement*. New York: Harper & Brothers, 1951. p. 172-185.)

Civil Service Assembly of the United States and Canada. *Employee Relations in the Public Service*. Chicago, Illinois: 1942. 246p.

Clapp, G. R. "What Price Ability in the Public Service?" *Personnel Administration*, 10:1-4, May 1948.

Duke, C. A., and Cummings, H. B., Jr. "How TVA Trains Its Engineers." *Electrical World*, 136:99-103, October 22, 1951.

Dunford, R. E., and Hultquist, K. B. "Personnel Testing in the TVA." *Public Personnel Review*, 5:133-139, July 1944.

Fredriksen, C. W. "Getting Support from Supervisors in Performance Reviewing." *Personnel Administration*, 12:8-10, January 1950.

Gant, G. F. "Unity and Specialization in Administration." (In *Conference on Science, Philosophy and Religion in Their Relation to the Democratic Way of Life*. 6th Symposium, August 23-27, 1945. 1947. p. 126-134.)

Greene, L. S. "Personnel Administration in the Tennessee Valley Authority." *Journal of Politics*, 1:171-194, May 1939.

McGlothlin, W. J. "Apprentice Program of TVA." *Personnel Administration*, 8:5-8, April 1946.

McGlothlin, W. J. "Employee Training in TVA During Wartime Expansion." *Public Personnel Review*, 4:244-253, October 1943.

Martinson, H. M. *The Effectiveness of Apprentice Training in the Tennessee Valley Authority.* Knoxville, Tennessee: August 1949. 180p. Thesis (M.S.)—University of Tennessee. Typewritten.

Tennessee Valley Authority. Division of Personnel. *Documentation of TVA Apprenticeship Program.* Knoxville, Tennessee: TVA, July 1952. 13p.

Tennessee Valley Authority. Division of Personnel. *Effectiveness of Apprentice Training in TVA.* Knoxville, Tennessee: TVA, December 1951. 93p.

Tennessee Valley Authority. Division of Personnel. *Personnel Administration in TVA; the Experience of 14 Years.* Knoxville, Tennessee: TVA, June 1947. 45p.

Tennessee Valley Authority. Division of Personnel. *Summary Description of Personnel Administration in TVA.* Knoxville, Tennessee: TVA, April 1951. 10p. mimeo.

U.S. Bureau of Apprenticeship. *Report on Apprentice Training Program of the Tennessee Valley Authority.* Washington: Apprentice-Training Service, 1947. 67p.

Williamson, M. M. "TVA Retirement System." *Tennessee Engineer,* 54:12-13, January 1951.

Young, C. H., and Martinson, H. M. "TVA's Training Program for Chemical Plant Operations." *Chemical and Engineering News,* 23:233-237, February 10, 1947.

POWER UTILIZATION

Bauer, John, and Costello, Peter. *Public Organization of Electric Power: Conditions, Policies, and Program.* New York: Harper & Brothers, 1949. 263p.

Clapp, G. R. "On Whose Side of the Bus Bar? The Experience of the Tennessee Valley." (In American Public Power Association. *Proceedings,* 1947. p. 53-62.)

Freeman, R. M. "Regional and River Valley Public Power Development." *Nebraska Law Review,* 30:401-415, March 1951.

Kampmeier, R. A. "Electric Power in the Tennessee Valley." *Tennessee Valley Engineer,* 12:2-7, February 1951.

Krug, J. A. "Testimony on the TVA Power Program." (In U.S. Congress. Joint Committee on the Investigation of the Tennessee Valley Authority. *Hearings* . . . 75th Congress. Washington: Government Printing Office, 1939. Pt. 12, p. 5189-5203, 5227-5451, 5495-5509.)

Martin, B. H., and Newberry, T. W. "Heating by Electricity in the Tennessee Valley Area." *Heating and Ventilating,* 45:57-63, May 1948.

Morgan, H. A. "Rural Electrification; a Promise to American Life." (In Third World Power Conference, Washington, D. C., 1936. *Transactions.* Washington: Government Printing Office, 1938. V. 8, p. 769-799.)

Pritchett, C. H. "Lessons of the TVA Power Program." *Public Affairs,* 9:98-103, Winter 1946.

Tennessee Valley Authority. *TVA Power—1952.* Knoxville, Tennessee: TVA, 1952. 19p.

Tennessee Valley Authority. Department of Power Utilization. *Electricity Sales Statistics,* Monthly Report No. 1 to Date. Chattanooga, Tennessee: TVA, 1935 to Date.

RECREATION

Howes, R. M. "TVA and Recreational Development in the Southeast." (In Institute on Regional Development of the Southeast, July 28-29, 1949. Knoxville, Tennessee: University of Tennessee, May 1950. University of Tennessee Record, Extension Series, V. 26, No. 2, p. 110-114.)

Lesure, T. B. "Thriving Vacation Area." *Travel*, 98:12-15, September 1952.

Lord, Russell. "TVA Playground." *Holiday*, 2:67-70, September 1947.

Nixon, H. C. *Tennessee Valley, a Recreation Domain*. Nashville, Tennessee: Vanderbilt University Press, June 1945. 22p. (Vanderbilt University. Institute of Research and Training in the Social Sciences. Paper No. 9.)

Simpich, Frederick. "Around the 'Great Lakes of the South.'" *National Geographic Magazine*, 93:463-491, April 1948.

Tennessee. Department of Conservation. *A Guide of the Great Lakes of the Tennessee, Paducah to Knoxville*. Nashville, Tennessee: 1950. 17p.

Tennessee Valley Authority. *Extent of Recreation Development and Use of TVA Lakes and Actual Lake Frontage Property*. Knoxville, Tennessee: TVA, 1947 to 1951.
Tabulations showing kinds and extent of recreation development and use by individual reservoirs and accumulated totals from 1947 to current calendar year; also comparative totals 1947 through 1951.

Tennessee Valley Authority. *Recreation Development of the Tennessee River System*. Washington: Government Printing Office, 1940. 99p. (76th Congress. House Document No. 565.)

Tennessee Valley Authority. *Recreation on TVA Lakes*. Knoxville, Tennessee: TVA, 1952. unp.
Folder with map and list of recreation and vacation accommodations and facilities on TVA lakes along with a brief description of kind and extent of recreation development occurring on the lakes.

Tennessee Valley Authority. *Scenic Resources of the Tennessee Valley; a Descriptive and Pictorial Inventory*. Washington: Government Printing Office, 1938. 222p.

U.S. President's Water Resources Policy Commission. *Report*, V. 2: "Ten Rivers in America's Future." Washington: Government Printing Office, 1950. p. 782-785.

APPENDIX B

STIMULATION OF LOCAL, STATE, AND PRIVATE INITIATIVE BY A FEDERAL REGIONAL AGENCY

Portions of the Testimony of Hon. Gordon R. Clapp, Chairman of the Tennessee Valley Authority, regarding the TVA's appropriation request for the fiscal year 1953, before a subcommittee of the House Appropriations Committee, (1952).[1]

In carrying out [TVA's statutory] responsibilities we have come year after year before this committee of the House, and the committee has been very understanding in appropriating money for what we have called the resource development program and for fertilizer and munitions research and the development program involving the chemical plants at Muscle Shoals.

In the careful administering of those programs we have been guided by two major concerns.

In the first place, we have done our best to do what we had to do directly in the most efficient manner possible, in an honest way, in an economical way and finding ways to cut costs wherever we could. I think our record on that is one that we have a right to be proud of, and we are proud of it.

The other thing that we have paid major attention to is how to set these programs of resource development into the economy of the region in such a way as to encourage local initiative. We looked forward to the time when the TVA, representing the Federal Government, would be

[1] U. S. Congress. House. Committee on Appropriations. Subcommittee on Independent Offices. Independent Offices Appropriations for 1953. Part 3. Hearings . . . 82d Congress, 2d Session. (Washington: Government Printing Office, 1952), pp. 1325-1409.

putting less money into many of these activities and the State and local agencies would be taking a larger proportion of the expense of those programs and would be staffing their own agencies to do things which TVA originally gave some impetus to in the beginning.

Now, to get concrete, the chemical plants that we took over in 1933, the ones that were built for wartime purposes in 1916 and 1917 and 1918, were turned into facilities for the production of phosphatic fertilizers. We developed new processes largely through the use of the electric furnace. We had to test those new fertilizers.

In the process of developing the test and demonstration programs, we got together with the State agricultural colleges and the extension services of the various States and asked them to share leadership in the programs with us.

This committee knows a lot of the history of that test and demonstration program. It knows that at one time we have as many as 30,000 test-demonstration farms using TVA materials under programs sponsored by the States, and reporting the results of those new types of fertilizers to TVA, so that its chemical research could adapt processes of manufacture to the problems and the soil.

As time has gone on we have reduced that program more and more, and we have called upon the States to assume more and more responsibility for it, and to give more and more leadership in its administration and execution.

The result is that, as you see in this budget proposal for 1953, the test-demonstration program is reduced to a still lower level of volume for 1953, calling for distribution of less fertilizer materials through the test-demonstration program. It calls for the assumption of more responsibility on the part of the State agencies to carry on this program and to make its results effective and applicable to the farm problems of the area as a whole.

Consider these facts: In fiscal year 1947 TVA spent approximately $640,000 for contractual payments to land-grant colleges for supervision of test demonstrations. Total TVA payments for this purpose are estimated at $318,000 in this budget for 1953. The number of extension workers in the valley States increased from 1,289 in 1934 to 2,468 in 1948. Average extension funds available per county in the valley States in 1949 were $20,520, an increase of 285 per cent over 1934. Within this total, State and college funds increased by 343 per cent to $5,204 in 1949 and county funds increased by 237 per cent to $4,025 in 1949. All of these percentage increases were greater in the valley States than in the other 41 States.

Likewise in forestry we have, in times past, spent money appropriated by this committee and the Congress, in getting people to plant trees to reforest large parts of the area and thereby contribute new products, increase the water holding power of the valley and cut down on erosion and siltation, which result in large waste of land and wealth.

The program as reflected here takes very little time on the part of the TVA staff in the promotion of tree planting; now citizens and organized groups and test-demonstration farmers and whole communities under the leadership of the State agencies in agriculture and forestry, allied with the bankers and with businessmen in local communities, are pushing those tree planting programs in greater and greater volume. TVA's role remains primarily that of operating a couple of seedling nurseries where we raise seedlings and turn them over to the States and to other agencies for distribution in these programs.

The States, in the meantime, are building up their seedling producing programs, so I think in 1953 their plans call for the production of some 150 million seedlings, whereas, a few years ago their production was practically nil.

In the meantime, we have worked with the States and the landowners of the area to get them to realize that it does not do much good, or make much sense to spend money, time, and labor planting trees if fires are going to burn them up.

We could have come to this committee year after year and urged Federal money for fire protection. We have not done so. There are Federal programs that operate in that field, but our special role in that particular problem has been to work with the States and in the counties getting the various landowners to realize that the business aspects of forestry cannot succeed commensurate with the great forest reserves in this region unless the landowners, out of their own pockets, support local programs of fire prevention and protection.

The result is that today 80 per cent of the forest lands of the Tennessee Valley region have some kind of protection, not paid for by the TVA, but paid for and operated and carried on by the States and local agencies.

Sixty-five per cent of the forest lands have what technical foresters call adequate fire protection.

Here are a few statistics on the decrease in the annual burn of timber of the area and the decrease in the acreage of burn: While forest-fire records are not complete for all counties, a survey in 1938 indicated an average annual burn of about 5 per cent in the Tennessee Valley. The estimated average burn in the valley in 1951 was approximately 1 per cent. However, the average annual burn varies from a low of 0.2 per cent in one area to as high as 10 per cent in some private nonprotected areas.

We have gone through some very risky seasons in the last few years with very dry fall months, and yet the widespread forest fires that used to curse the region have not occurred in as great volume or with as great frequency.

Now, the point that I would like to get across is that TVA in that field has concentrated on the idea of leading the way, suggesting the way to do things, using its small amounts of money to carry on demonstrations and to get States to harness their educational forces in working with the landowners, who, in the last analysis, are going to determine the kind of forests and forest management we will have.

That has left our staff, then, free again to move to the next type of problem, which is, with more trees, with more forests, with better growth, with better fire protection, how do you get better management of the forests and how do you get more economic benefit out of their croppage?

Consequently, in this budget proposal for 1953 the committee will note that there is more emphasis upon demonstrations of more efficient forest management; an example is sawmill operations. Sawmill operators are called together and come of their own volition to attend schools right on the site of somebody's sawmill. Here the experts explain how they can improve the efficiency of different types of sawmills, how large they should be, and how large a cut ought to be taken to increase the dollar value of forest raw materials consistent with forest conservation programs.

Similarly in the field of recreational development. It may seem at first glance that the TVA should be the last agency interested in recreational development, but, of course, as this committee and as many of you as individuals know from your own knowledge of the Tennessee Valley and other parts of the country, where you create lakes people will make use of them as recreational assets. That has been the case in the Tennessee Valley.

The TVA recognized that there would be a great byproduct value for recreation in building these dams and storing up these waters for navigation, flood control, and power.

Moreover, the TVA recognized, and called attention of the States in the region to the fact that there would be a great public demand for recreational facilities on these lakes. We suggested that the people would look to the States and to their own county and local governments for the development of parks and recreational areas.

The first reaction that we got years ago to the idea of capitalizing on the recreational value of these lakes was that TVA ought to do all of these things because local governments were not prepared to do the job. We did not agree that TVA should assume such a responsibility.

We saw, however, that it was going to be necessary and advisable to establish some demonstrations of what could be developed on these lakes in an economic way to serve as a guide to both private and to local public investment.

We set up some demonstration parks in connection with the reservations around our dams, and for a time we operated some of those parks. . . .

We were operating those so-called park facilities, not to make them a part of the permanent operating requirements of the TVA, but in order to suggest or demonstrate, both to private citizens and Government agencies in the valley and in the States, what could be done. As a result of that and other guidance, the State agencies have gone into that development, and as of now there are some 11 State parks on TVA lakes in the valley, whereas in 1933 there were no State parks.

There are more than 35 municipal and county parks on these lakes where local money, not TVA money, has gone into the development and establishment of the physical facilities.

The operating requirements are not on the TVA, they are on the State, the county, and municipal governments.

The demonstration parks that TVA established to make these lessons clear have now been turned over to the States either by straight transfer or long-term leasing arrangements thereby divesting the Federal Government of operating expenses and responsibility for this enterprise.

The same lesson can be pointed to in the field of malaria control. I dare say that when historians, at some future date, take a long look at the TVA program, one of the achievements they will cite, perhaps even more than the development of the power supply, which has been an extremely dramatic thing, and continues to be, is what has happened to malaria in the Tennessee Valley.

When you build a dam on a stream in a region that has a history of malaria you slow the flow of that stream, and you increase the conditions which are conducive to breeding malaria mosquitoes. If this is disregarded, then you get an endemic condition that just multiplies and becomes a curse upon the productive capacity of the people.

When TVA started out in 1933 the incidence of malaria in the Tennessee Valley along the southernmost stretches of the river ranged all the way from zero up to 65 per cent. I mean that 65 people out of 100 in some communities either had malaria or had a history of malaria infection. . . .

As the malaria control programs of the TVA and the States and local counties along the river have done their work, the incidence of malaria has gone down and down until in 1948, using the same sampling techniques that were used earlier, the incidence had dropped down to one-tenth of 1 per cent.

Since 1948 regular sampling methods that the counties and the States use have discovered no cases of malaria. . . .

The important point again in that is that the TVA, instead of undertaking to do the whole malaria control program itself, has worked with the States and helped them to train and to acquire more competent personnel for the public health job in those activities. TVA has turned over to those agencies the inspections, the mosquito count and inspection work, to test our malaria control measures in the operation of our reservoirs. We have also helped the State and local agencies to pioneer in some of the more advanced prevention techniques, such as the use of DDT in house paint, and new and more effective spraying methods.

The story that runs through all of these things in the resource development field is that the people in TVA—our division chiefs, our section chiefs, and the men working out in the counties and on the front line with the States—have, I think, been devoted to the idea that TVA's function is to help build up the State and local agencies to a point where they can do these things which TVA might otherwise have to do. . . .

The same point can be made in connection with TVA's work in exploration and research in the discovery and use of minerals.

The committee will note that this year the proposal for 1953 shows a very drastic reduction in what we are proposing to apply to mineral research. This is largely because the program has now reached the point where the States of North Carolina, Tennessee, Georgia, and Alabama, through their own staffs and their own programs—stimulated, in large part by money made available to the TVA through this committee and this Congress—can now carry on their programs in their own States under their own leadership with TVA counseling on special problems.

APPENDIX C

TVA AS A SYMBOL OF RESOURCE DEVELOPMENT IN MANY COUNTRIES

Portions of a Digest and Selected Bibliography of Information

Compiled January 1952
TVA Technical Library

I

Jordan River Development Plan
The DVC—India's Damodar Valley Corporation
Puerto Rico's Water Resources Authority
The Santa Corporation of Peru
The Niger Valley in French West Africa
Mexico's Papaloapan Basin
Brazil's Sao Francisco Valley
RIONE—On Uruguay's Rio Negro
The Snowy-Murray Project in Australia
Proposed YVA on the Yangtze
Uganda's Development Where the Nile Begins
Pilot Demonstration Projects in the Middle East
Chilean Development Corporation
The Scottish Highlands and Islands
India's MVP—The Mahanadi Valley Project
The Rhône Valley in France
El Salvador's Lempa Valley
Proposed Volta River Authority on the Gold Coast

II

Africa—Belgian Congo
  —Rhodesia
  —Union of South Africa
  —Valley of the Nile
Australia—Clarence River Scheme

Europe—Greece
  —Wales
Middle East—Iraq
  —Turkey
Southwest Asia—Afghanistan
  —Ceylon
  —India—The Ganges Basin
      —The Sutlej Development
      —The Machkund River
      —The Godavari River System
      —Smaller River Systems in Southwest
      —The Kistna River Valley
West Indies—Haiti—Artibonite Valley

FOREWORD

In a number of countries over the world TVA has become a symbol of the unified development of resources. In many instances, however, the symbol is used loosely to describe projects that resemble TVA only in some minor feature.

To provide some concept of the scope and magnitude of foreign projects or plans which have been influenced by the TVA example, the following digest of available material relating to TVA-like developments over the world has been prepared. For the purpose of this digest these developments—based on data available—have been divided into two classifications: (I) Developments which appear to approach within a reasonable degree the TVA conception of the development and utilization of resources. (II) Projects on which available data were meager or where in planning and development the TVA idea—although recognized —appears to have been used only to a limited extent.

This brief digest is not an all-inclusive listing of the many water resource developments influenced in some measure by TVA.

I

JORDAN RIVER DEVELOPMENT PLAN

Location

At the eastern end of the Mediterranean in an area encompassing the Palestine of Biblical times that extended from "Dan to Beersheba" there is a major engineering plan for the development of water resources. This proposed development has been called "TVA on the Jordan."

Scope and Salient Features

Palestine's area of slightly over 10,000 square miles is about one fourth that of the Tennessee Valley. However, unlike the Tennessee Valley, it is not entirely within one national boundary. Palestine today is comprised of the State of Israel and an area known as Arab Palestine now annexed to Jordan. The major water supply essential to the development originates in adjacent Lebanon, Syria, and Jordan. Cooperation between Israel and the adjacent Arab States would be absolutely essential to the successful execution of the proposed over-all plan; only small portions could be developed to an individual country's advantage without such cooperation.

The purposes of the plan are to supply Palestine's two chief economic needs: water for irrigated agriculture and power for industrial development. The northern or upper part of the area has a surplus of water over and above what would be needed to supply the local demands. If properly conserved, this surplus could be conveyed to other sections, particularly in the south where there are large areas of fertile land but little rainfall. By means of dams the waters of the upper Jordan and its tributaries could be stored and diverted as needed into a network of irrigation canals. In order to compensate the Dead Sea for the loss of these waters, sea water from the Mediterranean could be introduced starting at a point near Haifa and conducted through tunnels and canals down the below-sea-level Jordan depression to the Dead Sea. As this sea water dropped into the Jordan rift there would be almost 1,300 feet of effective fall for the development of electric power. The water supply of the main irrigation canal as it traversed the coastal plain area could be supplemented by the development of the underground water sources and springs along the coastal plain from the northern border with Lebanon south to the Egyptian border.

One of the major advantages of the program proposed is that the entire development was planned so that it could be progressively undertaken in eight successive stages or units, each of which would bring into use upon its completion reasonable additional acreages of land. Ultimately the entire water resources of Palestine would thus be developed for maximum profitable utilization. Irrigation as contemplated in the development program would be provided for at least 606,000 acres (the area now under irrigation in Israel is only 75,000 acres). The development would produce an estimated 660 million kilowatt-hours of hydro-electric energy per annum.

TVA Influence

James B. Hays, formerly Project Manager of the TVA's South Holston projects and an irrigation and power engineer of over 30 years' experience, became the Palestine Commission's Chief Engineer for the development plan and was assisted by an experienced Engineering Consulting Board which included C. E. Blee, Chief Engineer of TVA, and the late Col. Theodore B. Parker, former Chief Engineer of the TVA.

Bibliography

"Jordan Valley Authority—a counterpart of TVA in Palestine." W. C. Lowdermilk. (In his *Palestine, land of promise.* New York: Harper, 1944. p. 168-179.)

"TVA on the Jordan." G. W. Norris. *Nation,* 158:589-591, May 20, 1944.

"Waters of Jordan: A Jordan Valley Authority." *Time,* 47:90, April 8, 1946.

"Palestine's Jordan river valley plan emulates TVA development." E. E. Shalowitz. *Civil Engineering,* 17:529-531, September 1947.

"Land and the people." W. C. Lowdermilk. *Nation,* 165:360-361, October 4, 1947.

T.V.A. on the Jordan; proposals for irrigation and hydroelectric development in Palestine. J. B. Hays. Washington: Public Affairs Press, 1948. 114p.

"JVA to renew Palestine land." F.E.A. Thone. *Science News Letter,* 53: 186-187, March 20, 1948.

"Multiple-purpose river valley development—Palestine." M. L. Cooke. *Mechanical Engineering,* 71:131, February 1949.

"TVA's in the Middle East." Feliks Bochenski and William Diamond. *Middle East Journal,* 4:52-82, January 1950.

"Water problem in the Middle East." *Geographical Review,* 40:481-484, July 1950.

"TVA on the Tigris [Resource Development in the Middle East]." G. R. Clapp. *New Leader,* 33:6-8, July 22, 1950.

"Israel banks on its new immigrants." W. G. Bowman. *Engineering News-Record,* 146:26-30, March 22, 1951.

THE DVC—INDIA'S DAMODAR VALLEY CORPORATION

Location

Between the Himalaya Mountains and the Bay of Bengal lie India's two easternmost provinces—Bihar and West Bengal—where work is under way on the Damodar Valley development. First units of the thermal power stations were dedicated by Prime Minister Nehru and put into service in February, 1953.

The Damodar River joins the Hooghly—an important mouth of the Ganges—about 30 miles below the large port of Calcutta. To the east is the Pakistan province of East Bengal.

Scope and Salient Features

The 340-mile-long river with a drainage area of 8,500 square miles rises in the hills of western Bihar and flows generally southeast to the low-lying delta plains of the Ganges. The plan for this river calls for its unified multipurpose development by means of several dams which when completed will provide perennial irrigation to 750,000 acres and generate 300,000 kilowatts of electrical energy. By improving navigation facilities it will transform the river into an arterial waterway linking the Raniganj coal field with the port of Calcutta. By making cheap power available it will provide opportunities for establishment of new industries, facilitate industrial decentralization throughout the basin and thus contribute to the economic well-being of five million rural inhabitants and two million urban dwellers. The havoc periodically wrought by the torrential waters of the Damodar in their wayward rush to the sea will be minimized through flood regulation.

TVA Influence

In September 1948, V. S. Swaminathan stated in the *Fortnightly* (London): "To India 1947 was a banner year for two excellent reasons: the Dominions of India and Pakistan and, even more significant for economic and social reasons, the adoption of the draft constitution for the Damodar Valley Corporation (D.V.C.). This was modelled on the Tennessee Valley Authority by representatives of the Government of India, Bengal, and Bihar of the Inter-Provincial Conference held at New Delhi."

Prior to the formation of the DVC the central government of India secured Mr. W. L. Voorduin, formerly Head Planning Engineer of TVA, to serve on the Central Technical Board and prepare plans for unified river developments. In addition Ross M. Riegel, former Head Civil Engineer, and Fred C. Schlemmer, former Construction Project Manager of TVA, traveled to India to serve as consultants on this development. In October 1950, A. M. Komora, former TVA Construction Engineer, was appointed Chief Engineer of DVC.

The October, 1952, issue of the *Indian Journal of Power & River Valley Development* (Calcutta) is devoted entirely to the DVC. The editorial, "India and the TVA Method," discusses the application of the TVA idea to the problems of the subcontinent of India; other articles by Indian officials trace the origins and impact in India of the TVA example.

Bibliography

"Preliminary memorandum on the unified development of the Damodar river." Damodar Valley Corporation. Calcutta: August 1945. 40p.

"Developments beyond U.S. borders—India." *Engineering News-Record,* 138:4, January 2, 1947.

"India stakes her economic future on hydroelectric developments." J. K. Van Denburg, Jr., *Power,* 91:310-311, May 1947.

"Preliminary memorandum on the unified development of the Damodar river (abridged)." India. Central technical power board. Calcutta, 1948. 20p.

"India's TVA." V. S. Swaminatham. *Fortnightly* (London), 170 (ns 164): 180-186, September 1948.

Why the Damodar scheme deserves top priority among India's development projects. Damodar Valley Corporation. Calcutta: November 1948. 11p.

Mineral resources of the Damodar valley and adjacent region and their utilisation for industrial development (synopsis). V. R. Khedker. Calcutta: Damodar Valley Corporation, 1949. 24p.

"India taps enormous water and power resources." A. V. Karpov. *Civil Engineering,* 19:235-238, April 1949.

"Hydro-electric development in India." H. A. Sieveking. *Water Power,* 2:60-66, March-April 1950.

"Damodar valley—'Valles opima.'" William Kirk. *Geographical Review,* 40:415-443, July 1950.

"Damodar valley project, a survey of progress." *Indian Journal of Power & River Valley Development,* 1:9-21, December 1950.

Improved land use in the Damodar valley. Damodar Valley Corporation. Calcutta: January 15, 1951. 18p.

"Letter from India: India stakes future on her rivers—Damodar valley project." W. G. Bowman. *Engineering News-Record,* 146:34-35, March 1, 1951.

"India's TVA." W. G. Bowman. *Engineering News-Record,* 146:33-36, May 24, 1951.

"New projects—India." *Irrigation & Power,* 8:338-359, July 1951.

"Importance and necessity of combined resource development of a river valley multi-purpose project." Kanwar Sain. *Irrigation & Power*, 8: 499-506, July 1951.

PUERTO RICO'S WATER RESOURCES AUTHORITY

Location

The island of Puerto Rico—the middle link of the West Indian chain enclosing the Caribbean—is the location of a river development project which has been styled a "junior-sized TVA." The Puerto Rico Water Resources Authority, a government agency, is charged with the fullest development of the Island's water resources.

Scope and Salient Features

About 100 miles long from east to west and about a third as wide, Puerto Rico has an area one-twelfth that of the Tennessee Valley. Two recently completed hydroelectric projects—the Dos Bocas and Caonillas —are both located in the mountainous central western section of the island where the annual rainfall reaches 100 inches. These two projects provide a major source of the present more than 500,000,000 kilowatt-hours produced yearly by the Water Resources Authority. An additional 36,000,000 kilowatt-hours will be added with the completion of a series of four dams known as the Caonillas Extension Project. The largest hydroelectric project of all is still in the planning stage. This is the Lajas Valley power and irrigation project located in a mountainous area north of Ponce on the Island's south shore. The ultimate potential total water power that may be developed from the streams in the Island is estimated at 700,000,000 kilowatt-hours.

TVA Influence

The chief engineer of the "junior-sized" TVA in Puerto Rico is Carl A. Bock, formerly of TVA.

Bibliography

"Harness water power." *Science News Letter*, 54:132-133, August 28, 1948.

"Puerto Rico Builds a 'junior TVA.'" *Public Power*, 6:7, September 1948.

"Multiple-purpose river valley development—Puerto Rico." M. L. Cooke. *Mechanical Engineering*, 71:131-132, February 1949.

"Developments abroad—Power for Puerto Rico." *Engineering News-Record*, 143:53, August 18, 1949.

THE SANTA CORPORATION OF PERU

Location

In Peru—below the equator on the western bulge of South America—where the mighty Andes tower three to four miles above the Pacific is the Cañon del Plato (Duck Canyon) of the Santa River. In this gorge between the Black and White Cordilleras (mountain ranges) about 225 miles north of the Peruvian capital of Lima is a key project of the Santa Corporation which was formed by the Peruvian Government in 1943.

Scope and Salient Features

Rising in a rainy valley between the two overshadowing Andean ranges the Santa River reaches Peru's almost rainless Pacific coast through the Cañon del Plato where it falls 1400 feet in six miles. The waters impounded by the dam in the gorge are conveyed to a 125,000-kilowatt-capacity power plant through a pressure tunnel. In addition to power development the project is expected to add 25 percent to Peru's irrigated farming area. The development also includes the establishment of a port and industrial area on the coast at Chimbote near the mouth of the Santa.

TVA Influence

In 1942 the Peruvian Government requested the United States to send experts who could supervise this development project. It secured Barton M. Jones, civil engineer; Andrew Komora, construction engineer; and W. P. Fegley, electrical engineer, all former employees of TVA. Publicity regarding this Peruvian development has been titled by such designations as "Andean TVA," and "Peru's TVA."

THE NIGER VALLEY IN FRENCH WEST AFRICA

Location

South of the Sahara in Africa's western bulge, the Niger River flows in a 2,600-mile arc from the southwest to the southeast and then south into the Gulf of Guinea. On the middle Niger—near Timbuktu at the edge of the desert—is a development that has been called TVA's contemporary.

Scope and Salient Features

The Niger River, in centuries past, created a vast interior delta in what is now the center of the Sudan and filled it with alluvium. This vast region extending over a territory of several million acres is in the heart of French West Africa. Here exist all of the elements to provide a new and resourceful setting for a much more thickly settled population with an improved standard of living.

The earliest stage of the middle Niger development was the erection of a diversion dam at Sansanding nearly 300 miles upstream from Timbuktu. This structure was completed in 1941 and supplies a principal irrigation network over halfway to Timbuktu. The main canals are navigable throughout the year and are equipped with locks where necessary. In spite of the fact that World War II retarded the project, by 1945 approximately 50,000 acres formerly covered with jungle growth had been completely cleared, irrigated, and peopled with nearly 20,000 natives who produce ten to fifteen times more crops than prior to development. The area is being transformed into a productive region and its continued development could turn the Niger interior delta into the granary for this part of Africa. The development of the middle Niger could lead to the eventual development of its upper valley where sites for power and storage dams are found.

TVA Influence

Although the "Office du Niger" was established by the French Government in 1932, one year before TVA, its developments have been strongly influenced by what has been called its great American contemporary, the TVA. Mr. Maurice Rossin, chief of social and economic engineering of the Niger River Office is one of the many eminent French engineers and technicians who have visited and studied the TVA development.

Bibliography

"Travaux d'irrigation dans le Soudan, au moyen des eaux du Niger." Génie Civil, 100:177-184, February 20, 1932.

"Travaux d'irrigation dans la région du Macina, au Soudan, au moyen des eaux au Niger." Génie Civil, 101:602-605, December 17, 1932.

"West African possibilities." J. S. Huxley. Yale Review, ns 34, No. 2:255-269, [December] 1944.

"Niger valley." M. C. Rossin. Survey Graphic, 34:8-12, January 1945,

"Lesson of the Niger." New Republic, 112:249, February 19, 1945.

"Multiple-purpose river valley development—French West Africa." M. L. Cooke. Mechanical Engineering, 71:131, February 1949.

"French engineering news." Engineer, 191:808, June 15, 1951.

MEXICO'S PAPALOAPAN BASIN

Location

In Mexico—about 35 miles south of Vera Cruz—the Papaloapan River discharges into the Bay of Campeche. In the mountainous States of Pueblo and Oaxaca to the west and south, the tributaries of this river system rise near peaks over 10,000 feet high and drain precipitously from the mountains into the low-lying areas of the State of Vera Cruz. Less than 200 miles northwest of the center of the Papaloapan Basin is Mexico City.

Scope and Salient Features

The roughly rectangular Papaloapan Basin has an area of about 17,500 square miles and ranges in character from desertlike highlands to tropical junglelike lowlands where there is an average annual precipitation of over 100 inches (about twice that of the TVA region). As the streams of the system drop sharply from the highlands into the lowlands there are a number of waterfalls offering sites for water-power development. Investigations have so far revealed the feasibility of the Cerro Oro, Temascal, and Toro Bravo Dam sites, and construction of the Aleman Dam has already started at Temascal. These dams, with an installed capacity of 105,000 kilowatts could produce 500,000,000 kilowatt-hours per year.

The program for the Papaloapan Valley calls for flood regulation, navigation improvement, increased industrialization, promotion of agriculture, drainage of low lands, irrigation and power development, financing of public works and private industry for the public good, increasing public health standards, and expansion of the tourist industry. It is designed to bring prosperity to the Valley and to turn its tropical wildness into the agricultural and power-producing center of Mexico.

The region has many latent economic possibilities, but it also has many obstacles to be overcome. Proper sewage disposal, the guarantee of a potable water supply, swamp drainage, and preventive and corrective medicine are indispensable to the start of construction. Roads and docks must be built for the only means of transportation at present is the river.

TVA Influence

The Papaloapan Commission—often referred to as the Mexican TVA —was established by President Aleman in 1947 and its administration patterned, in many respects, after TVA. President Aleman and his Secretary of Hydraulic Resources, Engineer Adolfo Orive Alba, visited the TVA in 1947. They had been immediately preceded by a staff of five

Mexican engineering, geologic, and other technical experts who prepared a digest of TVA for the use of the President.

In the late summer of 1948 TVA's Chief Geologist, Berlen C. Moneymaker, at the request of the Mexican Government, joined other American consultants and collaborated on a geologic and engineering study of the Papaloapan Basin.

Bibliography

"Mexico planning vast program on pattern of TVA." Jeanne Bellamy. *St. Louis Post-Dispatch,* December 17, 1946.

Papaloapan en marcha. H. R. Couto. Mexico, D. F.: Editorial Stylo, 1947, 85p.

"TVA Mexican style." C. A. Vanderlip. *New York Herald Tribune,* October 13, 1947.

"Mexico's Papaloapan valley development." *Pan American Union Bulletin,* 82:49, January 1948.

"Método de los estudios económicos de la cuenca del Papaloapan." José Attolini. *Revista de Economia,* 11:8-12, April 15, 1948.

"TVA spirit reaches Mexican swampland." Reprint from *Christian Science Monitor. Knoxville News-Sentinel,* July 6, 1948.

Papaloapan, obra del Presidente Aleman. Mexico. Comision del Papaloapan. 1949. unp.

"Multiple-purpose river valley development—Mexico." M. L. Cooke. *Mechanical Engineering,* 71:131, February 1949.

"New day in Butterfly basin, Papaloapan valley development." R. W. Mulvey. *Reader's Digest,* 59:129-132, August 1951.

"Boom below the Border—Mexico's TVA." *U.S. News and World Report,* April 11, 1952, p. 30.

BRAZIL'S SAO FRANCISCO VALLEY

Location

For 1,000 miles northeast of Rio de Janiero, the Sao Francisco parallels the southeast coast of Brazil. Then—swinging sharply to the right—it plunges over the spectacular 275-foot Paulo Alfonso Falls and continues on to the South Atlantic 300 miles away. In this hook-shaped valley of the Sao Francisco River, another TVA-style development is coming into being.

Scope and Salient Features

The area encompassed by the proposed development is about 263,000 square miles and includes parts of five states: Minas Gerais, Bahia, Pernambuco, Alagoas, and Sergipe. It is sparsely inhabited and malaria is prevalent over a wide area. The potential resources of the area include gold, diamonds, iron, manganese, bauxite, phosphates, limestone, wheat and other grains, and cattle. The fight against malaria has already started. Other objectives of the development are the control of floods, improvement of waterways, production of electric power, and settlement of the sparsely inhabited area.

One of the largest of several planned power plants is already under construction at Paulo Alfonso Falls. In 1953, when the first generators are scheduled to be placed in operation, this plant will have an installed capacity of 120,000 kilowatts. Its ultimate capacity is 440,000 kilowatts.

In addition to the power plants the plan calls for 12 irrigation dams, 33 area hospitals, 3 health centers, 4 health outposts, 1 rural school for teachers, docks in 27 river ports, a river shipyard, 8 highways, several feeder roads, and a regional post office. By law enacted in 1946, 1 per cent of all national revenues is set aside for 20 years for development of the valley.

TVA Influence

In 1944 Dr. Apolonia Sales, Brazilian Minister of Agriculture at that time, visited the Tennessee Valley and was quoted as saying, "My main purpose in coming to Tennessee was to study TVA's dams and see how they could be applied in Brazil." In 1946, at the request of the Brazilian Government, Mr. Oren Reed, TVA construction engineer, studied plans and reports and made an inspection trip of the Sao Francisco area. His conclusions regarding the development were favorable. He stated that the project could be made self-liquidating without taking into account its many intangible values. When President Eurico Dutra of Brazil visited the United States in 1949 he visited and inspected the TVA development. A Brazilian publication reporting his visit stated that once the Sao Francisco project was finished it would, like the Tennessee, transform its valley into an area of economic opportunity.

Bibliography

"San Francisco, a multiple-purpose river." M. L. Cooke. (In his *Brazil on the March*. New York: McGraw-Hill, 1944. p. 193-208.)

"Brazil to Develop 'TVA' project on San Francisco river. *Engineering News-Record*, 134:626, May 3, 1945.

"Multiple-purpose river valley development—Brazil." M. L. Cooke. *Mechanical Engineering*, 71:130, February 1949.

"Vale do Sao Francisco e as obras do Tennessee." *Brasil Constroi*, No. 3:96-97, Julho 1949.

"Brazil plans huge 'TVA' development." C. R. Escudero. *Asheville* (N. C.) *Citizen,* August 1, 1949.

"Power for the bulge in Brazil." *Time,* 54:30, September 5, 1949.

"Power: Hub of South America's industrial development—Brazil." *Foreign Commerce Weekly,* 39:12-13, April 10, 1950.

"Public power said key to Brazil industry. Model for the world." *Nashville Tennessean,* November 26, 1950, and December 1, 1950.

"Brazil started on major power plan." *Engineering News-Record,* 147:50. November 22, 1951.

RIONE—ON URUGUAY'S RIO NEGRO

Location

Southwest across Uruguay—the smallest country in South America—the Rio Negro flows from Brazil on the northeast to the River Uruguay, the Argentine border, on the west. Argentina's capital city of Buenos Aires is less than 100 miles from the south. RIONE—for Rio Negro—is the name given the Uruguayan Commission undertaking the development of this river.

Scope and Salient Features

The 500-mile-long Rio Negro has a drainage area of 26,400 square miles. Average annual rainfall is almost equal to the 51-inch average in the Tennessee Valley, but rainfall over the Rio Negro watershed is subject to erratic fluctuations and there are periodic severe droughts. For this reason storage of water is of great importance to the successful operation of the development.

The ultimate development calls for four dams of which one, the Rincon del Bonete, is completed and has a power installation of 128,000 kilowatts. This project is practically in the center of Uruguay. When the others are completed, the installed capacity of the system will be nearly 500,000 kilowatts. Although power is the primary purpose of this development, other important purposes include flood regulation, navigation, and reclamation.

TVA Influence

The director of the work, Luis Giorgi, former dean of Engineering at the University of Uruguay, spent 14 months in the United States with several associates studying TVA and other projects. When the chief civil engineer of the project, Carlas A. Giavi, visited the United States in 1946 he stated that RIONE was an autonomous governmental organization comparable to TVA and that coupled with the dams would be a "broad reclamation project on the order of TVA. . . ."

Bibliography

"Hydro project solves Uruguay's war fuel crisis." Luis Giorgi and L. F. Harza. *Electrical World*, 123:78-81, February 17, 1945.

"Uruguayan multiple-purpose dam will double country's power." L. F. Harza and Luis Giorgi. *Engineering News-Record*, 134:772-775, May 31, 1945.

"Uruguay's big power development: Rio Negro power project." *Pan American Union, Bulletin*, 80:260-264, May 1946.

"Uruguay's Rincon del Bonete project supplies country's first hydro power." Luis Giorgi. *Civil Engineering*, 18:14-18, January 1948.

"Power: Hub of South America's industrial development—Uruguay." *Foreign Commerce Weekly*, 39:5-6, April 24, 1950.

"Hydro-electric development in Uruguay." K. E. Sorensen. *Water Power*, 3:411-418, November 1951.

THE SNOWY-MURRAY PROJECT IN AUSTRALIA

Location

In southeastern Australia are the Snowy and Murray Rivers and a major tributary of the Murray—the Murrumbidgee. All three rivers rise practically within sight of Mt. Kosciusko (el. 7,305 feet), the highest peak in the Australian Alps. For about 2000 miles the Murray flows westerly—forming for a good part of its length the boundary between Victoria and New South Wales. When it reaches South Australia it sweeps around to the southwest and discharges into the Great Australian Bight. The Snowy, on the other hand, dashes southerly from the mountains a comparatively short distance (about 300 miles) across New South Wales and Victoria to the Tasman Sea. The development under way on these three rivers has been called "The TVA Twin."

Scope and Salient Features

The largest public work yet conceived in Australia has as its objective the harnessing of practically all the headwaters of the Snowy and nearly half its total volume. Through a series of tunnels under the Australian Alps this water of the Snowy will be diverted to the Murray and Murrumbidgee, first for the generation of electricity—an installation of 1,-720,000 kilowatts is contemplated—and then for irrigation in the fertile but arid valleys to the west. The work is estimated to cost between

$544,000,000 and $640,000,000 and may take as long as 25 years to complete.

The 16 power stations to be built under the plan will be placed underground and scattered through inaccessible mountain country. Other features of the project include the building of 7 large dams, driving from 80 to 100 miles of tunnels through the Australian Alps, and the construction of some 500 miles of water canals. After the generation of power, the additional water from the Snowy will supplement the already existing and extensive irrigation developments on the Murray and Murrumbidgee. By means of a system of dams and reservoirs on the tributaries, and weirs on the main rivers, these two river systems are already regulated for most of their extent. Locks in the weirs below the confluence with the Murrumbidgee provide navigation on the lower reaches of the Murray.

TVA Influence

During the last several years, a number of Australia's engineers, regional development technicians, and government representatives have visited the TVA and studied its methods, plans, and accomplishments. As far back as 1944, delegates to the Murray Valley Regional Development Conference at Yarrowonga were advised by leading Australian officials—among them Dr. Evatt, at that time Federal Attorney General —that they were discussing means of promoting what might become the equivalent of the TVA in the Murray Valley.

In 1949 when the Snowy River diversion project was announced by the Australian News and Information Bureau in New York City, it was stated that engineers and technicians would be taken to Australia to plan the project and that Australia planned to ask TVA for the loan of TVA personnel needed.

Bibliography

"Plan to decentralise government." *Melbourne (Australia) Herald,* August 15, 1944.

"Model for development:" "Story of the TVA;" "TVA record of success:" "How the plan has worked;" "Regional plan in N.S.W.;" "Clarence-Snowy movements." *Melbourne* (Australia) *Age,* August 26, 28, 29, 1944.

Murray valley; a geographical reconnaissance of the Murray valley and a new design for its regional organization. J. M. Holmes. Sydney: Angus and Robertson, 1948. 280p.

"Snowy river." *Water Power,* 1:101-104, May-June 1949.

"Australia plans power project to double her electrical energy." R. L. Curthoys. *New York Times,* June 6, 1949.

"Hydro-electric developments in south-eastern Australia." *Engineer,* 187:628-630, June 10, 1949.

"Water power in Australia; Snowy river hydro-electric project." *Electrical Review* (London), 145:1129-1133, December 16, 1949.

PROPOSED YVA ON THE YANGTZE

China at the present time is in a confused, critical period of major transition which would appear to preclude for some time construction of large-scale developments such as this project on the Yangtze. However, it remains a much publicized possibility for the future and for this reason alone it is included in this digest.

Location

In northeastern Tibet, three miles above sea level and almost due west of Shanghai, the Yangtze starts on a winding, twisting, 3,200-mile course through the heart of China to the Yellow Sea. One of the largest rivers in the world, the Yangtze has been called "transportation lifeline, bottomless irrigation well, and pitiless waster of life and property." Chungking, Hankow, Nanking—all three are cities on the Yangtze which are important in Chinese affairs. In 1946, the preliminary studies of a plan to develop this major river were started. This work was suspended in 1947 and plans of the present Chinese Government regarding this development are not known.

Scope and Salient Features

The terms "gigantic" or "colossal" are not inappropriate to apply to the ambitious plans for the proposed Yangtze development. TVA is dwarfed in comparison. Within a 300-mile radius of the main dam site, more people than live in the entire United States would be affected. The river would be regulated the year round, permitting ocean-going ships to sail to Chungking, 650 miles from the coast. Hundreds of miles of canals would be excavated. Ten million acres could reap irrigation benefits. Floods in the 700,000 square miles drained by the stream could be minimized. According to J. L. Savage, Consulting Engineer, the key project of this proposed development, the 820-foot-high Yangtze Gorge Dam at the east end of the gorges near Ichang, could have an ultimate installed power capacity of 17,500,000 kilowatts. An additional 3,042,000 kilowatts could be provided by eleven projects on the tributaries.

TVA Influence

During the past years a large number of engineers with the National Resources Commission of China as well as the leaders of that and other organizations in Nationalist China interested in the TVA water control and regional development idea have visited the Tennessee Valley and conferred with TVA officials and engineers. A meeting of the National Resources Commission of the Chinese Government was held in Knoxville, Tennessee, during July 1943. Many publications describing the proposed Yangtze project point out its similarity to TVA and the designation YVA—after TVA—has frequently been applied to the proposed Chinese development program.

In 1946 the China Edition of *The Stars and Stripes* said in part: "Drawing on the idealism and practical experience of the TVA and the Reclamation Bureau projects . . . the Chinese are projecting a public works improvement surpassing anything ever built."

Bibliography

"China's TVA." A. C. Wehrwein. *Stars and Stripes* (China edition), 1:3 (magazine supplement), January 19, 1946.

"China plans an unprecedented dam for power, irrigation and navigation." *Engineering News-Record*, 136:310-311, February 28, 1946.

"China to build biggest dam; irrigation and hydroelectric power development; Yangtze valley." *Compressed Air Magazine*, 51:107-109, April 1946.

"Yangtze gorge project." Li, Mei-Yun. *National Reconstruction Journal*, 7:59-70, October 1946.

"Yangtze gorge project." J. L. Savage. *Midwest Engineer*, 1:30-34, May 1949.

UGANDA'S DEVELOPMENT WHERE THE NILE BEGINS

Location

In Uganda, astride the equator in east-central Africa, a dam is being built at Owen Falls on the Victoria Nile just after it leaves Lake Victoria. This lake, the largest in Africa, is an important source of the historically famous Nile of Egypt which enters the eastern Mediterranean far to the north.

Scope and Salient Features

The Owen Falls Dam is the first step in a contemplated African irrigation, power, and reclamation development. A joint project of British

Uganda and Egypt, it is estimated the proposed plan would increase the irrigable area of the Anglo-Egyptian Sudan from 862,000 to 2,500,000 acres, and also would reclaim thousands of acres of swampy land in the Southern Sudan region. By raising the surface of Lake Victoria by one meter (about 3.3 feet) the Owen Falls Dam will provide a storage capacity of about 56,000,000 acre-feet for power and river control. The ultimate installed power capacity of the dam will be 150,000 kilowatts. This power will aid in the industrialization of Uganda and will be supplied to parts of Tanganyika and Belgian Congo; the first power is scheduled for delivery in 1953 or 1954.

TVA Influence

In 1948 an extensive tour of the TVA development was made by a technical mission of the Uganda Protectorate Government. The objective of the mission—composed of Dr. K. A. Davies, Mr. H. G. Stent, Dr. A. J. V. Underwood and Mr. C. R. Westlake—was to discover from the experience of TVA how best the rock phosphates in the neighborhood of Owen Falls could be processed.

In newspaper accounts of the proposed development, it has been referred to as an African TVA that compares in size with its American prototype.

Bibliography

"Owen Falls hydro-electric scheme." *Engineer*, 186:38-40, July 9, 1948.
"African TVA." *St. Louis Post-Dispatch*, March 27, 1949.
"Uganda's resources." *Water Power*, 1:179, July-August 1949.
"Uganda hydro-electric scheme." *Electrician*, 143:1054, September 30, 1949.
"Contract let for hydro plant at headwaters of the Nile river." *Engineering News-Record*, 143:46-47, November 10, 1949.
"TVA's in the Middle East." Feliks Bochenski and William Diamond. *Middle East Journal*, 4:52-82, January 1950.
"Progress of the Owen Falls hydroelectric scheme." *Engineer*, 192:828-829, December 28, 1951.

PILOT DEMONSTRATION PROJECTS IN THE MIDDLE EAST

Location

Located at the eastern end of the Mediterranean from Turkey to Egypt are the Middle East States of Syria, Lebanon, and Jordan (including Arab-Palestine). For these countries the United Nations Economic Survey Mission for the Middle East has recommended "pilot demonstration" projects on the Orontes and Litani Rivers and the Wadis (rivers) Zerka and Qilt. The Orontes is a northerly flowing river in western Syria that crosses into Turkey where it sweeps around to the southwest past Antakya (early Antioch) and on into the Mediterranean near its northeast corner. The Litani flows across Lebanon from northeast to southwest and enters the Mediterranean about midway between Tyr and Saida (ancient Tyre and Sidon). The Wadi Zerka in Jordan flows from the east out of the high desert plateau into the Jordan River at a point due east of Tel Aviv, the new Israeli city on the Mediterranean. The Wadi Qilt, in Jordan's Arab-Palestine, enters the Jordan River just above the Dead Sea from beyond Jericho to the west.

Scope and Salient Features

The reclamation of the large swamps on the Orontes River in western Syria would open up a new farming area, provide flood control and electric power. Including 84,000 acres in the Ghab depression after drainage, the Orontes River project would add a total of 183,000 acres to the irrigated areas of Syria.

For the Litani River in Lebanon a complete engineering and geological survey is visualized with a view to developing this small but important river for electricity, irrigation, and domestic water supplies. The United Nations Mission's engineering consultants indicated that power potentialities of this river were in the neighborhood of 350,000 kilowatts, in terms of installed capacity. In a distance of 62 miles the Litani drops some 2,800 feet.

A dam on the Wadi Zerka in Jordan, it is estimated, could double the dry-season flow of this river and thereby double the irrigable land in its area. The scheme for the Wadi Zerka contemplates that the area be developed completely as a unit; that is, construction of all necessary roads into the area, provision of water for perennial irrigation, with necessary small check dams or principal gullies to minimize siltation, and afforestation work, terracing, and planting of fruit trees where this seems to be feasible.

The development contemplated for the Wadi Qilt in the Arab-Palestine part of Jordan is similar to that for the Wadi Zerka just described.

TVA Influence

Mr. Gordon R. Clapp, Chairman of TVA's Board of Directors, served as the head of the United Nations Economic Survey Mission for the Middle East. Van Court Hare, Office of Chief Engineer, served as a member of the Mission's engineering development staff which was headed by William L. Voorduin, formerly Head Project Planning Engineer of TVA.

Bibliography

"WPA for Mid-East is Clapp solution; 50,000 refugees to starve—unless: Transjordan king spurs development; Israeli show pride in rapid strides." Nat Caldwell. *Nashville Tennessean,* November 6, 7, 8, 9, 1949.

Final report. Part 2: Technical supplement. United Nations. Economic Survey Mission for the Middle East. Lake Success: December 1949. 74p.

"U. N. Economic Mission proposes Arab TVA (AP)." *Louisville Courier-Journal,* December 13, 1949.

"Approach to economic development in the Middle East: A Summary of the reports of the United Nations economic survey mission for the Middle East." G. R. Clapp. *International Conciliation,* No. 460:203-217, April 1950.

"Water problem in the Middle East." *Geographical Review,* 40:481-484, July 1950.

"TVA on the Tigris [Resource development in the Middle East]." G. R. Clapp. *New Leader,* 33:6-8, July 22, 1950.

CHILEAN DEVELOPMENT CORPORATION

Location

From Peru south to Cape Horn—where South America points to Antarctica—Chile stretches for 2,600 miles. From the towering Andean mountain ranges—two to four miles high—on the east, down to the Pacific on the west, averages not much more than 100 miles. This elongated country is the province of the Chilean Development Corporation.

Scope and Salient Features

The corporation, established in 1939, has made the production of electric power the principal feature of its development program—a program which will ultimately lead to a unified national development of the country's resources. In Chile, the rivers plunge down from great heights in the Andes directly into the Pacific Ocean, offering excellent sites for high-head hydroelectric power installations. Pilmaiquen, near Osorno, with 13,500 kilowatts, was the first to go into operation, and is now being expanded to 24,000 kilowatts. Abanico and Sauzal followed: Abanico, to supply the Concepcion zone with 129,000 kilowatts, is now partly in operation; Sauzal, south of Santiago, will supply 76,200 kilowatts. Other plants now being constructed, such as Cipreses and Los Molles, will add more than 100,000 kilowatts additional to the supply. Production of electric energy in Chile, as indicated by statistics recently released by the Chilean Statistical Bureau, increased from somewhat less than three-quarters of a billion kilowatt-hours in 1944 to well over one billion in 1948.

TVA Influence

A number of engineers and technicians of the Chilean Development Corporation—particularly during the first few years following its establishment in 1939—visited the TVA and conferred with members of its staff. Certain specialists of the Corporation remained with TVA for periods of 6 to 12 months.

In a 1947 publication of the International Labour Office entitled *The Chilean Development Corporation*, by Herman Finer. Mr. Finer makes several comparisons with TVA and states in one instance, ". . . the experience of other countries was readily applicable. An acknowledgment is made in this respect to the Tennessee Valley Authority." In April of 1950 President Gabriel Gonzalez Videla of Chile visited the TVA area.

Bibliography

Chilean development corporation; a study in national planning to raise living standards. Herman Finer. Montreal: International Labour Office. 1947. 83p.

"Chile builds her future: CORFU [Corporación de fomento de la producción], adventure in progress." Karna Steelquist. *Pan American*, p. 13-17, April 1950.

"Power: Hub of South America's industrial development—Chile." *Foreign Commerce Weekly*, 39:42-43, April 10, 1950.

THE SCOTTISH HIGHLANDS AND ISLANDS

Location

The Scottish Highlands and Islands from Loch Lomond north to the Shetlands comprise the service area of the North of Scotland Hydro-Electric Board established in 1943.

Scope and Salient Features

In addition to "being responsible for initiating and undertaking the development of all further means of generation of electricity by water power" within an area just over half that of the Tennessee Valley, the Board collaborates "in the carrying out of any measures for the economic development and social improvement" in this North of Scotland district. It is a region of heavy rainfall and swiftly rushing rivers. While there are many usable streams, they are mostly quite short, and the nature of the terrain forbids the construction of large reservoirs. At the end of 1949, nine hydroelectric schemes were under construction and two of these— the Sloy and Clunie projects—were almost ready to go into operation. The total capacity of the nine projects will be 428,450 kilowatts of which Sloy will develop 130,450 kilowatts and Clunie 61,200 kilowatts. Ten additional hydroelectric schemes promoted by the Board had not been started by the end of 1949; these ten will develop 203,800 kilowatts.

TVA Influence

The North of Scotland Hydro-Electric Board has been publicized as "a body similar to TVA which served in some ways as a model," and its development program has been variously referred to as "TVA for the Highlands," "TVA of Scotland," "Scotland's TVA," etc. One article regarding this development was headlined, "TVA Ideas Used in Harnessing Scottish Rivers." A number of engineers and technicians from the British Isles have visited TVA and conferred with members of its staff.

Bibliography

Hydro-electric development (Scotland) act, 1943. London: H. M. Stationery Office, 1943. 30p.

"TVA ideas used in harnessing Scottish rivers." David Nichol. *St. Louis Post-Dispatch*, September 1, 1946.

"Hydro-electric developments in Scotland." J. Henderson. *Engineering*, 164:333-335, 357-359, October 3-10, 1947.

"TVA for the Highlands." Keith Hutchison. *Nation*, 166:711-713, June 26, 1948.

"New heart in the Highlands." Andrew Dargie. *Rotarian*, 73:17-22, September 1948.

"Growing pains of TVA are felt in Scotland." *Memphis Commercial Appeal*, June 1, 1951.

"Electrical aspects of modern hydro-electric development in Scotland." T. Lawrie. *Engineering*, 172:313-315, September 7, 1951.

INDIA'S MVP—THE MAHANADI VALLEY PROJECT

Location

From India's Central Provinces, the Mahanadi River flows southeastwardly across the Province of Orissa into the Bay of Bengal. At Hirakud near Sambalpur in Orissa work was started late in 1949 on the first dam of the Mahanadi Valley Project (MVP).

Scope and Salient Features

This multipurpose—irrigation, power, navigation, flood control—project involves the erection of three dams. The development program provides for power generation, the construction of three canal systems for irrigation, and the dredging of a navigable canal from the sea to Cuttack at the head of the Mahanadi delta. In addition to providing power for Orissa Province, the project will supply power to parts of the Central Provinces and the Eastern States. The dam at Hirakud, the farthest upstream, will be followed by construction of dams at Tikarpara and Naraj. The power installations in the three dams, it is estimated, will have a total capacity of almost 900,000 kilowatts and the total area that will eventually come under irrigation is estimated to be about 2,500,000 acres.

TVA Influence

In 1949, Mr. Nityananda Kanungo, Minister of Development and Industries of the Province of Orissa, spent some time in the TVA area studying its plans, programs, and accomplishments in order to secure the benefit of TVA's experience for the Mahanadi Valley development. In 1950 Mr. J. N. Panda, an engineer of the Province of Orissa, made a study of the engineering and construction features of TVA.

In a letter dated May 4, 1951, to the TVA Chairman, Dr. H. B. Mohanty, Secretary to the Government of Orissa, requested information about TVA as "it is being used as a model in developing Mahanadi River."

Bibliography

"India stakes her economic future on hydroelectric developments." *Power*, 91:310-311, May 1947.

"India's TVA." V. S. Swaminathan. *Fortnightly* (London), 170 (ns 164): 180-186, September 1948.

"India taps enormous water and power resources." A. V. Karpov. *Civil Engineering*, 19:235-238, April 1949.

"Hydro-electric development in India." H. A. Sieveking. *Water Power,* 2:60-66, March-April 1950.

Mahanadi valley development. India. Central Water-Power, Irrigation & Navigation Commission (in its Quinquennial report, April 1945 to March 1950. Simla: Government of India Press, September 1950. p. 106-119).

"Letter from India: India stakes future on her rivers—the Mahanadi valley." W. G. Bowman. *Engineering News-Record,* 146:35, March 1, 1951.

"Hirakud dam progress." *Water Power,* 3:202, June 1951.

"First dams for India's great barren plateau." *Engineering News-Record,* 146:35-38, June 7, 1951.

"Importance and necessity of combined resource development of a river valley multi-purpose project." Kanwar Sain. *Irrigation & Power,* 8:499-506, July 1951.

THE RHÔNE VALLEY IN FRANCE

Location

From sources shadowed by the icy spires of the Matterhorn and the Jungfrau in Switzerland, the Rhône River starts on its way to the sunny Mediterranean by way of Lake Geneva. Leaving Lake Geneva it flows southwesterly into France until it reaches Lyon where it turns sharply south and finally reaches the sea near Marseille.

Scope and Salient Features

The development of the River Rhône in French territory has been described as perhaps one of the most ambitious series of civil engineering projects ever formulated in western Europe. Its purposes are power generation, navigation, and irrigation. The general plan for multiple-purpose development includes ten power plants on the upper Rhône, eleven on the lower Rhône, navigation from its mouth to Lake Geneva, and irrigation of the arid lower Rhône Valley. The development, rapidly nearing completion, will add 13 billion kilowatt-hours a year to France's supply of power, will increase the country's agricultural yield by 5 per cent, and will provide 354 additional miles of inland waterway.

TVA Influence

This development has been called "TVA for France" and publications describing it have compared it to TVA. A large number of French engineers, technicians, public officials, students, representatives of private concerns and other French organizations have visited and studied TVA during the past several years and are continuing to do so.

Bibliography

"Developments beyond U. S. borders—France." *Engineering News-Record*, 138:474-475, March 27, 1947.

"French hydroelectric program." G. Constantini. *Compressed Air Magazine*, 54:146-151, June 1949.

"Hydraulics on the Rhône." (In *Hydraulique et électricité françaises*. Grenoble: Houille Blanche, 1950. p. 101-150.)

"Some French schemes—a pictorial survey." *Water Power*, 2:72-76, March-April 1950.

"Billions of kilowatts for France; Rhône river valley project." *Life*, 28:27-33, June 26, 1950.

"Development of the River Rhône." *Engineer*, 190:549-551, 580-584, 617-619, 644-646, December 8-29, 1950.

"French Rhône scheme." *Water Power*, 3:79-80, February 1951.

"France's push for kilowatts pays off." W. G. Bowman. *Engineering News-Record*, 146:30-34, April 5, 1951.

"More power for France." *Engineering News-Record*, 147:64, September 13, 1951.

"Renaissance on the Rhône." W. G. Bowman. *Engineering News-Record*, 147:30-35, November 22, 1951.

"Europe's tallest dam rises in French Alps." W. G. Bowman. *Engineering News-Record*, 147:30-32, December 13, 1951.

EL SALVADOR'S LEMPA VALLEY

Location

This smallest country on the American continent, in Central America, is only about one-third the size of the Tennessee Valley. It is a region of mountains, hills, and upland plains and has a 160-mile shore line on the Pacific Ocean. The Valley of the Lempa River comprises, roughly, about one-third of the country's entire area.

Scope and Salient Features

For twenty-five years the people of El Salvador had been thinking and planning the development of the Lempa Valley until, in July 1951, construction started on the Guayabo Dam. This damming of the Lempa has been called, in effect, the basic engineering "cornerstone" of a vast plan for exploiting the river's resources. Up to 250,000 acres will be irrigated by a series of canals which will be constructed as a part of the valley development. The dam will have an initial power installation of 30,000 kilowatts with a planned ultimate installation of 75,000 kilowatts. In 1953, according to latest estimates, the hitherto wasted waters of the Lempa will finally turn the turbines at Chorrera del Guayabo. Many present industries are expected to improve technologically with the advent of the new electric power; still others are planned for development to satisfy the demand for important products. The government of El Salvador foresees a rise of factories and plants of many types: paper, varnish, oil, paint, soap, woven fabrics, fertilizers, milk derivatives, shoe leather and shoes, metal products, plastics, luggage, etc., will be produced. The results of the development through its electric power, its irrigation benefits, and its abundant supply of water have been described as a means of providing a higher standard of living and a future filled with constructive work for the people of El Salvador.

TVA Influence

This development has been publicized as a TVA-type project and visitors to TVA from El Salvador have inspected and studied the TVA development.

Bibliography

Electrificacion nacional de El Salvador en sus aspectos tecnicos y sociales. R. E. Lima. San Salvador: Conferencia Dictada en la Sociedad de Obreros de El Salvador Federada, 1945. 37p.

"Lempa river hydroelectric project." Foreign Commerce Weekly, 39:31, May 8, 1950.

"Power station of radical design proposed for El Salvador." K. E. Sorensen. Engineering News-Record, 144:44-45, June 15, 1950.

"Developments abroad—El Salvador hits the jackpot." Engineering News-Record, 146:54, February 8, 1951.

"Guayabo hydro-electric project." Water Power, 3:99-101, March 1951.

"TVA on the Lempa." José Gomez. United Nations World, 5:46-47, September 1951.

PROPOSED VOLTA RIVER AUTHORITY ON THE GOLD COAST

Location

The Gold Coast, so named from the grains of gold found in the sands of its rivers, is on the north shore of the Gulf of Guinea under the West African bulge. This British colony and protectorate is about twice the size of the Tennessee Valley, and the Volta River Basin with its tributaries, the Black Volta and the White Volta, comprise roughly one-half or more of its area.

Scope and Salient Features

Consultants to the Gold Coast Government recently issued a preliminary report on the development of the Volta Basin. This report covers aspects of hydroelectric power, irrigation and drainage, and river navigation. The primary purpose of the power development would be for the production of aluminum, and the report estimates that the Volta River could be harnessed to produce 545,000 kilowatts. The irrigation possibilities consider that 500,000 acres in the Accra Plains could be supplied by water brought in by canal from the reservoir created by a projected dam at Ajena. This would be a navigable reservoir 200 miles long with an area of 2,000 square miles. In addition to power, irrigation, and navigation, the scheme contemplates construction of roads and railroads, a new seaport, a very large aluminum works, and resettlement of 20,000 people.

TVA Influence

The Chief Secretary's Office of the Gold Coast Government at Accra, in May 1951, stated it was probable that in a short time a Volta River Authority would be established. Lists of TVA technical and other publications were requested.

Bibliography

"Gold coast survey." *Water Power*, 1:179, July-August 1949.
"Volta river survey." *Water Power*, 2:183, September-October 1950.
"Volta river project." *Water Power*, 3:203, June 1951.

II

AFRICA

Belgian Congo

A ten-year plan of the Belgian Government for the development of this nearly one million-square-mile area in the heart of Africa envisions an eventual development along TVA lines in the naturally favored areas, as in the area below Stanleyville. The Belgian Congo—stretching from the Atlantic to Lake Tanganyika—comprises about two-thirds of the Congo River Basin; the other third is to the north in French Equatorial Africa. A principal tributary source of the Congo rises in the mountains near Lake Albert, one of the sources of the Nile, but whereas the Nile drains north to the Mediterranean, the Congo drains west to the South Atlantic just a few degrees south of the equator.

The most valuable resources—copper, cobalt, manganese, and uranium—are centralized in the area near Elizabethville, its northern neighbor Jadotville, and the expanding uranium community of Shinkolobwe. The chief diamond country is in the upper Kasai (Tschikapa) River region.

Rhodesia (Northern and Southern)

Rhodesian developments that are under way or proposed in the valley of the Zambesi in southern Africa are expected to exercise a marked influence on the economic and industrial development of large territories bordering the Zambesi River. This major river drains easterly across southern Africa and enters the Indian Ocean near the south end of the Mozambique Channel. The governments of Northern and Southern Rhodesia (protectorate and self-governing colony respectively of the British Commonwealth) are considering proposals for harnessing the Zambesi River at Kariba gorge. On the Zambesi, which separates the two countries, are the Victoria Falls, described as the greatest natural spectacle in southern Africa. For Southern Rhodesia a large scheme on broad TVA lines has been announced, and a pilot scheme is understood to have been started for the Sabi-Lund development, a three-dam project for power and irrigation.

Union of South Africa

Officials of the Union Government have announced that South Africa is to have its River Valley Authority on the TVA pattern. A number of dams are contemplated and schemes for the Fish, Sundays, Orange, Vet, Sand, Caledon, Riet, Nagalies, and Modder Rivers mentioned. Work on the Orange River project has recently been started.

The Union of South Africa with an area of nearly a half million square miles occupies the south end of the African continent.

Valley of the Nile

The Nile, over 4,000 miles long, has a basin embracing more than a million square miles. Portions of Anglo-Egyptian Sudan, Egypt, Ethiopia, Kenya and Uganda lie in this historic valley and studies, plans, and schemes for its integrated development have been the subject of much discussion among the interested governments. The latest maps also indicate that parts of the Belgian Congo and Tanganyika are invaded by the upper reaches of the Nile system. The Owen Falls project in Uganda is included with the developments in the first classification described in the preceding pages. An agreement has been reached between Egypt,

Britain, and Ethiopia for the construction of a dam at Lake Tana, the source of the Blue Nile in Ethiopia. Other projects on the upper reaches of the Nile are being studied. The Aswan Dam in Egypt has been regulating the Nile for a number of years and further development of the lower Nile is being accomplished by the Egyptian Government.

AUSTRALIA

Clarence River Scheme

The Clarence River is in the northeast corner of New South Wales where the continent of Australia bulges eastward into the Pacific. The proposed scheme includes a series of multipurpose dams for power production, flood regulation, irrigation, and navigation. Progressive development of the Clarence, beginning with the building of a 220-foot dam at the Clarence gorge, would add 300 miles of navigable river channel and unlock the door of 3,000 square miles at present inaccessible. It would eliminate the frequent devastating floods; irrigate 100,000 acres of fertile flats; and generate continuously at least 125,000 kilowatts of electric energy. Publicity relating to this project mentions TVA as a model for development.

EUROPE

Greece

Full development of Greece's river resources, including construction of hydroelectric projects, has been recommended by a United Nations investigating committee. Greece, with the guidance of the United Nations, is urged to undertake flood regulation, drainage, and irrigation projects. Publicity states this program amounts to a little TVA for Greece. In 1950 it was announced that Greece and Turkey were planning a large-scale program of land reclamation and flood control along the banks of the River Eros which roughly marks the boundary between the two countries.

Occupying the southern peninsula of the Balkans, Greece stretches down into the Mediterranean between the Aegean and Ionian Seas. In area, Greece is comparable in size to the Tennessee Valley.

Wales

There has been publicity and promotion by Welsh organizations for a TVA-type of development in Wales. At the present time there are being investigated two extensions to existing schemes and six new major projects. The proposed extensions are at Dolgarrog and Maentwrog and would increase the output by 36,000,000 kilowatt-hours annually. The new hydroelectric projects are at Upper Conway, Mawddoch, Rheidol, Snowdon, Ffestiniog, and Nant Ffranoon. The annual output of these six projects, it is estimated, would be about 520,000,000 kilowatt-hours.

Wales, an integral part of Great Britain, has an area about one-fifth that of the Tennessee Valley. A number of British government officials, engineers, and technicians have visited the TVA and inspected its projects and discussed its program with TVA staff members.

MIDDLE EAST

Iraq

Iraq, the major part of which is in the valley of the historic Tigris and Euphrates Rivers (ancient Mesopotamia), has plans for flood regulation and irrigation projects on this river system. The two rivers enter Iraq from Turkey and Syria to the northwest and flow southeasterly across the country to empty into the head of the Persian Gulf. The Iraq plan has been described as a project that is essentially an expansion and adaptation along the lines of TVA. The site of Babylon of Old Testament times is in Central Iraq.

Turkey

This country, the greater part of which occupies the large peninsula formed by the Mediterranean, Aegean, Marmara, and Black Seas, is developing a multiple-purpose program for power, flood regulation, and irrigation. Among the rivers to be developed are the Sakarya, the Eros between Greece and Turkey, and the Gediz. Several former TVA engineers and geologists have made investigations in Turkey, and on some of the Turkish projects these former TVA employees will have charge of the design and construction work.

SOUTHWEST ASIA

Afghanistan

To the northwest of India and Pakistan beyond the famous Khyber Pass lies this extremely mountainous country. It has plans for the development of the Helmand River and its tributary, the Arghandab, for power and irrigation purposes. The valley of the Helmand runs southwesterly through the middle of Afghanistan, and the river has its sources in the towering Hindu Kush mountains to the northeast. James B. Hayes, former TVA project engineer, was connected with the Afghanistanian project as chief engineer in that country for the American contractor.

Ceylon

The government of Ceylon has river development plans involving several projects on the island, which is not quite two-thirds the area of the Tennessee Valley. Plans for two of the projects have reached the stage where construction has started on one—Gal Oya—and is expected to start on the other—Walawe Ganga—in 1950. Gal Oya Dam on the Gal Oya River in southeast Ceylon will be 154 feet high and irrigate 100,000 acres; its power capacity will be just under 10,000 kilowatts. Walawe Ganga Dam on the river of the same name in southern Ceylon will be 110 feet high and have a power capacity just over 10,000 kilowatts.

The island of Ceylon lies in the Indian Ocean just southeast of the southern tip of India. Technicians and students from Ceylon have visited TVA and detailed information—including technical reports—regarding the TVA development has been sent to Ceylonese officials in response to their requests.

India

In addition to the Damodar and Mahanadi valley projects already being developed along TVA lines, many of the major multi-purpose developments proposed for the rivers of India are mentioned in publicity as having similarity to TVA.

The Ganges Basin—The proposed developments are on tributaries of the Ganges. This major stream discharges into the head of the Bay of Bengal after sweeping southeastwardly across northern India in the shadow of the Himalayas along India's northeast border.

The Sutlej Development—The Sutlej River cuts westwardly through the Himalayas into northern India from Tibet. It then crosses into Pakistan where it joins the Indus, which continues on southwestwardly to the Arabian Sea near Karachi. Two projects are now under way:

Bhakra on the Sutlej River—560-foot dam—850,000-kilowatt capacity —1,500,000-acre irrigation area.

Nangal on the Sutlej River—144,000-kilowatt capacity.

The Machkund River—The Machkund River is a relatively short stream draining southeastwardly into the Bay of Bengal in east-central India.

The Godavari River System—The Godavari River drains southeast-wardly almost all the way across central India from near Bombay on the west coast into the Bay of Bengal on the east.

WEST INDIES

Haiti

Publicity relating to the development of the Artibonite Valley states that it is to be patterned after the TVA. Haiti is about one-fourth the area of the Tennessee Valley and occupies the western third of the island known as Hispaniola; the other two-thirds of the island constitute the Dominican Republic. The island lies between Cuba to the northwest and Puerto Rico to the southeast; the island of Jamaica is to the west.

Index